The Pioneer Settlers
Unsung Heroes
of Our Past

In First-Hand and Early Writings

Compiled and Edited by:

DONNA L. PRESTON

ISBN: 978-0-578-77963-8
Printed in the United States of America

All photographs are by the author.
Other book by the author:
"Spirital Maturity: The Normal Christian Life."

Book design by TeaBerryCreative.com

Table of Contents

The American Revolution

CONTENTS

The Northwest Territory

CONTENTS

CONTENTS

CONTENTS

PART 1

The American Revolution

"In the beginning of the contest with Britain when we were sensible of danger, we had daily prayers in that room for Divine protection.

Our prayers were heard, and they were gratiously answered.

All of us who were engaged in the struggle, must have observed frequent instances of a superintending Providence in our favor."

—BENJAMIN FRANKLIN

CHAPTER 1

Theater of Early Adventure

"THE BARK CANOE"

By James Hall

"THE FRENCH, WHO FIRST EXPLORED OUR NORTHERN FRONTIER, ascended the great chain of Lakes to Huron and Michigan, and afterwards penetrated through Lake Superior to that remote wilderness where the head branches of the St. Lawrence interlock with those of the Mississippi.

Adopting and probably improving the bark canoe of the natives, they were enabled to traverse immeasurable wilds which nature had seemed to have rendered inaccessible to man by floods of water at one season, and masses of ice and snow at another; by the wide spread lakes and ponds and morasses, which in every direction intercepted the journey by land, and by the cataracts and rapids which cut off the communication by water. All difficulties vanished before the efficiency of this little vessel. Its wonderful buoyancy enabled it, though heavily freighted, to ride safely over the waves

of the lakes. Even in boisterous weather, its slender form and lightness of draught permitted it to navigate the smallest streams, and
pass the narrowest channels; while its weight was so little that
it was easily carried on the shoulders of men from one stream
to another. Thus, when these intrepid navigators found the river
channel closed by an impassable barrier, the boat was unloaded,
the freight which had previously been formed into suitable packages for the purpose, was carried round the obstruction by the
boatmen. The boat itself performed the same journey, and then
was again launched in its proper element. So also, when a river
had been traced up to its sources, and no longer furnished sufficient water for navigation, the accommodating bark canoe, like
some amphibious monster, forsook the nearly exhausted channel
and traveled across the land to the nearest navigable stream. By
this simple but admirable contrivance, the fur trade was secured,
the great continent of North America was penetrated to its center
through thousands of miles of wilderness, and a valuable staple
brought to the marts of commerce.

If we regard that little boat as the means of bringing to market this great mass of the treasurers of the wilderness, we may
well remark that never was an important object effected by means
so insignificant. But the human labor, and peril, and exposure—
the courage, the enterprise, and the skill employed, were far from
insignificant. The results were great. Besides the vast trade which
was developed, the interior of a great Continent was explored,
the boundaries between two empires were traced out and inci-
dentally established. An intercourse with the Indian tribes was
opened, and valuable facts were added to the treasures of science.
And all this was accomplished, not by the power of an empire,

not by the march of a conqueror impelled by military ambition or the lust of conquest—not by a lavish expenditure of money, or the shedding of human blood—but by the action of humble individuals acting under the great stimulus of exploration, adventure and commercial enterprise." —James Hall: *The West, Its Commerce and Navigation 1848*

"THE LEGEND OF NORTH BEND"
[Along the Ohio Shore-line]
By James Hall

"It will be recollected, that when the shores of the Ohio River were first explored by the adventurous pioneers, as villages were found upon them; not a solitary lodge was seen along its secluded waters. The numerous and war-like tribes whose battle-cry was often heard on the frontier, inhabited the tributary branches of the Ohio; leaving the immediate shores of that river an untenanted wilderness, rich in the glorious productions of nature, and animated only by the brute and the wild bird; by the lurking hunter and the stealthy war-party.

A few adventurous pioneers from Pennsylvania, Virginia, and North Carolina, had crossed the Alleghenies and settled at different place far distant from each other, but these also were inland as respected the great River; the civilized man avoiding its dangerous shores on the one side, from an instinct similar to that which induced the Indian to shun a residence upon them on the other.

All the tribes inhabiting the country north of the Ohio were at that time hostile to the American people, and beheld with great jealousy these migrations into the west that indicated an intention to plant a civilized population on this side of the mountains. The agents also of a foreign (British) power, which saw with dissatisfaction the growing prosperity of the United States, deemed this a favorable moment to unite the savage tribes against our young republic, and they were accordingly instructed to address such arguments to the chiefs who would be likely to effect that object. Councils were accordingly held, and arms and trinkets distributed by those adversaries. In consequence of these efforts, the hostile feelings of the savages, already sufficiently bitter, became greatly excited, and at the period of which we write, a war with the combined forces of the north-western tribes seemed inevitable.

The policy of the American government was pacific. They did not aim at conquest. They desired to extend to the savages within their borders the same justice by which their foreign relations were intended to be governed. Difficult as this proposition might seem, it was not deemed impracticable. That the enterprising and intelligent population of the United States would spread out from the seaboard over the wilderness; that the savage must retire before civilized man; that the *desert* must be reclaimed from a state of nature, and be subjected to the hand of art, were propositions too evident to be concealed or denied. Had the government been disposed to perpetuate the reign of barbarism over the fairest portion of our country, it could not have enforced its decree for a purpose so inconsistent with the interests of the people, and the spirit of the age. But it never was intended that the Indian should be driven from his hunting grounds by violence, and while a necessity, as strong as the law of nature…gave dominion to art, industry, and religion, it was always proposed that the savage should be removed by negotiation, and a just price given for the relinquishment of his possessory title.

Had these counsels prevailed, humanity would have been spared the anguish and humiliation for acts of deception, and weeping over scenes of bloodshed. They did not prevail: the magnanimous policy of the government remained unaltered, but many individuals have committed deep wrongs against the Indians while the latter, misled to their ruin by foreign interference, spurned at the offers of conciliation; the acceptance of which would have insured to them the strong protection of the nation." —James Hall, *Sketches of History,* 1857

"THE MISSISSIPPI VALLEY"
By M. E. Thalheimer

"North and south through the interior of this Continent stretches an immense plain, twelve hundred miles in width; the home in ancient times of vast herds of bison. Through this plain, flows the longest River in the world measuring more than two thousand miles from the head of its longest branch. It receives 57 other rivers from East and West. The natives called it Miche Sepe, the Father of Waters.

The soil of this valley is very fertile, and a great writer has declared it to be 'the most magnificent dwelling-place prepared by God for man's abode.'

The Iroquois excelled all the northern Indians in the arts of war and government. Knowing well the advantage of their position on the great waterways which lead to the interior of the continent, they made themselves feared by all their race. From Canada to the Carolinas, and from Maine to the Mississippi, Indian women trembled at the name of the Ho-de-no-sau'-nee. (People of the Long House, the name the Iroquois called themselves). Even the bravest warriors of other tribes went far out of their way in the wintry forests to avoid meeting them.

Within sixty years from the coming of the white man, the Iroquois had destroyed the Hurons; their own nearest kindred and bitterest foes, the Eries and Neutrals about Lake Erie, and the Andastes of the upper Susquehanna; while they had forced a humiliating peace upon the Lenape, or Delawares, the most powerful of the Algonquins, and had driven the Ottawas from their home upon the river which bears their name. Though then at the height of their power, they numbered only 1,200 fighting men of their own race, but they had adopted a thousand young warriors from their captives to fill the vacancies made by war and sickness....

In 1681, William Penn obtained from King Charles 11 a tract of land west of the Delaware River, instead of a large sum of money which the king owed Penn's father. Buying land of the Swedes, who had already bought it of the Indians, he laid out Philadelphia. In August of that year, it contained only three or four cottages; two years later, it numbered six hundred houses, and had a school and a printing press. The Lenni Lanape of the surrounding region had been so humbled by the Iroquois that they were not able to make war. Their hearts were touched, moreover, by the kind and just words of Penn, and the treaty which they made with Penn under the great elm tree at Shackamizon was, "The only Indian treaty never sworn to and never broken."

CHAPTER 2

Quakerism and Spiritual Advancement

"WILLIAM PENN"

By J. Bourne and E. Benton

"WILLIAM PENN WAS THE MOST PROMINENT QUAKER IN ENGLAND...He was the son of Admiral Penn who was a favorite with King Charles II. The old admiral was at first enraged when his son became a Quaker, but finally forgave him. On the death of the admiral in 1670, William inherited the family estate.

Six years later Penn purchased a share in New Jersey which had already become a refuge for distressed Quakers who settled mostly along the Delaware River. Many Puritans had also come in from Connecticut and had selected farms in northern New Jersey.

Meanwhile Penn had become interested in another form of colony building which he called his *Holy Experiment*. As King Charles owed him money borrowed from his father, Penn asked for a grant of land west of the Delaware and north of Maryland. He proposed to call the country...Sylvania. The king granted the land and insisted, in honor of Admiral Penn: *Pennsylvania.*

Penn expected to find many settlers among the persecuted Quakers, but he wished also to obtain other industrious persons. In order to attract them to his colony, he prepared an *Account of the Province of Pennsylvania* which he sent to many places in the British Isles. He had it translated into French, German and Dutch, so that enterprising Europeans might come to America and join the colony.

Penn was proprietor of his colony. Through councils and assemblies, he planned to share the management of the colony with the settlers. In the laws which he drew up, he showed that he was far ahead of most men of his day. For example, prisoners were not to be tormented and starved as they were in English prisons at that time, but were to be fed and clothed.

The Founding of Philadelphia in 1682

Quakers from his own neighborhood in England arrived. Others of the early settlers came from Wales and Ireland...The first party of colonists selected a site for a town about one hundred and twenty miles up the Delaware River. Broad streets and squares were laid out in a grove of pine trees on a low bluff along the river front. Penn called his town Philadelphia, a Greek word meaning, "Brotherly love."

'Penn drew settlers from many parts of Europe. All forms of belief were free in Pennsylvania. Superstitions were met by that calm good sense which is their only cure. Only one trial for witchcraft ever took place: the prisoner, a Swede, was set free after trial, though censured for disorderly conduct.' —*Thalheimer*

Penn's colony grew rapidly. As the lands about Philadelphia were soon taken, later comers scattered along the Delaware River within the limits of Delaware and eastern Pennsylvania.

One of the earlier settlers wrote an account of his experiences:

'I settled upon my tract of land which I purchased of the Proprietor…and set up a house and a corn mill which was very useful to the country for several miles around. But there not being plenty of horses, people generally brought their corn on their own backs many miles. I remember one man who had a bull so gentle that he used to bring his corn on him instead of on a horse or on his back.'

Penn was obliged to return to England in 1684. Most matters of government were left to the colonists.

'The colony flourished; their proprietor became poor. He had spent all his fortune in carrying on his great *Experiment*. Many settlers refused to pay the low rent which he asked. He went to jail in his old age for debt.' —*Thalheimer*

'The Colony of Pennsylvania was founded on principles of greater freedom than any of the others. It was in Philadelphia that the delegates of the Colonies discussed and signed The Declaration of Independence' —*Everit Brown*

Among the earlier bands of settlers were twelve or thirteen German families, mostly weavers. They bought a tract of land a few miles north of the town, and began the settlement known as *Germantown.*

The first settlements had been made on the coast or on the banks of some bay or river at a place which sea-going ships might reach. As the population increased, the better lands soon were taken up, and newcomers as well as enterprising young men and women of the older settlements, left the coast and moved farther up the rivers.

German and Swiss Emigrants

Events in England and Europe continued to drive many persons to America. Thousands emigrated from Germany and Switzerland...

Most of the Germans went to Pennsylvania. By the opening of the Revolutionary War, over 100,000 Germans lived in Pennsylvania, and made up more than a third of the population...From Pennsylvania, many Germans moved southward along the Appalachian ridges until they reached the fertile lands of the beautiful Shenandoah Valley in Virginia...

Many Scotch-Irish went to America because the Irish woolen industry was ruined by English laws which prevented the export of Irish woolen goods.

It was not long before the foremost emigrants were pushing westward into the valleys sloping into Tennessee. Among those who came from Pennsylvania was the father of Daniel Boone...

Scotch-Irish people formed fully a third of the settlers of Pennsylvania, Delaware and North Carolina, and a half of South Carolina. Germans and Scotch-Irish emigrants soon filled the back country with little settlements. Their eyes ever turned toward newer lands beyond the ridges which hemmed them in. They were the first to bear the brunt of Indian attacks."

"THE NATURE OF QUAKERISM"[1]

By Howard Brinton

"The Society of Friends (Quakers) began in the middle of the Seventeenth Century as part of the religious revolution...The type of Quakerism described here is that which prevailed through the first two centuries of the Society's existence...

The primary doctrine of the Society of Friends declares that the presence of God is in everyone who comes into the world; is felt at the apex of the human soul, and that man can therefore know and heed God directly, without any intermediary in the form of church, priest, sacrament, or sacred book. God is for man both immanent and transcendent. *Immanent* because He is not mechanically operating on man from without, but sharing in his life; *transcendent,* for the Divine Life extends infinitely beyond and above all human life.

Many figures of speech are used to designate this Divine Presence: Light, Power, Word, Seed of the Kingdom, Christ within, that of God in every man.

He was the true light that lights everyone who comes into the world. —John 1-9

---

1   Permission to quote from the article, courtesy of Pendle Hill.

God dwells in man to guide him and transform him into the likeness of His Son. Man's endeavor should be to merge his will with the Divine Will as far as he is able to comprehend it, and by obedience to the Divine Will, to become an instrument through which God's power works upon the world. To seek such a goal is to seek to be an embodiment of Divine Life. In this search, man's life acquires unity and purpose.

Such a doctrine is not peculiar to Quakerism nor even to Christianity. It has existed in various forms in all the great religions of the world. In different ages and in different places, the experience of the Presence of God has been described in essentially the same terms. This in itself is evidence of its validity and reality. All human beings have had some measure of this experience, whether they are aware of its nature or not. All persons are therefore infinitely valuable, and all can be appealed to as capable of right action...

There has been much individual philanthropy in the *Society of Friends*. During and after almost every war in Europe and America for the past three centuries, *Friends* have been engaged in some form of relief work...

Friends gave up their slaves in America nearly a century before the Civil War.

In Colonial America, they were in control politically for a long period of time in four of the Colonies: Pennsylvania, New Jersey, Rhode Island, Delaware, and for a short period in North Carolina. They did much to prepare the way for democracy.

As one fixed price for an article of merchandise was more honest and simpler than haggling over the price, Quaker merchants initiated the one-price system. Simplicity was mainly propagated by integrity in business dealings and plainness of living." —*H. Brinton*

George Fox, Founder of the Quaker Religion

"Many *Friends* that were tradesmen of several sorts, lost their customers at first, for the people were shy of them and would not trade with them; so that for a time some *Friends* could hardly get money enough to buy bread. But afterwards, people came to have experiences of their honesty and faithfulness: that they kept to a word in their dealings, and would not cozen and cheat, and if a child was sent to their shops for anything, he was as well-treated as his parents.

Then the lives and conversation of *Friends* became a witness of God to the people, and things altered so that all the inquiry became: where to find a draper or a shop-keeper, or a tailor, or a shoemaker, or any other tradesman that is a Quaker. In so much that *Friends* had more trade than many of their neighbors. Then the envious professors altered their note, and began to cry out, "If we let these Quakers alone, they will take the trade of the Nation out of our hands." — *The Journal of George Fox*

GEORGE WASHINGTON'S *reply to an address sent by the Religious Society called Quakers from their yearly meeting... September 28, 1789:*

"Your principles and conduct are well-known to me, and it is doing the people called Quakers no more than justice to say that, except their declining to share with others the burden of the common defense, there is no denomination among us who are more exemplary and useful citizens."

"ROBERT BARCLAY" (1648-1690)

By Rufus Jones

"Robert Barclay, a Scotchman of distinguished family and of refined and extensive learning, became the greatest early interpreter of the Quaker conception, publishing the first edition of his *Apology for the True Christian Divinity, of a People called Quakers* in 1678. It was an epoch-making book both for the challenge it made to Christian scholars everywhere, and even more for the effect it produced during the next two centuries upon *Friends* themselves." [Barclay became Governor for life of the provinces of New Jersey.]

(from) An Apology for the True Christian Divinity...

Proposition II: Of Immediate Revelation

ROBERT BARCLAY: "Let such know, that the secret light which shines in the heart, and reproves unrighteousness, is the small beginning of the revelation of God's Spirit which was first sent into the world to reprove it of sin. (John 16-8)...And as by forsaking iniquity by minding this light in their own consciences, one comes to be acquainted with that Heavenly *Voice* in thy heart...I say, you shall feel the new person, or the Spiritual birth which has its Spiritual sense...but till then, the knowledge of things Spiritual is but as an historical faith."

Propositions V and VI: Of Universal and Saving Light:

..."That God, in and by this Light, calls, exhorts and strives with everyone in order to save them; which as it is received and not resisted, works the salvation of all, even of those who are ignorant of the death and sufferings of Christ, and of Adam's fall. Therefore, it is a constant incitement and provocation, and lively encouragement to everyone, to forsake evil and to choose that which is good...

There was hardly a man found in any place on the earth, however barbarous and wild, but has acknowledged, that at some time or other, he has found something in his heart reproving him for some things evil which he has done; threatening a certain horror if he continued in them, as also promising and communicating a certain peace, as he has given way to it and not resisted it. It wonderfully shows the excellent wisdom of God by which He has made the means of salvation so universal and comprehensive; that it is not needful to recur to those miraculous and strange ways seeing, according to this most true doctrine, the *gospel* reaches all of any condition, age or nation...

The Scriptures everywhere declares the mercy of God to be, in that He invites and calls sinners to repentance, and has opened a way of salvation for them; so that though those men be not bound to believe the history of Christ's death and passion who never came to know of it, yet they are bound to believe that God will be merciful to them, if they follow His ways; and that he is merciful unto them in that he reproves them for evil and encourages them to good.

This Light or Grace is a real Spiritual substance which the soul of man is capable to sense and apprehend, from which that real, Spiritual inward birth in believers arises, called *the new creature*, *the new person* in the heart. This seems strange to carnal-minded men, because they are not acquainted with it, but we know it, and are sensible of it by a true and certain experience; though it be hard for a person in the natural wisdom to comprehend, until he comes to the experience in himself.

This then, is the day of God's gracious visitation to thy soul, which if resisted not, shalt be happy forever...There is a 'will' raised in him, by which he comes to be a co-worker with the Grace; for according to that of Augustine, 'He that made us without us, will not save us without us.'

And the Lord said unto Cain, 'Why art thou wroth? And why is thy countenance fallen? Thou shall be accepted, if thou doeth well.' ...He gave a day of visitation to the old world: And the Lord said, 'My Spirit shall not always strive in man.'

...There can be no other true use assigned *the Ministry* but to lead people out of sin into righteousness. If these ministers assure us that we need never expect to be delivered from sin, do not they render their own work needless? What needs preaching against sin, for the reproving of which all preaching is, if it can never be forsaken?

...**SOCRATES** was informed by the Light in his day of the falsity of the heathen gods.

...Some confiding in an external barren faith, think all is well if they do but firmly believe that Christ died for their sins: past, present and to come; while in the meantime He is daily resisted in appearance in their hearts and minds. Blessed are they who daily go on forsaking unrighteousness. In due time they will be conquerors." —Robert Barclay

SOCRATES' MESSAGE regarding the *Light*: "The Divine Voice has been constantly with me all through my life till now, opposing me in quite small matters if I were not going to act rightly." —*The Apology of Socrates*

…"Minutes before his execution, Socrates said, 'I say, let a man be of good cheer about his soul. When the soul has been arrayed in her own proper jewels of temperance, and justice and courage, and nobility, and truth—she is ready to go on her journey when the hour comes." *(from) Plato's Phaedo*

Notable Persons of former times with sayings or poems:

1. CLEMENT OF ALEXANDRIA "A noble hymn of God is an immortal man established in righteousness, with truth engraved in his heart." (180 A D)

2. SEBASTIAN CASTELLIO "His emphasis is always on the heart's experience of God. He was extremely sensitive to the Divine Voice within his soul." (R. Jones)

3. JOHN MILTON "Obedience to the Spirit of God, rather than to the fair seeming pretense of men, is the best and most dutiful order that a Christian can observe."

    "And chiefly thou O Spirit, that dost prefer,
    Before all temples, the upright heart and pure…
    Instruct me, for Thou know'st, Thou from the first
    Was present: What in me is dark, illumine; what is low,
    raise… —*Paradise Lost.*

4. JOHN G. WHITTIER "One faith alone so broad that all mankind
    Within themselves, its secret witness find,
    The soul's communion with the Eternal Mind."

5. JEANNE GUYON "If people once came to know the operations of the Lord in souls wholly resigned to His guiding, it would fill them with reverential admiration and awe…

    If we walk uprightly, He will never fail us. He would sooner do miracles for us."

6. MARCUS AURELIUS "But my good friend, consider whether goodness and nobility are not something different from saving and being saved."

7. PLATO "The Earth, the Sun and Stars, and the Universe itself, and the charming variety of the seasons, demonstrate the existence of a Divinity."

"WHERE ARE THE QUAKERS NOW?"
By Rufus Jones

"A few words perhaps ought to be written on the unhappy and disastrous separations in American Quakerism. The first one of importance occurred in Philadelphia in 1827 when the *Friends* of Pennsylvania and New Jersey divided into branches: popularly known as The *Orthodox* and the other, *Hicksite*. The former emphasizes the Inner Light of the individual. The other tendency: Elias Hicks of Long Island instigated a powerful *Evangelical* message, and thereby a new church and title was formed: "*The Evangelical Friends* Church.""

CHAPTER 3

Advancing Spiritually

By Donna Preston

A Scripture from Daniel: 12-3, "Those who turn many to righteousness, will shine as the stars forever and ever." There are one hundred and sixty-seven listings in one concordance for *Righteousness.* Evangelicals tell us that God imputes His own righteousness to believers, yet many Scriptures speak otherwise: Psalm 106-3: "Blessed are they that do righteousness at all times." Psalm 18-20: The Lord rewarded me according to my righteousness."

When *repentance* and *placing trust* in the Lord as one's "personal Savior" are preached as fulfilling all requirements for salvation, then diligence toward self-improvement, the basic factor in advancing Spiritually, may lessen or subside. Paul wrote to Timothy, "My own son in the faith…lead a peaceable life in all uprightness and honesty; for this is good and acceptable to God, who would have everyone saved." (So like a microcosm of the New Testament).

Prevailing beliefs must be evaluated Scripturally, prior to or in accordance with the forward advance. Untruths are powerful, making a person less involved, increasingly docile, and at peace when they should be active, inquisitive and upward-striving.

There is a dependency that is, unintentionally perhaps, thrust upon a religious people who, in their hearts want to do what is right, and are capable of advancing on their own; yet not on their own exclusively perhaps, but how is it that the highest level and most intricate of God's creation; made in His own image, are urged toward mediocrity because substantial numbers from the pulpit; preachers from whom wisdom is anticipated, are saying, in essence, "Let God do it." "You cannot change yourself. "You are prone to sin." "You need God to impute His righteousness to you." Your works are useless."

The fine attribute of being *justified* is weakened by a quaint, yet vague and misleading definition: "To be justified means, just-as-if-I'd-never sinned…"

KARL ADAM: "Justification is not a mere covering over of sin. It is the communication of a true inward righteousness. It is sanctification."

GEORGE BERNANOS: "Truth is meant to save you first, and the comfort comes afterward."

"By their fruits you will know them," which may refer to good works, and/or the higher qualities of goodness and integrity, fine-tuned over time; the best of works since other people find inspiration being near those of honest heart and good intentions.

The abundance of admonitions to *do right* and *avoid wrongdoing* are something of a so-called *broad-brush word-painting* throughout the New Testament, Psalms and Proverbs.

Clergy would better serve their congregations by developing more sermons based on the New Testament, and dwell less often and less intensely on the Old Testament during these upheaval times, unless specifics would teach listeners regarding "transformation," or "become a new creature" that PAUL trended upon and in a variety of ways. He often said things like: "Strive for the mastery," "Increase in stature," "Press toward the mark for the high calling of God." He seemed to shun *the ordina*ry for himself, as well as for the 'churches.'

Those *"seekers after truth"* which truly does describe everyone attending church services, await in anticipation of being informed of the most important matters. It is a serious disservice to flatter them that God loves them unconditionally; that they cannot change themselves, and the most preposterous of all: that a person becomes a *saint* the moment they *"accept the Lord as Savior."*

One preacher told his audience of believers: *Jesus is your friend, and He wants to do great things for you.*

Teach them rather how to advance to greater heights such as, *"Grow* in favor with God and 'man.'" Only then by *trials* leading to Spiritual maturity, will the *blessings flow as* preachers promise."

"You should walk and please God that you may abound yet more and more."

"Those who receive Him have the power *to become* the sons of God." This is, in fact, looking toward the future; with a degree of inner workmanship needed in the interim. (See Romans Chapter 8 on 'sons'.)

It is not uncommon for an entire sermon to be preached on a, one-size-fits-all *Forgiveness* lecture. "God forgives all your sins," a preacher said, "in fact He doesn't even remember them, and neither should you." That is quite a reckless statement, unless time is spent on the subject of *Reparations or Restitution*. Hard and fast rules cannot be applied to all situations; therefore, Paul wrote in his letter to the ***Colossians 3-25:*** ... "He that does wrong, shall receive for the wrong he has done; and there is no respect of persons with God."

If a person collects about three to five Scriptures on the same subject, and then looks closely at them, he might have a general idea of the truth meant to be conveyed. For example, with a concordance look up, "rich." It is as difficult for a rich man to enter Heaven as it is for a "camel to pass through the eye of a needle." And a milder one: "Tell the rich to be rich in good works...that he may lay hold on eternal life." In Luke's gospel, are four other Scriptures on the subject of "rich." Coleridge wrote in his book, *Aids to Reflection*, "Everyone should have a spirit of inquiry when studying the Bible." They should refrain from exploiting that seemingly *perfect* Scripture such as the blanket statement, "He forgives all of our sins." All the while, there may be victims of that 'forgiven' individual who await some form of justice.

MATTHEW 5-23,24: "If thou bring thy gift to the altar, and there remember that thy brother hath *a matter* against thee; leave there thy gift before the altar, and go thy way; first be reconciled to thy brother, and then come and offer thy gift."

Becoming convinced, after decades of the same doctrine; that a person need do no more than commit to a trust in the Lord in order to qualify for eternity; has had the effect of complacency set-tling in, carelessness in conduct and conversation, and an unearned confidence; which may in time, lead to a plethora of "*Whys*" seek-ing answers:

"Why doesn't God answer my prayers!?" Why doesn't God give me something to do?" "Why can't I have more of the Holy Spirit?

Those grievances are *unfulfillment* crying out, and the intellect and one's future destiny yearn for an authentic substance the 'heart' can assent to; that all-important and cherished fact of *knowing they are being guided into the unbiased, life-saving, life-enhancing Truth.*

"If thou would seek after God betimes; if thou were pure and upright, surely now He would awaken for thee." (Job 8-5)

Such brief counsel, and yet one that may explain why prayers go unanswered. To reflect on the innocent *goodness* of childhood, is to understand the Scripture, "The pure in heart will see God "… And then may they apprise their own disposition, acts and/or mis-deeds to determine what corrections are needed; having the effect perhaps of kindling the interest of the Divine Power toward them. "He hears the prayers of the righteous."

2 CHRONICLES 19-3, "Nevertheless there are good things found in thee. Thou hast prepared thy heart to seek God."

THOMAS A' KEMPIS, "Christ will come unto thee, and show thee His consolations, if thou prepare for Him a worthy mansion within thee."

ZEPHANIAH 2-3: "Seek righteousness that it may be, you shall be hid in the day of the Lord's anger."

"Labor to become acceptable to Him." "Be you transformed by the renewing of your mind," "If you keep my Commandments, you will abide in my love." "The effectual fervent prayer of a righteous person avails much."

"The Scriptures are profitable…
for instruction in Righteousness."
Righteousness is the key subject in Paul's Epistle to *the Romans*.

The following Scripture in Peter's second Epistle, reveals requirements for salvation that reach significantly beyond the accepted norm of "believing," or "trusting in the Lord."

2 PETER 1 "He gives us all things that pertain to life and godliness; therefore, giving all diligence, add to your faith: virtue, and to virtue, knowledge, and to knowledge, temperance, and to temperance, patience, and to patience, goodness, …kindness and…charity. If these things are in you and abound, you will never be unfruitful… If you do these things, you will never fall, for so an entrance shall be opened unto you into the everlasting Kingdom of our Lord."

Tabitha was known for "good works and alms deeds which she did." She died, and was restored to life by Peter, who had kneeled and prayed to God.

"Peter said, 'Tabitha, rise.' When she saw Peter, she sat up. He gave her his hand, and lifted her up. And then he called the saints and widows and presented her alive." (Book of Acts)

"Good Works" (and how their image took a down-turn.)

It is far better to be over-prepared than to find oneself overly confident that salvation is to be gained at so little cost in effort or inconvenience. *James* stated: "What does it profit though a person says he has faith and has not works; can faith save him?" Also: "A person is justified by works and not by faith only." The value placed on good works is that of *dismissive* in some circles, and the following Scripture is the one most often blamed:

TITUS 3-5: "Not by *works of righteousness* we have done, but according to His mercy, He saved us…" (Those 'works' refer to *the Jewish Law*).

ACTS 10-34: "Of a truth, I perceive that God is no respecter of persons, but in every nation, he that fears Him and *works righteousness* is accepted of Him."

TITUS 3-8: "These things I will that thou affirm constantly, that they who have believed in God might be careful to maintain good works. These things are good and profitable unto men."

One of *the best* Scriptures to clarify that *not of works* refers to the Jewish Law, includes in the same sentence, a positive reference to *good works*, thus the distinction is made:

"By grace are you saved through faith, and that not of your-
selves, it is a gift of God, *not of works*, lest anyone should
boast, because we are his workmanship created unto <u>good
works;</u> which God has ordained that we should walk in
them." (Ephesians 2: 8-10)

ROMANS' CHAPTERS 3 AND 4 expound on faith compared to the
works of the Law, and those "works of the Law," stated as *not of
works*, are often applied to <u>good works</u>.

Positive references to good works and fruit bearing are numerous throughout the New Testament and Psalms.

On the Imputation of *Righteousness*

A few words on the popular notion that we must have God's righteousness "imputed" to us.

SCRIPTURES THAT REFUTE THIS: "The fruit of the righteous is a
tree of life." "The righteous person regards the life of his animals."
(They protect small dogs from the anguish of toy-like handling by
young children). "It shall be *our* righteousness if we do those things
that He commands of us." (Such as:) "Fathers do not provoke your
children, lest they become discouraged."

ROMANS 4: "Abraham was reckoned the father of all those that
believe, that righteousness might be *imputed* to others also who
walk in the steps of that faith of Abraham..."

ABRAHAM'S *WALK:* JAMES 2: "Was not Abraham justified by works when he had *offered Isaac, his son, upon the altar?* See how faith wrought with his work and by works was faith made perfect, and the Scripture was fulfilled which says, 'Abraham *believed* God and it was *imputed* unto Him for righteousness.' You see then how that by works a person is justified, and not by faith only."

(Believing and obeying are sometimes used signifying the combination is assumed): 1 PETER 2-8: "Unto you who *believe*, he is precious, but unto the *disobedient*...a stone of stumbling.".

HEBREWS 11-8: "By faith Abraham, when he was called to go out into a place which he should after receive for an inheritance, *obeyed* not knowing whither he went."

In studying even lightly, the New Testament, a person learns that the *way to Salvation* has many directives, and is not limited to a sentence here or there, removed from its rightful place; separated from the ongoing subject at hand, and thereafter extolled as a stand-alone doctrine to be added to other Scriptures retrieved in the same manner; with the result of a handy list Scriptures with which to preach Salvation or to *Witness for Christ*.

JOHN 3-16: The Most Famous and Most Often-Quoted Scripture

"For God so loved the world that He gave His only begotten Son, that whosoever believes in Him should not perish, but have everlasting life."

JOHN 3-16, 18 *Believing* being considered the essence of salvation: Not giving attention to JOHN 3-19, 20, 21 diminishes somewhat the full definition of 3-16 and 3-18 which states 'He that believes on Him is not condemned, but he that believes not is condemned already'...and the above three Scriptures: *"And this is the condemnation: that Light is come into the world, and people loved darkness better than light because their deeds were evil, but he that does good, comes to the light that his deeds may be manifest; that they are approved of God."*

This clarification places goodness on a level equal to and imperative to the that of believing.

Other Scriptures in the GOSPEL OF JOHN that reveal responsibilities for salvation; other than, or in accordance with *believing*:

JOHN 5-25, 29: "The hour is coming when the dead will hear the voice of the Son of God, and all in the graves shall come forth...Those who have done good unto the resurrection of life."

JOHN 8-51: "If a person keeps my sayings, he will never see death."

JOHN 10-27: "My sheep hear my voice, and I know them and they follow me, and I give unto them eternal life."

1 John 5-13

1 JOHN 5-13: One of the main Scriptures incorporated by proponents of "Believing saves."

The following, *1 John 5-13*, is toned down by the qualifier, "does His will," as noted in *1 John 2-17.*

1 JOHN 5-13: "These things I have written to you that believe on the name of the Son of God; that you may know that you have eternal life."

1 JOHN 2-17 "The world passes away, but he that *does the will* of God abides forever."

3 JOHN: "Beloved, follow not that which is evil, but follow that which is good. He that does good is of God."

The Philippian 'keeper of the prison' (another popular doctrine).

'ACTS' 16-30, 32: The *Jailor* asked: "Sirs, what must I do to be saved?" And they said, **"Believe on the Lord Jesus, and thou shalt be saved, and thy house."** And they spoke unto them the word of the Lord and to all who were in his house. (*The word spoken*, certainly must have addressed other requirements that Paul included in his Philippian Epistle)

PAUL'S *Epistle to the Philippians:* 2-12-13: "As you have always obeyed… work out your own salvation; for it is God working in you, both to will and to do of his good pleasure."

PREACHERS SHOULD REFRAIN FROM PROMOTING the THEORY that *BELIEVING SAVES SOULS.*

Each person, when approached by those who say they are *witnesses for Christ,* should be prepared as enlightened educators in their own right. "There are apostles, there are teachers," who were not obscure or reclusive in such matters. A few relevant Scriptures committed to memory, will give pause to those so firmly equipped with one-line Scripture 'gems,' ready at a moment's notice to "save souls for Christ."

> *The electrician was packing his tools, ready to leave, when he said, "You know, you have to be born again if you want to be saved." She replied, "Those who do righteousness are born again." He said, "Yeah, will, people say a lot of things." She said, "It's in John's Epistle."*

A Collection of Relevant Counter-Scriptures
"Not everyone who says, 'Lord, Lord' will enter the Kingdom of Heaven, but they who do the will of my Father who is in Heaven." (Matthew 7)

"You believe there is one God, thou doest well, the devils also believe and tremble, but will thou know, O vain man, that faith without works is dead?" (James 2)

"Charge them that are rich in this world...that they do good, are rich in good works, ready to distribute, willing to communicate... that they may lay hold on eternal life." (1 Timothy 6)

"To those, who in well-doing seek immortality, Eternal life." (Romans 2)

"Know you not that the unrighteous will not inherit the Kingdom of God?" (1 Corinthians 6

"The grace of God that brings Salvation has appeared unto all, teaching us that denying ungodliness, we should live soberly and righteously in this present world." (Titus 2)

In the following instructions to **TIMOTHY** on responsibilities for salvation, Paul did not address *believing; rather, he was firm about goodness and integrity being essential traits.*

1. "Son Timothy, lead a quiet and peaceable life in all godliness and honesty, for this is good and acceptable to God who would have everyone saved.
2. Bodily exercise profits for a little time, but goodness is profitable unto all things, having promise of the life that now is, and of that which is to come.
3. Follow after righteousness, goodness, faith, patience, gentleness; laying hold on eternal life."

JOHN WESLEY

Out of his early life and teaching.

"He that believes not is condemned already, and so long as he believes not, that condemnation cannot be removed...Whatever good works he may do, it profits not; he is still under the curse until he believes in Jesus. He has no righteousness at all antecedent to this, but faith is imputed to him for righteousness the very moment he believes. He counts us righteous from the time we believe in Him; treats us as though we were guiltless and righteous. God sanctifies as well as justifies all them that believe in Him. The righteousness of Christ is imputed to every believer."

(The above commentary on Salvation-by-believing, has been valid and in working mode for two centuries, yet the following *omnipresent* gospel instruction by Jesus Himself, does not seem to spark a dispute, at least not in recent times.)

MARK 10-17: "And when He was gone forth into the way, there came one running and kneeled to Him and asked, 'Good Master, what shall I do that I may inherit *eternal life?*' Jesus said unto him...Thou know the commandments. Do not commit adultery, do not kill, do not steal, do not bear false witness, do not defraud others. Give to the poor and you shall have treasure in Heaven."

WESLEY...
Advanced in Spiritual Insight

"Everyone has some measure of that Light; some faint glimmering ray which sooner or later, more or less, enlightens every person who comes into the world. And everyone, unless he is of that small number whose conscience is seared with a hot iron, feels more or less uneasy when he acts contrary to the light of his own conscience.

Therefore, inasmuch as God works in you, you are now able to work out your own salvation. Since He works in you of His own good pleasure, both to will and to do, it is possible for you to fulfill all righteousness.

God works in you; therefore, you must work. You must be workers together with Him, otherwise He will cease working. Even St. Augustine makes that just remark, 'He that made us without ourselves will not save us without ourselves.' He will not save us unless we fight the good fight of faith, and lay hold on eternal life."

'ROMANS' CHAPTER 6
6-23 is perhaps second only to John 3-16 of Scriptures to "lead others to Christ."

"Since Christ died for our sins, we should reckon ourselves dead unto sin. As He was raised from the dead, we should reckon ourselves alive also, and walk in newness of life."

Many people take Chapter 5 as the end of the matter on salvation; now having a Savior who paid for our sins, reconciling us to God, and that all we need to do now is to receive Him into our hearts.

THE EVANGELICAL STATEMENT: "Salvation is a gift offered to every sinner, but it is a gift that must be received. *Romans 6-23 says: 'The wages of sin is death, but the gift of God is eternal life through Jesus.' In order to be saved, you must personally receive Jesus as your Savior.'"

Omitted or slighted is a very important condition in this Chapter: *"Yield to (follow) righteousness; righteousness leads to holiness and holiness (goodness) leads to Eternal life."* To increase in righteousness, is to advance toward salvation. To assume a *gift* without some responsibility, can lead to stoicism, a pseudo-confidence, and/or a half-hearted commitment.

FROM PETER'S EPISTLE: "**He bore our sins on the tree that we should live unto righteousness**; for the eyes of the Lord are over the righteous…and He hears their prayers. And who will harm you if you follow that which is good."

WILLIAM LAW: "It would be strange to suppose that mankind were redeemed by the sufferings of their Savior, to live in ease and softness themselves."

"ON 'ROMANS' CHAPTER 6"
By Martin Luther

"Throughout our lives, we shall be kept fully employed with our own selves, taming our body… controlling its members till they obey, not the passions, but the Spirit…It is one thing to be provoked of temptation, and yet not willing to yield to it. To walk after the leading of the Spirit…is optimum."

'ROMANS' CHAPTER 7

Paul (and St. Augustine)

Gaining the **VICTORY OVER SIN** was his goal. The deliverance from the temptation to sin, and not the deliverance that forgiveness implies, was his heartfelt desire.

He had the will, but the 'performance' thereof eluded him. He yearned for that *righteousness which leads to eternal life.*

PAUL WROTE: "The good that I would do, I do not; The evil I would not do, that I do....I delight in the law of God after the inward man, but I see another law in my members, warring against the law of my mind, and bringing me into captivity to the law of sin which is in my members... Oh, wretched man that I am, who will deliver me from this body of death? I thank God through Jesus. So then with *the mind I serve God, but with the flesh, I serve sin.*"

"The walk in newness of Life" (Chapter 6), now advances to, "Serve in newness of the Spirit." (Chapter 8)

RABBI NAHMAN OF BRATSLAV: "By withdrawing into dialogue with God, man can attain the complete abandonment of his passions and evil habits..."

GALATIANS 5-6: "Walk in the Spirit, and you will not fulfill the deeds of the flesh."

JOHN EVERARD: "If you turn the man loose who has found the living Guide with him, then let him neglect the outward if he can."

EVANGELICAL INTERPRETATION OF CHAPTER 7:

"Who will deliver me? ...I thank God, through Jesus (His sacrifice saves, they emphasize, rather than the Holy Spirit as their guide advancing toward righteousness.)

"Sin is inevitable," they say, and quote *1 John: "If we say we have no sin, we lie."* Believers are advised to: "Lay your sins at the feet of Jesus because His blood cleanses us from all sin."

John's Epistle reveals that a tendency to sin can be overcome.
"Everyone who does righteousness is born of God."
"Whosoever is born of God does not commit sin."

ST. AUGUSTINE (BY JOHN LORD): "Augustine...had a double nature; strong yet sensual from his sins. *The law of his members warred against the law of his mind.* In agonies he, (quoting Paul), cried out, 'Oh wretched man that I am! Who shall deliver me from the body of this death?'"

AUGUSTINE'S BOOK, "CONFESSIONS OF AUGUSTINE": "...And Thou sent Thine hand from above, and drew my soul out of that profound darkness. My mother, thy faithful one, weeping to Thee for me... For she, by that faith and Spirit which she had from Thee, discerned the death wherein I lay, and thou heard her, O Lord, Thou heard her, and despised not her tears, when streaming down, they watered the ground...."

I read that section [Romans 13:13,14] on which my eyes first fell. 'Not in rioting and drunkenness, not in chambering and wantonness, not in strife and envying, but put on the Lord Jesus, and make no provision for the flesh.'"

(John Lord continued): "Augustine lived the doctrines that he preached. He became affable, courteous, accessible, full of sympathy and kindness...He ascribed all his triumphs to Divine assistance, and his mother's prayers."

'ROMANS' CHAPTER 8

Furthering Paul's determination to gain the victory over sin, and resolving finally: "With the *mind*, I serve God..."

CHAPTER 8: "There is therefore now no condemnation to those who walk, not after the flesh but after the Spirit."

A BRIEF SUMMARY OF CHAPTER 8:

"You are not in the flesh but in the Spirit, if the Spirit of God dwells in you.

And if Christ is in you, the Spirit is life, [active] because of righteousness [advancing]

We are debtors not to live after the flesh, but if you, through the Spirit, do mortify the deeds of the body, you shall live; for as many as are guided by the Spirit of God, they are the sons of God.

The Spirit itself bears witness with our spirit, that we are the children of God; and if children, then heirs of God and joint-heirs with Christ.

The Spirit makes intercession for us according to the will of God.

The Spirit helps our infirmities."

EVANGELICAL BELIEFS:

"Appropriating the gifts of God are their reward for repenting and placing their trust in Jesus as their "personal Savior."

They are proclaimed to be Saints *as believers* by preachers, who assure them that the Holy Spirit dwells within them… (although in Chapter 6, "Yielding to or obeying righteousness leads to holiness and eternal life,") Their emphasis being placed firmly on 6-23: the *gift*.

In "Mortifying the deeds of the body" and, "The Spirit is life because of righteousness," they say that Jesus imputes His own righteousness to believers. They accept as is conveyed in sermons, that being led by the Spirit, they are "sons or daughters of God, and joint-heirs with Christ."

MANY DO QUESTION those assurances that the Holy Spirit is guiding them; acknowledging having had no consciousness of Jesus' presence. A common reply from the pulpit is, "You cannot rely on your feelings."

(There are many people who seem to 'do by nature,' those things which are right and acceptable and good.)

1 JOHN: "He that keeps His Commandments, dwells in Him and He in them, and hereby we know he abides in us, by the Spirit He has given us."

BLAISE PASCAL: "It is the heart that experiences God and not the reason. Those to whom God imparts Spiritual insight are very fortunate and justly convinced."

MARY WOOLEY: "I cannot quite understand how a person can face life without a belief in a Supreme Power, a personality where communion can be a real thing."

'ROMANS' CHAPTERS 9 AND 10

CHAPTERS 9 AND 10 were written by Paul, *exclusively* for his brethren, *the Israelites*, who were content to abide in their Law's ordinances; presuming by doing so, they were "fulfilling all righteousness."

Paul saw 'grave' misconceptions in this, stating, "I have great heaviness and continual sorrow in my heart, for I could wish myself were accursed from Christ for my brethren, my kinsmen. The Gentiles... have attained to the righteousness which is of faith, but Israel has not attained to righteousness. Why? Because they sought it by the works of the Law."

In keeping the subject of *righteousness* in the forefront, Paul's quest now, above all, was to direct his brethren on the pathway to righteousness by faith.

Paul wrote, "The word is nigh unto thee, in thy mouth and in thy heart; that is the word of faith which we preach: *10-9,10 "That if thou shall confess with thy mouth the Lord Jesus and shall believe in thy heart that God has raised Him from the dead, thou shall be saved. For with the heart a person believes unto righteousness."*

It is not *confessing and believing* that *saves* a person, but righteousness advancing in the Spiritual walk; which is exactly what 'faith' presumes. As stated in Chapter 8: "If you, through the Spirit [in cooperation with], 'mortify' the deeds of the body, then 'The Spirit is life' (alive within) because of righteousness [ever more advancing].

Paul alluded to the fact that faith (believing) presumes righteousness. In his letter to the Corinthians: "Be not unequally yoked together with unbelievers, for what fellowship has righteousness with unrighteousness."

(FROM) PAUL'S LETTER TO THE EPHESIANS
Providing more detail on the Spiritual walk

"We both, Jew and Gentile, have access by one Spirit unto the Father. The building, fitly framed together, grows unto a holy Temple for a habitation of God through the Spirit...Walk not as other Gentiles in the vanity of their minds, their understanding darkened; alienated from God...having given over to lasciviousness. You are not so, learned Christ, if that you have heard Him, and been taught by Him. Put on the new person created in righteousness...Put aside malice, wrath, stealing, lying, clamor, evil speaking; for no unclean person has any inheritance in the Kingdom of God. Grieve not the Holy Spirit.

Walk as children of light; for the fruit of the Spirit is in all goodness and righteousness and truth, proving what is acceptable to the Lord. Walk circumspectly as the wise."

(FROM) RALPH W. EMERSON'S 1837 DIVINITY SCHOOL ADDRESS

"The Divine Bards are the friends of my intellect, of my virtue. They admonish me that the gleams which flash across my mind are not mine, but are of God. That they had the like, and were not disobedient to the Heavenly vision. Noble provocations go out from them inviting me to resist evil, to subdue evil, and to be; and thus by his holy thoughts Jesus serves us and thus only. To aim to convert a person by miracles, is a profanation of the soul. Only by coming again to oneself or to God in themselves, can they grow forevermore. It is of low benefit to give me something; it is of high benefit to enable me to do somewhat of myself. The time is coming when all people will see that the gift of God to the soul is not a vaunting, overpowering, excluding sanctity, but a sweet, natural goodness. A goodness like thine and mine, and that invites thine and mine to be and to grow."

WILLIAM KINGSLAND: "Intellect, we shall put in its proper place as complementary to the subjective life of the Spirit."

(FROM) ROMANS CHAPTERS 12,14
A Conclusion

"I beseech you therefore brethren, …that you present your bodies a living sacrifice, holy and acceptable unto God, and be not conformed to the world, but be transformed that you may prove what is that good and acceptable will of God."

12-3: "Abhor that which is evil, cleave to that which is good…Be not slothful in business; provide things honest in the sight of all."

12-23: "Be not overcome of evil, but overcome evil with good."

14-10,11,12: "We shall all stand before the judgment seat of Christ. For it is written, 'As I live, saith the Lord, every knee shall bow to me, and every tongue shall confess to God.' So then, every one of us shall give an account to God."

"STRIVE FOR THE MASTERY"

…Need not pertain only to lofty endeavors. The pathway toward the higher level of a Spiritual nature, is in doing what is right even in matters seemingly small, but consequential.

"One in five children diagnosed with cancer, will not survive:" A prominent announcement by the Cancer Society. That is an emergency call.

People seek hope, so where do they turn? The next line of defense is THE FAMILY, and looking within is where they should have been in trusting themselves to act rightly; with prevention uppermost, at all times.

Store bathroom and kitchen cleaners on a metal shelf unit in the garage in easy reach, perhaps. Identify particle board, or veneers, glues, carpet backing, even magazines that may be subtly emitting chemical odors and clean, isolate, replace or perhaps seal them. Change air in the house often. Wash new clothing two or more times and air them outdoors until free of suspicious scents.

Healthier Children

Place a shield of protection, first by apprising the quality of food consumed on any given day. How many *chips* or sugary pastries or frosted-type cereals take valuable internal space that organic fruit; and a fine stew; several fresh vegetables and chunks of meat in a stir-fry; or other hearty meals should take. A burger patty and French toast with maple syrup in the morning will prevent mid-morning hunger pangs and address *attention deficit syndrome* the natural way.

Closer monitoring and interceding where needed, may change the direction from an underweight, pale, low in energy; perhaps irritable child to one who becomes more interested in life around him.

Throughout three-quarters of the span of U.S. history, **the backyard garden** was the norm rather than the exception, and often, the family owned a cow. A boy would call for the neighborhood cows in the morning, lead them to pasture, and drive them home again at evening-time for milking. Those who did not have cows bought milk from those who did.

Even young children will take pride that their efforts helped to create a garden. New sights for them:

Those cucumbers and zucchini they see in the grocery, actually were attached to vines that spread about the garden patch. Green beans dangle from a bush, or another type will climb a trellis. Tomatoes are juicer than store-bought, add color, and how nice that carrots, radishes and onions can be pulled knowing that the soil is 'pure,' The lettuce row looks fresh and bright and no 'recalls' await them.

Green caterpillars will be found feeding on cabbage or broccoli leaves. Children can place them in a container, (a screen on top) with the leaves. They will form a chrysalis and during a week or so, transform into white ('sulfur') butterflies. After hatching, they flutter about the yard for a day or more.

In consuming better quality food, there should be reduced or eliminated allergies, higher energy levels, fewer colds; perhaps an improvement in grades. (And money saved on packaging).

No one really knows what all nutrients are lost in commercially-produced food trucked about, or how GMOs affect food quality and safety. Gaining experience in gardening, raising enough to freeze certain items, and pride is earned, because when scarcities occur, they will be heads-up toward independence.

"Be humble," the preachers tell us, but Shakespeare said: "Self-love my liege, is not so great a sin as self-neglecting."

"INCREASE IN STATURE"

It takes work staying mentally active if retired or unemployed. We are advised to "labor to become acceptable to Him." "Grow in favor with God and man." "Become a new person" "Increase in stature" "Grow in righteousness." If the mind fails, and is due to non-compliance in the things a person should be doing to stay mentally strong, then the prognosis is predictable; the above exhortations lie inert, unfulfilled.

A person can be in assisted living, and read interesting, somewhat challenging books or articles; thereby having something to say to staff or family; and she/he is still in the 'battle of life,' contributing tokens of a pleasant personality.

In order to thwart the decline in mental acuity: *mental exercise and nutritious food, along with optimum posture,* top the list of primary interceptors to dementia.

Zealousness is not too emphatic a word for implementing all that can be done. It is crucial, it is life-saving, and it is primarily the responsibility of the afflicted person before forgetfulness becomes irreversible; and the burden falls on family and society.

Everyone knows when his/her memory is slipping, and would do well in thwarting those mundane reflections on the past that do not stimulate formation of new brain cells, nor do repetitive reminiscences, along with other poor health habits preserve old brain cells.

(FROM) THE BOOK OF PROVERBS:
"The heart of him that *hath understanding*, seeks knowledge."
"...A person of knowledge increases strength."
"Knowledge is pleasant to thy soul."

MEMORIZE several lines of poetry, and recite them when waiting in line. With practice, a person will be able to take on additional lines; a sign memory is improving.

READING helps to intercept a decline, but books on compact disc (or cassette tape) are perhaps the most useful, even are therapeutic, and require concentration in order to steadily listen. Libraries have extensive collections, with shelf units set aside for CDs and DVDs. Choose interesting titles, and the attention will be less likely to stray.

POSTURE: Tilt backward a little; straightening when you notice that slouching causes pressure on the diaphragm. Deeper breathing will result, and the pulse seems stronger.

DAYLIGHT is healthful; houses can be dark. Sit outside in fresh air, and exchange the air throughout the house often. Wear non-restrictive, natural clothing. Avoid 'pretzel'-like positions of the limbs such as folding the arms and pressing them close to the middle when lying on the back or side. The wisest-seeming guests on news shows will look straight on, without head gestures or throwing their arms about.

PREFER SUBSTANTIAL FOOD of good quality throughout the day. Pots of stew and stir-fried vegetables, with chunks of meat are easy to prepare. Jars can be filled with soups and stew for the freezer.

THE BEST NEWS is that new brain cells actually can form. That revelation should spark motivation to cherish them, feed them well, give them plenty of exercise, and more may form to cope with the increased 'work load' of fine listening, interesting reading, and relaxing music.

"…UNTO THE EXAMPLE AND SHADOW OF HEAVENLY THINGS" (HEB. 8-5)

"That they may increase more and more."

"Put off the old, and take on the new, created in righteousness."

"He hath shown His people the power of His works."

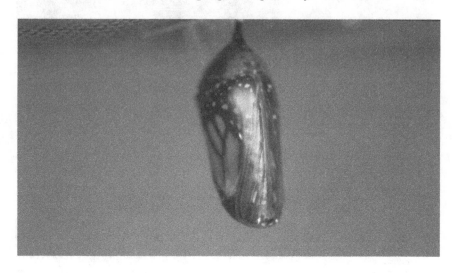

"Be you transformed; proving that good and acceptable will of God."

"In a twinkling of an eye...the earthly shall put on the Heavenly."

*Monarch butterflies raised from caterpillar stage,
and photographed by the author.*

CHAPTER 4

Territorial Expansion

"THE NORTHWEST TERRITORY"

By E.O Randall

"No portion of the United States presents more of romantic interest or historic importance than the part known as The Northwest Territory. Out of it were carved the States of Ohio, Indiana, Illinois, Michigan, and Wisconsin. It is the territory bounded by the Ohio River on the east and south, the chain of Great Lakes on the North and the Mississippi River on the west. ...The French were first on the ground, and said it belonged to them. In 1534 Jacques Cartier sailed from France across the Atlantic and up the St Lawrence River. In 1608 Sam Champlain, a famous French navigator, ascended the St. Lawrence, and sailed across the Great Lakes. Many French voyagers followed. In 1608 Champlain established a colony at Quebec, and in 1620 King Louis XIII of France appointed him Governor of Canada. Other French adventurers now pushed on west from Lakes Huron and Michigan to the Illinois and Mississippi Rivers; the latter of which they descended to its mouth at the Gulf of Mexico.

And then the vast territory embraced within the triangle of the Great Lakes on the North, the Mississippi on the west and the Allegheny Mountains on the east was claimed by France, by right of discovery and exploration.

Lasalle Lays Claim by Exploration:

'This ninth day of April, sixteen hundred and eighty-two, I, in virtue of the commission of His Majesty which I hold in my hand...have taken, and do now take, in the name of His Majesty and of his successors to the crown, possession of this country of Louisiana, the seas, harbors, ports, bays, adjacent straits, and all the nations, people, provinces, cities, town, villages, mines, minerals, fisheries, streams and rivers comprised in the extent of the said Louisiana... —Sieur de La Salle: 1682—*La Salle claims the Mississippi Valley for France.*' [1682: The same year Philadelphia was founded by William Penn.]

Meanwhile the Englishman, the foe of the Frenchman, was slowly but surely getting a firm foothold on the American shore. In the year 1498, more than a third of a century before Jacques Cartier's little vessel plowed its way up the St. Lawrence, and before Columbus had made his last voyage, the Cabots: John and Sebastian, father and son under Henry V11 of England, coasted along the continent of North America, and claimed it by discovery. In 1607 the Jamestown Colony became the first permanent English settlement in America. This was just one year before Champlain established his French Colony at Quebec. The other English settlements known as the New England Colonies rapidly followed. The charters and patents for these English colonies granted by the English sovereigns gave the colonies the land, not only along the Atlantic coast, but also west as far as those lands extended. Both France and England therefore, claimed the same territory; the great triangle described above. It was to be a neck and neck race between the Frenchman and the Englishman for the Northwest Territory...

The French commander now ordered troops from Montreal into the Ohio Country, at the same time the royal Governor Dinwiddie of Virginia, sent a detachment of English soldiers to build a fort on the Ohio near Pittsburg to keep out the French...Nothing but war could settle the dispute. The French and Indian War followed. It lasted seven years: from 1756 to 1763.

NATHANIAL AMES, *AMERICA IN 1758:*
(Two years into the war):

"The present state of North America: That fertile country to the west of the Appalachian Mountains is of larger extent than all of France, Germany, and Poland, and all well-provided with rivers, a very wholesome air, a rich soil; in fine, the garden of the world! Time was when we might have been possessed of it. At this time two mighty kings contend for this inestimable prize. Their respective claims are to be measured by the length of their swords.

Our numbers will not avail till the Colonies are united. If we do not join heart and hand in the common cause against exulting foes, it may really happen, as the Governor of Pennsylvania told his assembly: 'We shall have no privilege to dispute about, nor a country to dispute in.'

...The English won, and by the Treaty of Peace signed at Paris, in 1763, France surrendered to the English...the country south of the Great Lakes and east of the Mississippi River. Thus, the Northwest Territory became English property.

The New England Colonies now expected this territory would be divided up among the Connecticut, Massachusetts, New York, Virginia and other Colonies who claimed strips of it from the Atlantic to the Mississippi. But England said 'No'. In short, the American Colonists were barred out of the rich Ohio Valley and the Great Northwest. That England did this was one of the causes of the Revolution. A part of that war took place in the Northwest Territory, particularly in the Ohio Valley, where the British induced the Indians to side with them and attack the American frontiers."
—E. O. Randall. *The Northwest Territory*

The Proclamation of 1763
"On this Proclamation, King George 111 forbade his American subjects on the seaboard....to extend their boundaries beyond the mountains; nor were they to enter that territory which they had spilled their blood to win from the French. The frontiersmen would not brook such restrictions, and the southern part of the forbidden land slowly slipped away from the British by "Manifest Destiny," that is, by a natural working of forces that could not be checked. In the 'back country' of Pennsylvania, Virginia, and the Carolinas... down these valleys and mountain passes, and over the Cumberland Mountains, by way of the Cumberland Gap, sturdy pioneers from the Colonies...took up their march." —Emerson Fite

"THE BRITISH COLONIES IN 1763"

By Emerson Fite

"With few roads and bridges, communications between the various sections was difficult. People stayed at home perforce. Upset vehicles, stage coaches and horses stuck in the mud, overturned ferry boats, and uncomfortable inns on the way were generally sufficient obstacles to all but the most necessary travel.

…Said Benjamin Franklin in London to prospective emigrants to his native land. 'Much less is it advisable for a person to go thither who has no quality to recommend him, but his birth in Europe. Indeed, it has value; but it is a commodity that cannot be carried to a worse market than to that of America where people do not inquire concerning a stranger, 'What is he'? But, 'What can he do? If he has any useful art, he is welcome; if he exercises it. If he behaves well, he will be respected by all that know him'…

On the seaboard and the East, agriculture was well-nigh universal. The New Englanders on their barren and rocky farm, raised the simple necessities of life, but could boast of no great staple New England crop.

New England was a land of villages and small farms. There, the one long village street was usually found, bordered by farmhouses, with the farms stretching back on both sides of the street: The ever-present meetinghouse, where the church-going habits of the people encouraged sociability as well as piety; the town hall, with its frequent public discussions, the village store, the inn, the schoolhouse, and frequently the blockhouse for refuge in case of threats by Indians.

The New Englander found fishing one of their most profitable occupations. A nearer market for their fish than Europe was gradually developed in the West Indies.

Another American industry in the Colonial period was shipbuilding; centered mainly in New England where the pine forests furnished excellent masts for ships. Here the royal navy of England looked for timber for manufacture of its vessels.

A traveler who visited New England in 1759 stated that, from the small towns along a single river in New Hampshire, two hundred vessels were launched annually. Many of these were owned and manned; as well as built in New England, and sailed from Boston, Salem, Newburyport, and the other seaboard towns."

—E. Fite

"The last war had settled forever the question as to what language, religion, and civilization should dominate the Continent of North America, with the effect of establishing more friendly relations among the Colonies in showing their strength and the necessity for united action."

—E. Brown

"BRITISH ACTS TO RAISE MONEY AND TIGHTEN CONTROL OVER THE COLONISTS"

"The British statesmen determined to centralize control of its enlarged empire in London more than ever by sending forth to the colonies, royal officials of new and greater powers; to station more British soldiers in the different parts of the empire, and in the Parliament in London, to pass more stringent colonial laws; all despite the fact that the colonists preferred to have things continue in the old way without new reminders of Great Britain's power over them.

NAVIGATION LAWS: To stop the practice of merchants trading with the fleets and garrisons of the French, the courts issued writs of assistance which were general search warrants authorizing the customs officials to search any house or building for smuggled goods....

THE SUGAR ACT OF 1764: The Molasses Act of 1733 was succeeded by the Sugar Act of 1764, which placed new duties on coffee, pimento, wines, silks, linens and sugar. Strict measures were taken to enforce the law...Offenders were to be tried in the admiralty courts without a jury.

THE STAMP ACT: Parliament passed the Stamp Act of 1765, which the British historian Lecky characterized as 'one of the most momentous legislative acts in the history of mankind.' This *Act* required the Americans to place stamps, which were to be purchased from the government, upon legal documents of various kind; upon newspapers, pamphlets, almanacs, playing cards, and many other articles... The Americans of 1765 flatly refused to have anything to do with a tax imposed on them by the British; that no taxes be imposed upon them, but with their own consent.

On the day when the *Act* was to go into effect, flags were hung at half-mast, shops were closed, bells were tolled, and copies of the Stamp Act were hawked about the streets bearing the inscription, *The folly of England and the ruin of America.*

Few stamps were sold. Merchants...ceased importations from Britain, until finally at the wish of the British commercial classes, who feared the loss of the entire American trade if the colonies were further exasperated, the Act was repealed.

THE DECLARATORY ACT accompanied the Repeal Act to the effect that Great Britain had full power to make laws, "To bind the Colonies and people of America, subjects of the Crown of Great Britain, in all cases whatsoever."

Great Britain turned to new tariff taxes in 1767, and by *the Townshend Acts* added tea, glass, lead, paper and a few other things to the list of articles upon which the Americans were to pay an import tax. In one year, importations from Great Britain fell off one-half... John Dickinson wrote: 'Let these truths be indelibly impressed upon our minds: that we cannot be happy without being free...'

By virtue of the Quartering Act passed in 1765...the colonies were required to provide for the accommodation of British regulars, who were to be sent to America in greater numbers...Late in 1768 the King sent two regiments to Boston...

On the night of the fifth of March, 1770, a crowd of men and boys began to harass and insult a handful of red-coated soldiers on guard in one of the principal streets...hurling snowballs, or stones...until the soldiers opened fire. Five of the harassers were killed and six wounded. The soldiers were tried and were acquitted. (*The Boston Massacre*).

When a consignment of tea arrived in Boston Harbor, citizens joined in a mass meeting, which voted unanimously that the tea be taken back to England. When more than two weeks had passed and the tea ships still lay at the wharf, a large town meeting came together in Old South Meetinghouse in Boston, and demanded that the governor order the tea be taken away...The governor sent his refusal...A shout of fifty passing 'Indians' was heard outside the door, and the crowd filed out of the meetinghouse to the wharf and stood in silence for three hours in the darkness of the night while the *Indians* pitched three hundred and forty chests of tea into the ocean in the famous *Boston Tea Party;* the date was nine days before Christmas, 1773...

Said an English writer upon hearing of the occurrence, 'Beware little town; count the cost, and know well if you dare to defy the wrath of Great Britain, and if you love exile, and poverty, and death rather than submission.'

THE INTOLERABLE ACTS: When Parliament met in March 1774, it passed a number of 'Acts' for the punishment of Massachusetts:
1. The Port of Boston was to be closed to trade until the tea destroyed should be paid for.
2. *Town meetings*, which the king's ministers unjustly called 'hotbeds of discussion and disobedience,' were forbidden to convene without the governor's permission.

3. Public buildings designated by the governor were to be used as barracks for the troops."

—E. Fite

THE FIRST CONTINENTAL CONGRESS MET ON SEPTEMBER 5, 1774: "Expressions of sympathy now came to Massachusetts from all over the Colonies...John and Samuel Adams of Massachusetts, George Washington and Patrick Henry of Virginia, and others respectfully petitioned the king to put an end to their grievance; specifying thirteen acts of Parliament which they deemed *infringements and violations of their rights*. They urged on all the Colonies, the adoption of the *American Association* for the boycott of British trade, both import and export, and after a six weeks' session, adjourned."

—David S. Muzzey

"DANIEL BOONE'S VIEW OF KENTUCKY"
By Cecil B. Hartley

..."It was not till the 1st of May, 1769, that the party were able to set out, as Boone in his autobiography expresses it, *in quest of the country of Kentucky.*

It was more than a month before these adventurers came in sight of the *Promise land.* We quote from *Mr. Peck's* excellent work, the description which undoubtedly formed the authority on which the artist relied in painting the engraving of: *Daniel Boone's first view of Kentucky:*

'It was the 7th of June, 1769 that six men, weary and way-worn, were seen wending their way up the steep side of a rugged mountain in the wilderness of Kentucky...

Toward the time of the setting sun, the party had reached the summit of the mountain-range up which they had toiled for some three or four hours, and which had bounded their prospect to the west during the day. Here, new and indescribable scenery opened to their view. Before them for an immense distance as if spread out on a map, lay the rich and beautiful vales watered by the Kentucky River; for they had now reached one of its northern branches. The country immediately before them, to use a western phrase, was rolling, and in places, abruptly hilly, but far in the vista was seen a beautiful expanse of level country over which the buffalo, deer and other forest animals, roamed unmolested, while they fed on the luxuriant herbage of the forest. The countenances of the party lighted up with pleasure; con-gratulations were exchanged, the romantic tales of Finley were confirmed visually, and orders were given to encamp for the night in a neighboring ravine. A large tree lay in a convenient position for the back of their camp. Logs were placed on the right and left, leaving the front open where fire might be kindled against another log, and for shelter from the rains and heavy dews, bark was peeled from the linden tree...

The buffaloes were found in great numbers feeding on the leaves of the cane, and rich fields of clover.'

...First came the hunter and trapper to trace the river courses, and spy out the choice spots of the land; then came the small farmer and the hardy adventurer to cultivate the rich plains discovered, and lay the nucleuses of the towns and cities which were so soon and so rapidly to spring up, and then came the surveyor to mark the boundaries of individual possessions and give civil shape. Kentucky now began to have a society...

The period in which Daniel Boone commenced the settlement of Kentucky, was the most eventful one in the history of our Country. In the year 1775, hostilities between Great Britain and her American Colonies commenced at Lexington and Concord, and the whole country was mustering in arms at the time when Boone and other western emigrants were forming settlements four hundred miles beyond the frontiers of Virginia and the Carolinas. That very early town they named Lexington was being settled and formed when the pioneers received news of the *Battle at Lexington*."

—Cecil B. Hartley

"THE FORTITUDE OF DANIEL BOONE"

By James Hall

"We should exceed our limits and unnecessarily shock the feelings of the reader, if we should detail all the achievements of Boone; the privations of himself and his companions, and the barbarities of their unrelenting foes. He continued to sustain himself in the midst of danger, displaying in every emergency that consummate skill and patient courage which elevated him above ordinary men, and distinguished by a gentleness of manners, and a benevolence of heart and action; which secured the affections of his friends, and won respect even from his ferocious enemies.

From this time, the forests of Kentucky began to be rapidly peopled. The settlers came in small parties, and spread over the whole country; each little colony erecting its own fort, and appointing its own leader. The Indians continued to harass them. The latter were now more than ever inflamed with rage and jealousy against the Americans by the arts of the British agents who supplied them with arms and ammunition; bribed them to hostility by valuable presents, and poisoned their minds by incendiary speeches. The whole district of Kentucky exhibited scenes of bloodshed.

The name of Boone is the most conspicuous among the pioneers, because he was the earliest adventurer to the shores of the Ohio, and continued longest to brave the perils of the forest. But there were others who were superior to him in education and strength of mind, and his equals in every other respect. Boone was remarkable for the perfect equanimity with which he bore every trial. Never greatly excited, he was never alarmed nor despondent. Others were allured to the wilderness by ambition or cupidity in the pursuit of wealth, or lands or fame, but he seems to have enjoyed the life of the pioneer, and to have dwelt in the woods from choice.

There were others who hunted down the Indians with rancorous hatred. Boone only defended himself against their assaults, and never troubled his head about them while they let him alone. He was good-humored, social, and disposed to live in quiet. Love of peace, rather than fondness for war, made him a dweller on the frontier, and when the restraints of society pressed around him, when the cavils of the neighborhood became vexatious, or any other cause rendered his residence disagreeable, his simple remedy was to plunge farther into the woods. He was abstemious in his habits, and a close observer of nature; and without any brilliancy or much grasp of intellect, he had a great deal of that practical good sense which may be supposed to have existed in the mind of a person of even temperament, who thought much, spoke little, and acted with deliberation; whose whole life was a series of journeying, danger, and vicissitude, and whose vigilant eye was constantly employed in watching the appearances of nature, the habit of animals, the changes of the season, and the movements of hostile men.

These are the characteristics of the backwoodsman; they were strongly developed in all those that accompanied or followed Boone, but in him they were less adulterated, because his mind was not distracted by the passions and cares that perplex other men." —James Hall

BENJAMIN FRANKLIN
Autobiography

"God has been very good to us in many respects. Therefore, let us enjoy His favors with a thankful and cheerful heart, and as we can make no direct return to Him, show our sense of His goodness to us by continuing to do good to our fellow creatures...The friendships of this world are changeable, uncertain transitory things, but His favor, if we can secure it, is an inheritance forever....

The unsettled state of the ministry ever since the Parliament passed the *Stamp Act* had stopped all proceedings in public affairs and ours among the rest. Every step in the law, every newspaper, advertisement and almanac was to be severely taxed, falling particularly hard on us lawyers and printers. They could not hurt us without hurting themselves. All our profits centered in England,

and the more they took from us, the less we could lay out to them. I was a member of the Assembly of Pennsylvania when this notification came to hand. I took every step in my power to prevent the passing of the Stamp Act, but the tide was too strong against us...The spirit of the people was violently against everyone they thought had the least concern with the Stamp Law...."

Two weeks after my exam before the government, I was made very happy by a vote of the Commons on February 22, 1766 for the repeal of the mother of mischiefs, *the Stamp Act*. The House of Commons, after a long debate, came to a resolution. Great honor and thanks were due to the British merchants trading to America; all of them being our zealous and indefatigable friends...

I often wished that I were employed by the crown to settle a colony in Ohio; that we could do it effectively and without putting the nation to much expense. What a glorious thing it would have been to settle in that fine country, a large strong body of religious and industrious people! What a security to the other Colonies, and advantage to Britain by increasing her people, territory, strength and commerce. Might it not have greatly facilitated the introduction of pure religion among the heathen, if we could by such a colony show them a better sample of Christians than they commonly saw in our Indian *traders*, the most vicious and abandoned wretches of our nation! In such an enterprise I could have spent the remainder of my life with pleasure...

In 1767, some incidents revived the contest between the two countries, creating great disorder in public affairs. In the same session with the Stamp Act, an act had been passed to regulate the *quartering of soldiers* in America, with a clause directing that empty houses, barns, etc. should be hired for them, and that the respective provinces where they were, should pay the expense and furnish the firing, bedding, drink and other articles to the soldiers, gratis. But the New York Assembly refused to do it. This proposal caused great mischief and alienation of the affection of the people of America toward the British Empire...

America, an immense territory; favored by Nature with all advantages of climate, soil, great navigable rivers and lakes, etc. was destined to become a great Country; populous and mighty, and would in less time than was generally conceived, be able to shake off any shackles that might be imposed on her, and perhaps place them on the impostors. In the meantime, every act of oppression soured their tempers, lessened greatly if not annihilated the profits of British commerce with them, and hastened their final revolt. For the seeds of liberty are universally sown there, and nothing could eradicate them...

In 1773 I opposed, without success, *the tax on tea.* The act passed in spite of me. The tea was burnt in Boston...Parliament, incensed, closed the port and by various acts took away privileges; forbidding fishing etc. I could not but see with concern the sending of troops to Boston; their behavior to the people there gave me infinite uneasiness as I apprehended the worst of consequences, a breach between the two countries...

I found at my arrival, all America from one end of the thirteen United Provinces to the other, busily employed in learning the use of arms. All trade and business, building, improving, etc. being at a stand-still, and nothing thought of but arms. The attack upon the country people near Boston by the army had roused everybody, and exasperated the whole continent. The tradesmen of Philadelphia were in the field twice a day with the utmost of diligence; all being volunteers. We had three battalions, a troop of light horse and a company of artillery who made surprising progress. The same spirit appeared everywhere and the unanimity was amazing. Our Army that was already formed would soon consist of above 20,000 men…

The Congress met at a time when all minds were exasperated by the perfidy of Gen. Gage, and his attack on the country people: the burning of houses, and our seaport towns, and other treacherous conduct without the least necessity. They barbarously plundered and burnt a fine, undefended town, opposite to Boston, called Charlestown, consisting of about 400 houses, many elegantly built…In this ministerial war against us, all Europe was conjured not to sell us arms or ammunition that we would be found defenseless, and more easily murdered."

Franklin's Reflections on Religion and Conduct

"Doubtlessly faith has its use in the world. I do not desire to see it diminished, nor would I endeavor to lessen it in any person. But I wish it were more productive of good works than I have generally seen it: I mean real good works: works of kindness, charity, mercy and public spirit; not holiday keeping, sermon reading or hearing, performing church ceremonies, or making long prayers, filled with flatteries and compliments, despised even by wise men, and much less capable of pleasing the Deity. The hearing and reading of sermons may be useful, but if men rest on hearing and praying as too many do, it is as if a tree should value itself on being watered and putting forth leaves though it never produced any fruit.

Jesus thought much less of these outward appearances and professions than many of his modern disciples. He preferred the *doers* of the word to the mere *hearers*. …Those who gave food to the hungry, drink to the thirsty, raiment to the naked, entertainment to the stranger, and relief to the sick, though they never heard of His name, He declares shall in the last day be accepted; when those who cry, "Lord, Lord," who value themselves on their faith and great miracles, but have neglected good works, shall be rejected. May I govern my passions with an absolute sway; Grow wise and better as my strength wears away. With courage undaunted may I face my last day. A man is not completely born until he be dead. Why then should we grieve? I feel a growing curiosity to be acquainted with some other life, and can cheerfully and with filial confidence, resign my spirit to the conduct of that Great and Good Parent of mankind, who created it, and who has so graciously protected and prospered me from my birth to the present hour."

—Benjamin Franklin

ABIGAIL ADAMS
In a letter to her husband, John

"This intelligence will make a plain path for you, though a dangerous one. I could not join today in the petitions of our worthy pastor for a reconciliation between our no longer parent state, but tyrant state, and these Colonies. Let us separate: they are unworthy to be our brethren. Let us renounce them; and instead of supplications, as formerly, for their prosperity and happiness, let us beseech the Almighty to blast their counsels, and to bring to naught all of their devices."

CHAPTER 5

The Point Pleasant Victory

"THE BATTLE OF POINT PLEASANT"
By Landon Bell

"Lord Dunmore, Governor of Virginia from 1772 to 1776 was suspected of playing double. While efforts were being made by the First Continental Congress in autumn 1774, to resist the encroachments of Great Britain against the Colonies, the Indians were committing depredations along the western frontiers, and the indignation of the people compelled their reluctant governor to take up arms and march against the very Indians whom he was suspected of having incited to the hostility.

Dunmore marched his army in two columns. The one under Andrew Lewis he sent to the junction of the Great Kanawha with the Ohio River [Point Pleasant] while the other he led to a point higher up on the Ohio River, with the alleged purpose of destroying certain Indian towns, and then joining Lewis at Point Pleasant.

The real purpose, however is suspected to have been the concentrating of the entire Indian force against Lewis.

Attacks on settlers were so severe, that in one year, one thousand settlers returned East. Frontiersmen were not preparing to enter the War for Independence; instead they were bound by fear for themselves and their families to remain and defend their small vulnerable homes in back country clearings.

During an Indian congress on the banks of the Scioto River in the autumn of 1774, united were: Shawnees, Delawares, Wyandots, Mingoes, Miamis, Ottawas, Illinois and others in the great Northwestern Confederacy; the most powerful that ever menaced the frontiers or confronted English civilization in America. At its head was placed the famous Shawnee chieftain, Cornstalk.

All day long that Sunday...October ninth...with silent tread they approached the Ohio River, and late in the evening halted in the dense forest in the valley of Champaign Creek in Gallia County, Ohio, and distant about three miles above the mouth of the Great Kanawha River. Soon after dark the warriors began crossing the Ohio River on rafts, seventy-nine of these having been prepared previously. Before morning they were all on the southern bank, distant about three miles from Camp Point Pleasant and were ready to proceed to action."

COLONEL FLEMING'S ACCOUNT OF THE BATTLE

'This morning before sunrise, two men came running into Camp and gave information that a considerable body of Indians were encamped about two miles up the Ohio River. The drums beat to arms; 150 men were ordered out of each line, and were to march against the enemy in two columns. They marched pretty briskly about one hundred to two hundred yards apart up the Ohio River about a half a mile, when all of a sudden the enemy, lurking behind bushes and trees, gave a heavy fire which was briskly followed by a second and third and returned again by our men with much bravery and courage.

This attack was attended with the death of some of our bravest officers and men, also with the deaths of a great number of the enemy. Immediately after the fire upon the right line, succeeded a heavy one on the left and a return from us ... The men were forced to quit their ranks and fly to trees. In doing this the enemy made a small advance and forced our men of both lines to retreat the distance of perhaps one or two hundred yards under heavy fires attended with dismal yells and screams from the enemy. About this time, they were succored with a detachment from the camp. This reinforcement from the camp, and our men found their strength much increased and making a fierce onset, forced the enemy from their stations, and caused them to retreat by degrees about a mile, giving them many brisk fires... An advantage being gained about one o'clock, all the efforts of the enemy to regain it proved fruitless. ...The steadiness of our men defied their most furious essays... About an hour by sun we were in full possession of the field of battle: Victory having now declared in our favor.'

LANDON BELL ADDRESS CONTINUES: "Gen. Andrew Lewis' defeat of the tribes under Cornstalk in October, 1774 kept the frontier quiet for about three years. This enabled the settlements at Boonesborough and Harrodsburg and other stations in Kentucky to become established, and these in turn furnished a base from which G. R. Clark made his campaign into the Ohio and Illinois Country, (1778-1779). 'Western' Virginia, early in the war, had recruits that went over the mountains to join Washington's regiments in the East.

The more the Revolutionary struggle is studied, the more important become the operations upon the western front during the Revolution. We have heard too little of George Rogers Clark and his men who held the foes at bay upon the western front, and Clark and his men in the Revolution could not have achieved what they did, and could not have made themselves masters of the western front if it had not been for the breaking of the Indian power at Point Pleasant. If they had not done what they did, Washington could not have triumphed."

—Landon Bell

ACTIVE, BRAVE YOUNG FELLOWS

PENNSYLVANIA "On Friday evening last, arrived at Lancaster, Pennsylvania on their way to the American camp, Captain Cresap's company of riflemen consisting of 130 active, brave young fellows; many of whom have been in the late expedition against the Indians. They bear in their bodies, visible marks of their prowess, and show scars and wounds which would do honor to Homer's *Illiad*. With rifles in their hands, they assume a kind of confidence. These men have been bred in the woods to hardships and dangers from their infancy...

This morning they will set out on their march for Cambridge."

—*Pennsylvania Journal* August 23, 1775

"THE VICTORIES ON THE KANAWHA AND THE WATAUGA"

By David Muzzey

"Indeed, it is a matter of history that these Point Pleasant men were on nearly every battlefield of the Revolution. And one of them, when sixty-three years of age, led the Americans in the Battle of the Thames, in 1813...

If the latter victories (Saratoga and Yorktown) decided that America should take her place among the Nations of the World, the former victories proclaimed that the new Nation would not be content to be shut up in a little strip of seacoast, but had begun facing westward to possess the entire Continent."

Site of the Battle of Pt. Pleasant

"THE SCOTCH-IRISH"

By James Hall

"There was another class of settlers who followed close upon the footsteps of the pioneers. They found here, rich valleys clothed with verdant grasses and herbage, over which herds of buffalo and deer still grazed, and where game of various kinds abounded. These were favorite hunting grounds of the Indians, who came from the west, across the mountains, at certain seasons of the year in search of game, and who were not disposed to submit tamely to the intrusion of the white people. None could live here but hardy men who were willing to fight, and ready at all times to defend themselves. And thus lived those sturdy Scotch-Irish emigrants.

They endured the privations, and learned the habits of the American backwoodsmen. Thoughtful and austere, industrious and conscientious, they found no pleasure in the hunter's life, which they pursued only so far as their necessities required, preferring to the quiet labors of the farm. But they belonged to a brave, high-spirited race...

The church and the school house were among the earliest structures in every neighborhood. While yet there were no wagons, no roads, nor saw-mills; buildings of solid stone were erected for public worship.

In Dr. Foote's *Sketches of Virginia*, we find the following graphic passage, illustrative of the habits of this people:

'From the time Mr. Cummings commenced *preaching* at Sinking Spring, up to about the year 1776, the men never went to church without being armed, and taking their families with them. On Sabbath morning during this period, it was

Mr. Cummings' custom, for he was always a very neat man in his dress; to dress himself, then put on his shot-pouch, shoulder his rifle, mount his horse, and ride off to church. There he met his gallant and intelligent congregation; each man with his rifle in his hand. When seated in the meeting-house, they presented altogether a most solemn and singular spectacle.

Mr. Cummings' uniform habit before entering the church, was to take a short walk alone while the congregation were seating themselves. He would then return, and at the door hold a few words of conversation with some one of the elders of the church, then would gravely walk through this crowd, mount the steps of the pulpit, deposit his rifle in a corner near him, lay off his shot-pouch, and commence the solemn worship of the day.'

Among their other sterling qualities, the Scotch-Irish were patriotic, and not only the people, but their ministers, entered zealously into the cause in the American Revolution." —James Hall

Hocking Hills, in Ohio

CHAPTER 6

Opening Scenes of The Revolution

PATRICK HENRY'S SPEECH

"Has Great Britain any enemy in this quarter of the world to call for all this accumulation of navies and armies? No, sir, she has none. They are meant for us: they can be meant for no other. They are sent over to bind and rivet upon us those chains which the British ministry has been so long forging. And what have we to oppose them? Shall we try argument? Sir, we have been trying that for the last ten years.

Sir, we have done everything that could be done to avert the storm which is now coming on. We have petitioned—we have supplicated—we have prostrated ourselves before the throne, and have implored its interposition to arrest the tyrannical hands of the ministry and parliament. Our petitions have been slighted: our supplications have been disregarded, and we have been spurned with contempt from the foot of the throne...There is no longer any room for hope. If we wish to be free—if we mean to preserve inviolate those inestimable privileges for which we have been so long contending—if we mean not basely to abandon the noble struggle in which we have been so long engaged, and which we have pledged ourselves never to abandon until the glorious object of our contest shall be obtained—we must fight!—I repeat it, sir, we must fight! An appeal to arms and to the God of Hosts, is all that is left us!

They tell us sir, that we are weak—unable to cope with so formidable an adversary. But when shall we be stronger? Will it be the next week, or the next year? Will it be when we are totally disarmed, and when a British guard shall be stationed in every house? Shall we acquire the means of effectual resistance by lying supinely on our backs, and hugging the delusive phantom of hope until our enemies shall have bound us hand and foot? Sir, we are not weak, if we make a proper use of those means which the God of Nature hath placed in our power.

Three millions of People, armed in the holy cause of liberty, and in such a country as that which we possess, are invincible by any force which our enemy can send against us. Besides, sir, we shall not fight our battles alone. There is a just God who presides over the destinies of nations, and who will raise up friends to fight our battles for us. The battle sir, is not to the strong alone; it is to the vigilant, the active, the brave. Besides sir, we have no election if we were base enough to desire it; it is now too late to retire from the contest. There is no retreat but in submission and slavery; our chains are forged! Their clanking may be heard on the plains of Boston! The war is inevitable, and let it come! I repeat, sir, let it come!

It is vain sir, to extenuate the matter. Gentlemen may cry, Peace, Peace! But there is no peace. The war is actually begun! The next gale that sweeps from the North will bring to our ears, the clash of resounding arms! Our brethren are already in the field! Why stand we here idle? What is it that gentlemen wish? What would they have? Is life so dear, or peace so sweet, as to be purchased at the price of chains and slavery? Forbid it Almighty God! I know not what course others may take, but as for me: *Give me liberty or give me death!*"

LEXINGTON AND CONCORD

(Note by author Watson): "It is thought, a work upon the plan of the *Campfires of the Revolution* will bring the doings and the scenes of the *trying time* more vividly before the mind than the common history. Here we have the actual incidents of various battles... told as if by eye-witnesses and in familiar, easily comprehended language of the farmer and mechanic, soldiers of the American army. No later achievements of a more dazzling character should withdraw the admiration and the gratitude of the American people from those iron-nerved patriots who, destitute of most of the requisites of an army, conquered only because they were determined to conquer...Their history affords the brightest examples for the imitation of those who would be truly brave and patriotic."

By the Patriots:
"Tell us about Concord, Ben" said Stuart, addressing Hadley. "I wish I had been there with you." 'You may well wish that,' was the reply. 'It was a glorious day; and the neighbors rose in their strength to show the murderers of our people who was going to be master.

Things went on bad enough for more than a year, but we didn't get to blows with the soldiers, because the time hadn't come. Our great men had determined not to strike the first blow, and not to take the second, without putting one in between.

The battle, you know took place on Wednesday. Well, on the Saturday previous, Dr. Warren observed a great stir among the soldiers, and before night a good number of them were off duty, and pretending to drill. But this was only a sham to deceive us. Dr. Warren however watched them close enough, and about midnight what should be behold but the sailors getting the boats ready to cross over toward Concord. Then it was he felt sure that no time was to be lost, so he sent Colonel Revere to tell Mr. Adams and Mr. Hancock to take care of themselves.

These three talked over the matter together at Lexington, and it was agreed that when Revere went back to Boston, he should make signals to let the surrounding country know if the rascally soldiers were going to attack them. If the soldiers should march out by Roxbury, a light was to be hung in the North Church steeple, but if they crossed in their boats to the country, there were to be two lights.

All day on Monday and Tuesday, our men were busy picking up information about what the soldiers intended to do, but the busiest time was yet to come. All the town was in alarm; folks left their own houses and ran to others whenever anybody arrived with fresh news. No one talked loud, but only whispered. Few men worked on those two days, but you might see crowds on the corners, speaking low, rolling their eyes like mad men; clenching their hands as firm as iron... A good number, not knowing what might happen, were busily engaged in hiding their little notions where they thought the soldiers couldn't get at them.

After some time, the fears of the people increased. An order came on Tuesday that no one should leave Boston that night, but Warren had just sent Colonel Revere and Mr. Dawes to warn the whole neighborhood. They didn't forget to hang the lanterns in the steeple either, and it was a sight to make one hold his breath to see those two dim lanterns burning in the darkness to warn the people of their danger. I was going home that night after being out to buy some flour, and the first thing I saw on looking toward town, was the lights in the steeple. Thinks I to myself, 'there's news, sure enough', and home I hurried to Lexington, as fast as my horse could trot. Pretty soon Colonel Revere rode into the town giving the alarm wherever he went, and stating that the soldiers were crossing Charlestown Neck.

While the news was spreading through the town, Mr. Dawes arrived. Both of them had been chased by the British...At one o'clock on Wednesday morning they started for Concord, and our prayers went with them, but you remember they were both taken on the road. The British left Revere behind, fearing they would be pursued. And they had good cause to fear; for the whole country was by this time alarmed, and the militia preparing to fight the minute the first gun should be fired.

Nor had they to wait long. At five o'clock on Wednesday morning, a man on horseback, without cap or coat, galloped into Lexington shouting that the British were coming up the road. Some called to him to stop; but he rushed on in that mad way toward Concord. Then it was that the blood boiled in our veins. We remembered the insults and threats which had been heaped upon us so long, and swore that they should be revenged that day...The women hurried from house to house, gathering muskets for the militia and carrying ammunition.

At last the drum beat to arms. We seized our muskets and rushed to the green. Captain Parker drew us up, seventy strong, in double rank; telling us to fight bravely in the cause of freedom. It was only a little while after that, the clouds of dust in the road told that the enemy were coming. Then we heard their drums beating and saw the bayonets peeping out from the dust. One company after another came in sight until our little party looked like a mere handful, compared to them...Our hearts were beating, but not with fear: no, we would have been cut to pieces before one of us would have acted cowardly! But what could seventy men do against nearly a thousand? Their leader galloped up like a madman; cursing, shouting and ordering us to disperse. All at once they poured a volley upon us. How many fell, I had no time to find out..."

"But where were they first checked?" asked Green.

'Not till they got to Concord. It was then seven o'clock. All the militia in town were drawn up on the hills; and the news of the affair at Lexington filled them with fury. The enemy marched to the storehouses, broke them open, and began the work of destruction. The flour was emptied into the river; the ball, which we had gathered with so much care, stolen or sunk in wells, and our two cannon, battered and abused till they were unfit for use. We let them do it all quietly, but swore that every pennyworth should be taken out of their red jackets. Next, they began to break up the bridges, and this was more than we could bear. We were getting stronger every minute; for the farmers came up, and all the towns were ringing their bells, and sending messengers in every direction, to get up a general rising. I had joined the party on the hills. We couldn't wait any longer, but down we went with gallant Davis at our head waving his sword, and calling on us to strike for freedom, but not to give the first blow. Near the bridge they fired upon us again, and Davis, with another man, fell dead. We flung back a volley that made the old hills echo, and half a dozen of Gage's men dropped. They wheeled and fired again, and we did the same till the guns cracked merrily all around, and we saw them falling as our men did at Lexington. The enemy didn't stand it long, but went back to the town in a greater hurry than they had quitted it. But we were after them in hot pursuit... You may believe it cheered our hearts as we chased the cowards, to see the old men, too feeble to fight, and wives and mothers, at the windows encouraging us to push on...

...Militia came on as though they were springing from the ground, and the sides of the road blazed with one sheet of fire after another. O! It was glorious to be in that chase—glorious! Remember, boys, how often we were insulted by Gage, and called 'rebels,' or Yankees,' by his men! Yes, and cowards, too—cowards! The blood boils at the word! And then our bleeding men behind us! It was glory, I say, lads, to chase the rascals like deer up the road, and make them feel that 'rebels' could fight as well as they!'

..."Did you get home safe?" asked Green.

'We didn't go home at all,' Hadley replied. 'I tell you, old man, the whole country, for miles around, was in arms. Our men were out in all directions spreading the glorious news that a battle had been fought, and that the red-coats had got a thrashing. It was sunset before we chased them into Cambridge; yet, when I stood on one of the neighboring hills, I could hear the old drums beating far off, and see signals shot up by parties that were hurrying on to help us.

Next day, old Putnam joined us, and began to put things to rights. He had left his plough in the furrow on hearing of the battle, and rode a hundred miles to join us.'

—Henry C Watson

… "Upon the whole, Lord North's troops have had a severe drubbing, and when we consider the disparity of numbers and discipline, we have reason to acknowledge the interposition of Heaven on that memorable day." *Dunlap's Pennsylvania Packet*, May 1, 1775.

"After the Battle"
By A Minuteman

"A most confused array in which many, new to the bitter taste of battle, shot off their guns in each direction. Fear was not apparent in our ranks, and my heart swelled with pride, and the more so when I spied youthful Connister, a bullet in his arm, and yet manfully holding away the tears. We did better on the retreat of the Lobsters, and behind walls, our few riflemen made slaughter with them. But we are prone to favor the quick, bury the dead and make merry over our triumph. I much fear however that this is a long and painful war upon which we embark.

I kissed goodbye and blessed be to my good wife and four little ones. God help them, and then went with the company in the direction of Boston Town. The roads are crowded with men bearing arms, and no good will or token for the oppressors. Our company is calm and marches brisk; with muskets and the blunderbuss and plenty of shot."

—Ephraim Banks, *Concord Farmer*

A Citizen-Patriot

"The morning after the Battle of Lexington, nearly one hundred militiamen stopped at Colonel Pond's house. They had marched all night, were covered with dust, and were faint from fatigue and hunger. The mistress of the house was unprepared for so large a party. Her husband was absent with his own militia. She had one assistant. They put a brass kettle over the fire, filled it with water and Indian meal. In the barnyard were ten cows. Military guests milked cows, while others stirred the pudding. A store nearby was visited which had brown earthen dishes and pewter spoons."

—*Women of the Revolution*

A Newspaper Article

"The proceedings of April nineteenth have united the Colonies and Continent, and brought in New York to act as vigorously as any other place whatsoever, and has raised an army in an instant which are lodged in the several houses of the towns round Boston till their tents are finished, which will be soon. All that is attended to, besides ploughing and planting is making ready for fighting...We have a fine spring; prospects of great plenty, and are in no danger of starving through the cruel acts against the New England governments. The men who had been used to fishery, a hardy generation of people, Lord North has undesignedly kept in the country; giving strength to our military operations, and assisting as occasion may require. Thanks to a superior Wisdom for his blunders. The

(British) general is expecting reinforcements, but few have arrived as yet. The winds, contrary to the common run this season, instead of being easterly, have been mostly the reverse."
    —*New York Gazette and Weekly Mercury*, June 19, 1775

Amish farm in central Ohio

CHAPTER 7

The War for Independence Gains Momentum

"ETHAN ALLEN TAKES FORT TICONDEROGA"

By Ethan Allen

"Ever since I arrived to a state of manhood, and acquainted myself with the general history of mankind, I have felt a sincere passion for liberty. The history of nations, doomed to perpetual slavery in consequence of yielding up to tyrants their natural-born liberties, I read with a sort of philosophical horror; so that the first systematical and bloody attempt at Lexington to enslave America, thoroughly electrified my mind, and fully determined me to take part with my Country. And while I was wishing for an opportunity to signalize myself in its behalf, directions were privately sent to me from the then colony of Connecticut to raise the Green Mountain Boys, and if possible, with them surprise and take the fortress, Ticonderoga. This enterprise I cheerfully undertook, and after first guarding all the several passes that led thither, to cut off all intelligence between the garrison and the country, made a forced march from Bennington, and arrived at the lake opposite to Ticonderoga on the evening of the ninth day of May, 1775 with two hundred and thirty valiant Green Mountain Boys. It was with the utmost difficulty that I procured boats to cross the lake, however I landed eighty-three men near the garrison, and sent the boats back for the rear guard commanded by Col. Seth Warner.

The men being at this time, drawn up in three ranks, each poised his firelock…The garrison being asleep except the sentries, we gave three huzzas which greatly surprised them…One of the sentries made a pass at one of my officers with a charged bayonet, and slightly wounded him…I demanded of him the place where the commanding officer kept. He showed me a pair of stairs in front of a barrack which led up to a second story; to which I immediately repaired, and ordered the commander to come forth instantly, or I would sacrifice the whole garrison; at which the Capt. came immediately to the door with his breeches in his hand. When I ordered him to deliver to me the fort instantly, he asked me by what authority I demanded it. I answered him, 'In the name of the Great God, and the Continental Congress.' …With my drawn sword over his head, again demanded an immediate surrender of the garrison; with which he then complied, and ordered his men to be forthwith paraded without arms, as he had given up the garrison.

In the meantime some of my officers had given orders, and in consequence thereof, sundry of the barrack doors were beat down, and about one third of the garrison imprisoned which consisted of a commander, a conductor of artillery, a gunner, two sergeants, and forty-four rank and file; about one hundred pieces of cannon, one thirteen inch mortar, and a number of swivels. This surprise was carried into execution in the gray of the morning of the tenth day of May, 1775. The sun seemed to rise that morning with a superior luster, and Ticonderoga and its dependencies smiled on its conquerors who tossed about the flowing bowl, and wished success to Congress, and the liberty and freedom of America."

—1775 Ethan Allen, Commandant
of the Green Mountain Boys

THE BATTLE OF BUNKER HILL

*An account of this battle is given by a gentleman in
Providence, Rhode Island, to his friend in New York.*

"On the evening of the 16th of June, Colonel Putnam took possession of Bunker Hill with about two thousand men, and began an entrenchment which they had made some progress in. At eight in the morning a party of Regulars landed at Charlestown, and after plundering it of all of its valuables, set fire to the town in various places. Under cover of the smoke, a body of about five thousand men marched up to our entrenchments, and made a furious and sudden attack. They were driven back three times, and when they were making the third attack, one of our people imprudently spoke aloud that their powder was all gone, which being heard by some of the regular officers, thereby encouraged their men to march up to the trenches with fixed bayonets, on which our people were ordered to retreat which they did with all speed till they got out of musket-shot. They then formed, but were not pursued. In the meantime, six men-of-war and four floating batteries were brought up, and kept up a continual fire on the causeway that leads on to

Charlestown. Our people retreated through the fire, but not without the loss of many of the men. The brave Doctor Warren is among the killed, and Colonel Gardner is wounded. We left six field-pieces on the hill. Our people are now entrenched on Pleasant Hill within cannon shot of Bunker Hill. The loss of the King's troops must be very considerable, the exact number we cannot tell. Among the slain is Major Pitcairn. If our people had been supplied with ammunition, they would have held possession most certainly. Our people are in high spirits, and are very earnest to put this matter on another trial."

—*Massachusetts Rivington's Gazette*, June 29, 1775

GENERAL WASHINGTON TAKES COMMAND OF THE MILITIA

JUNE 20, 1775, PENNSYLVANIA "This morning the three battalions of Philadelphia, and the liberties; together with the artillery company, a troop of light-horse, several companies of light infantry: rangers and riflemen, in the whole about two thousand, marched out to the commons, and having joined the brigade, were reviewed by General Washington, who is this day, appointed Commander-in-Chief of all the North American forces by the honorable Continental Congress.

They went through the manual exercise, firings and maneuvers with great dexterity and exactness."

—*Rivington's Gazette*, June 29, 1775

"DORCHESTER HEIGHTS"

By Hon. J. T. Headley
(Including) Washington Irving

"On the first day of January 1776, the National Flag of thirteen stripes was hoisted for the first time over the American army…The symbol of liberty, it was to move in front of Washington's battalions to victory or in defeat." —Headley

> "At length the camp was rejoiced by the arrival [from Fort Ticonderoga] of Colonel Knox with *that noble train of artillery* consisting of a long train of sleighs drawn by oxen, and bringing more than fifty cannon, mortars and howitzers; besides supplies of lead and flint. The zeal and perseverance he had displayed in his wintry expedition across frozen lakes and snowy wastes, won him the entire confidence of Washington." —Irving

"All this time the two armies lay only a mile apart, in full view of each other's operations. As the winter passed on, the British began to feel the want of provisions. Houses were torn down by the Brits to furnish fuel for their soldiers. The winter had been so mild, that but little ice had formed in the waters around Boston, but at length, in the middle of February, it froze hard enough to bear troops.

A Council of War however, decided that an attempt was too dangerous. Washington nevertheless resolved to take possession of Dorchester Heights, and plant his batteries above the town.

The better to conceal his purpose, and make it appear that an attack on the line was about to be made, Washington on the 2nd of March, opened a tremendous cannonade, the heavy metal reaching even into the city and shattering the houses. The British replied, and the two armies thundered on each other all night. The next night, Washington again opened his heavy batteries. On Monday night while the deafening explosions were filling the inhabitants of Boston with terror, he ordered that two thousand men march swiftly across the neck and occupy the heights.

The wife of John Adams, Abigail, knew that a general action was meditated, and wrote, 'I have been in a constant state of anxiety…It has been said tomorrow and tomorrow for this month, and when the dreadful tomorrow will be, I know not. But hark! The house this instant, shakes with the roar of cannon. I went to bed after twelve, my heart kept pace with them all night. 'Tis now an incessant roar—How many of our dear countrymen must fall!'

'Dorchester Heights will become a second Bunker Hill, and the rebels must be driven from them, or the city abandoned,' said Howe." —Headley

"Washington, not doubting that the enemy would storm his works, had therefore planned an assault on the city from the opposite side when it took place. Two columns of two thousand men, were to embark in boats near the mouth of Charles River, cross under cover of the fire of three floating batteries, land in two places in Boston, secure the strong posts, force the gates and works at the Neck, and let in the Roxbury troops." —Irving

"Howe prepared to storm the American works, and commanded Earl Percy with three thousand men to attack them without delay. Washington anticipating this, galloped to the heights and gazed on the preparations for battle going on in the enemy's camp. He did not doubt for a moment of winning a glorious victory.

With three thousand men and Percy at their head, the British were marched to the shore with orders to rendezvous at Castle William, (a fortified island for jumping off), and when night came on, mount to the assault. The hills around were covered with spectators...But toward night a heavy wind arose rendering it impossible for the boats to land, and while the troops stood awaiting the orders to advance, the night came on dark and stormy. The rain fell in torrents, and they returned drenched and chilled to camp. All the next day the storm continued to rage." —Headley

"That day was equally unpropitious. The storm continued with torrents of rain. The attack was again postponed. In the meantime, the Americans went on strengthening their works. By the time the storm subsided, General Howe deemed them too strong to be easily carried. The attempt therefore, was relinquished altogether." —Irving

"Washington, disappointed in not bringing on an engagement, returned to camp, and Howe began to make preparations for his departure. At length the army, numbering all told about eleven thousand men were taken aboard the transports—whose sails were soon moving down the bay. The American army no sooner saw the enemy in motion, then it paraded at Cambridge and entered the deserted works of the British.

'A wind more violent than anything I ever heard,' was the verdict of one British soldier."

—Headley

"Providence Rides a Storm"

..."Although the great storm of March 5-6, 1776 gets little attention in the American historical saga; surely it was one of the most crucial events in the entire American Revolution. Had rain, and wind and thunder not intervened, there would have been on Boston Neck such a battle as the Continental Army actually was to fight only once: at Fort Washington in upper Manhattan, where the entire American force that was engaged, would fall to the enemy...

The troops Washington had intended to land in Boston could never have regained their boats. They would have been trapped, forced either to annihilate the British or to face total defeat themselves.

General Washington wrote of that storm, 'It was a remarkable interposition of Providence.'"

— James Flexner

CHAPTER 8

The Battle of Long Island

By Washington Irving

THE DECLARATION OF INDEPENDENCE

"The British fleet, bearing the army from Boston had disappeared from the coast. 'Whither they are bound, and where they next will pitch their tents,' writes Washington, 'I know not.' He conjectured their destination to be New York, and made his arrangements accordingly, but he was mistaken. General Howe had steered for Halifax; there to await the arrival of strong reinforcements from England...We have a lively picture of the State of New York, *in letters* written at the time:

'When you are informed that New York is deserted by its old inhabitants, and filled with soldiers from New England, Philadelphia, Jersey, etc., you will naturally conclude the environs of it are not very safe from so undisciplined a multitude as our provincials are represented to be, but I do believe there are very few instances of so great a number of men together, with so little mischief done by them. They have all the simplicity of plowmen in their manners, and seem quite strangers to the vices of older soldiers. They have been employed in creating fortifications in every part of the town...'

Washington arrived at New York on the 13th of April, 1776. Many of the works which Lee had commenced were by this time finished; others were in progress. It was apprehended the principal operations of the enemy would be on Long Island...in the neighborhood of Brooklyn...

Washington at that time was not aware of the extraordinary expedients England had recently resorted to against the next campaign. Four thousand Hessians had entered the British service...They were to be paid seven pounds, four shillings and four pence sterling for every soldier furnished by them, and as much more for every one slain.

'We expect a bloody summer in New York and Canada,' writes Washington to his brother Augustine, 'and I am sorry to say that we are not, either in men or arms, prepared for it. However, it is to be hoped that if our cause is just, as I most religiously believe it, the same Providence which has in many instances appeared for us, will still go on to afford His aid...'

On the 29th of June an express from the look-out on Staten Island announced that forty sail were in sight. They were, in fact, ships from Halifax bringing between nine and ten thousand of the troops recently from Boston; together with six transports filled with Highland troops that had joined the fleet at sea.

While city and country were thus agitated by apprehensions of danger, both internal and external, other arrivals swelled the number of ships in the bay of New York to one hundred and thirty men-of-war and transports. They made no movement to ascend the Hudson, but anchored off Staten Island where they landed their troops, and the hillsides were soon whitened with their tents.

Washington beheld the gathering storm with an anxious eye, aware that General Howe only awaited the arrival of his brother the admiral to commence hostile operations.

While danger was gathering round New York, and its inhabitants were in mute suspense and fearful anticipation, the General Congress at Philadelphia was discussing within closed doors, what John Adams pronounced—

'The greatest question ever debated in America, and as great as ever was or will be debated among man.'

A resolution passed unanimously on the 2nd of July, 1776:

'That these United Colonies are, and of a right ought to be free and Independent States.'

'The 2nd of July will be the most memorable epoch in the history of America,' said Adams. 'I am apt to believe that it will be celebrated by succeeding generations as the great anniversary festival. It ought to be commemorated as the day of deliverance by solemn acts of devotion to Almighty God. It ought to be solemnized with pomp and parade, with guns, bells, bonfires and illuminations from one end of this continent to the other; from this time forth forevermore.'

In the steeple of the State House was a bell imported twenty-three years previously from London...It bore the portentous text from Scripture:

'Proclaim liberty throughout all the land, unto all the inhabitants thereof.'

A clang from the bell gave notice that the bill had passed.

On the 9th of July, Washington caused **THE DECLARATION OF INDEPENDENCE** to be read at six o'clock in the evening, at the head of each brigade of the army.

BOSTON, JULY 21, 1776: Abigail Adams' letter to her husband: "Last Thursday after hearing a very good sermon, I went with the multitude into King Street to hear the Proclamation for Independence read and proclaimed. Some field-pieces with the train were brought there. The troops appeared under arms, and all the inhabitants assembled there when Colonel Craft read from the balcony of the State House the Proclamation. Great attention was given to every word. As soon as he ended, the cry from the balcony was, 'God save our American States,' and then three cheers which rent the air. The bells rang, the privateers fired, the cannon were discharged, the platoons followed, and every face appeared joyful. Mr. B. then gave a sentiment, 'Stability and perpetuity to American Independence.'

After dinner, the King's Arms were taken down from the State House, and every vestige of him from every place in which it appeared, and burnt in King Street. Thus ends royal authority in this State. And all the people shall say, 'Amen!'"

In the course of a few days arrived a hundred sail with large reinforcements; among which were 1000 Hessians and many more reported on the way. Attacks of the enemy were now without question. Some of Washington's ablest advisers questioned the plan of remaining in New York where they might be entrapped; endangering the loss of the army and its military stores. During early August and late July, ships of war continued to arrive and landed on Staten Island. Clinton and Cornwallis came and brought 3000 troops.

Many of the yeomen of the country, thus hastily summoned from the farm, were destitute of arms; in lieu of which they were ordered to bring with them a shovel, spade or pickax; or a scythe straightened and fastened to a pole.

'The men turn out of their harvest fields to defend their country with surprising alacrity. The absence of so many of them at this time when their harvests are perishing for want of the sickle, will greatly distress the country'. —(a citizen)

'The women tilled the ground, planted, mowed hay, gathered the harvest and assisted in manufacturing ammunition. They too were marked out for the enemy's vengeance.' —Women of the Revolution

(Irving's narrative concludes): Reports from different quarters gave Washington reason to apprehend that the design of the enemy might be to land part of their force on Long Island, and endeavor to get possession of the heights of Brooklyn which overlooked New York; while another part should land above the city...Thus, various disconnected points distant from each other, and a great extent of intervening country had to be defended by raw troops against a superior force; well-disciplined and possessed of every facility for operation by land and water."

—Washington Irving

LETTERS TO NEWSPAPERS FROM TWO SOLDIERS

The First Soldier, New York, August 22, 1776

"This night we have reason to expect the grand attack from our barbarian enemies; the reasons why, follow: The night before last a lad went over to Staten Island, supped there with a friend, and got safe back again undiscovered. Soon after he went to General Washington, and upon good authority reported that the English army, amounting to fifteen or twenty thousand, had embarked and were in readiness for an engagement; that seven ships of the line and a number of other vessels of war, were to surround this city and cover their landing; that the Hessians, being fifteen thousand, were to remain on the island and attack Perth Amboy, Elizabethtown Point, and Bergen while the main body were doing their best at New York. Also, that the Highlanders expected America was already conquered, and that they were only to come over and settle on our lands, for which reason they had brought their churns, ploughs, etc.

Last evening, in a violent thunder storm, one man ventured over...informs, that last night the fleet was to come up, but the thunder storm prevented it. The truth of this appears from the circumstance of about three thousand red coats landing at ten o'clock this morning on Long Island, where by this time it is supposed our people are hard at it...

The thunder storm of last evening was one of the most dreadful we ever witnessed. It lasted from seven to ten o'clock. Several claps struck in and about New York. Many houses were damaged and several lives lost. Three officers; a captain and two lieutenants, belonging to Colonel McDougal's regiment, were struck instantly dead. The points of their swords for several inches were melted. When God speaks, who can but fear?"

—*The Pennsylvania Journal*, August 26, 1776

The Second Soldier, New York, August 30, 1776

"About twelve o'clock last Monday night, we were alarmed by the return of some of our scouting parties who advised us that the English were in motion, and coming up the island with several field-pieces, on which near three thousand men were ordered out, consisting chiefly of the Pennsylvania and Maryland troops; to attack them on their march...About sunrise the next morning, we came up with a very large body of them.

The enemy then advanced to us, upon which Lord Sterling, who commanded, drew us up in a line, and offered them battle in the true English taste. The British army then advanced within about three hundred yards of us, and began a very heavy fire from their cannon and mortars; for both the balls and shells flew very fast, now and then taking off a head. Our men stood it amazingly well—not even one of them showed a disposition to shrink... We stood from sunrise till twelve o'clock, the enemy firing upon us the chief part of the time, when the main body of their army, by a route we never dreamed of, had entirely surrounded us and drove within the lines, or scattered in the woods all our men except the Delaware and Maryland battalions. Thus situated, we were ordered to attempt a retreat by fighting our way through the enemy who had posted themselves, and nearly filled every field and road between us and our lines. We had not retreated a quarter of a mile before we were fired upon by an advanced part of the enemy, and those upon our rear were playing upon us with their artillery. Our men fought with more than Roman virtue, and would have stood until they were shot down to the man. We forced the advanced party which first attacked us to give way; through which opening we got a passage down to the side of a marsh seldom before waded over, which we passed and then swam a narrow river all the time exposed to the fire of the enemy. The companies commanded by Captains Ramsey and Scott were in the front, and sustained the first fire of the enemy when hardly a man fell.

The whole of the right wing of our battalion, thinking it impossible to march through the marsh, attempted to force their way through the woods where they were almost to a man, killed or taken. The Maryland battalion has lost two hundred and fifty-nine men, amongst whom are twelve officers... Many of the officers lost their swords and guns. We have since entirely abandoned Long Island, bringing off all our military stores.

Generals Sullivan and Stirling are both prisoners; Colonels—-are also taken. There are about a thousand men missing in all; we took a few prisoners. By a lieutenant we took, we understand they had about twenty-three thousand men on the island that morning. Most of our generals were on a high hill in our lines viewing us with glasses. When we began our retreat, they could see the enemy we had to pass through, though we could not. Many of them thought we would surrender in a body without firing. When we began the attack, General Washington wrung his hands, and cried out, 'Good God, what brave fellows I must this day lose.'

I had the satisfaction of dropping one of the enemy the first fire I made; I was so near that I could not miss. I discharged my rifle seven times that day as ever I did at a mark…"

—*Freeman's Journal*, September 28, 1776

"BRITISH GENERAL HOWE'S ACCOUNT"

Includes the following:

"The force of the enemy detached from the lines where General Putnam commanded, was not less, from the best accounts I have had, than ten thousand men…Their loss is computed to be about thirty-three hundred killed, wounded, prisoners and drowned, with five field-pieces and one howitzer taken.

On the part of the King's troops, five officers, and fifty-six non-commissioned officers and rank and file are killed. Twelve officers, and two hundred and forty-five non-commissioned officers and rank and file are wounded…

On August 29th at night the rebels evacuated their entrenchments and Red Hook with the utmost silence, and quitted Governor's Island the following evening leaving their cannon and a quantity of stores in all their works. At daybreak on the 30th, their flight was discovered.

The inhabitants of Long Island, many of whom had been forced into rebellion, have all submitted, and are ready to take the oaths of allegiance." —*Upcott IV*, 401

"THE PATRIOTS RETREAT ACROSS THE EAST RIVER"
By W. Irving

"The morning broke dreary. To appearance, the enemy were 20,000 strong. They were proceeding to entrench themselves, but were driven into their tents by a drenching rain.

New regiments from Philadelphia and Fort Washington arrived, about 800 men. Also Col. Glover's Massachusetts regiments composed of Marblehead fishermen and sailors.

The main body of the enemy kept within their tents until the latter part of the day when they began to break ground as preparing to approach.

A dense fog over the island appeared. During the morning Mifflin and Reed rode to the western outposts. While they were there, a light breeze lifted the fog temporarily from a part of the New York Bay, and revealed the British ships at their anchorage opposite Staten Island. There appeared to be an unusual bustle among them. Boats were passing to and from the admiral's ship as if seeking or carrying orders. Some movement was apparently in agitation. The idea occurred that the fleet was preparing to come up the bay at the turn of the tide and anchor in the East River. In that case the army on Long Island would be completely entrapped.

'Their fleet had been ordered to act in concert with the land force, and attacking the batteries on shore, pass up the East River, and so separating the main American army in New York from that in Brooklyn. A strong east wind surged all day down the East River holding back the ships with its unseen hands.' —J.T. Headley

Troops were fatigued, dispirited and exposed to weather. It was resolved to cross with the troops to the city of New York that very night. 9000 men with all the munitions of war were to be withdrawn from before a victorious army encamped so near that every stroke of spade and axe could be heard. Never did a retreat require greater secrecy. The retreating troops were to be embarked and conveyed across a strait three quarters of a mile wide. Some of the vessels had to be brought from a distance of 15 miles. They were all at Brooklyn at 8 o'clock in the evening, and put under the management of Col. Glover's amphibious Marblehead regiment.

The embarkation began. A strong wind from the northeast, and the boats with oars were insufficient to convey the troops, while those with sails could not make headway against the wind and tide.

The fog that prevailed all this time seemed almost *Providential*. While it hung over Long Island, and concealed the movements of the Americans, the atmosphere was clear on the New York side of the river. *The wind died away; the river became so smooth that the rowboats could be laden almost to the gunwale, and a breeze sprang up for the sailboats.* The whole embarkation of troops, artillery, ammunition, provisions, horses and carts was successful, and by daybreak the greater part had safely reached the city. Washington crossed the river with the last troops.

The fog had cleared sufficiently for the Brits to see the last boats half way across the river. The enemy now had possession of Long Island. British and Hessian troops garrisoned the works at Brooklyn."

—Washington Irving

TALLMADGE ACCOUNT OF THE RETREAT; RESCUE OF HIS HORSE

"Our entrenchment was so weak that it is most wonderful the British general did not attempt to storm it soon after the battle in which his troops had been victorious.

General Washington was so fully aware of the perilous situation of this division of his army that he immediately convened a council of war; at which the propriety of retiring to New York was decided on.

To move so large a body of troops with all their necessary appendages across a river a full mile wide with a rapid current in the face of a victorious, well-disciplined army nearly three times as numerous as his own, and a fleet capable of stopping the navigation so that not one boat could have passed over, seemed to present the most formidable of obstacles.

On the evening of the 29th, by 10 o'clock, the troops began to retire from the lines in such a manner that no chasm was made in the lines, but as one regiment left their station on guard, the remaining troops moved to the right and left and filled up the vacancies, while General Washington took his station at the ferry and superintended the embarkation of the troops.

It was one of the most anxious, busy nights that I ever recollect, and being the third in which hardly any of us had closed our eyes in sleep, we were all greatly fatigued. As the dawn of the next day approached, those of us who remained in the trenches became very anxious for our own safety, and when the dawn appeared there were several regiments still on duty. At this time a very dense fog began to rise and it seemed to settle in a peculiar manner over both encampments. I recollect this peculiar Providential occurrence perfectly well, and so very dense was the atmosphere that I could scarcely discern a man at six yards distance. ...

Finally, the second order arrived for the regiment to retire, and we very joyfully bid those trenches a long adieu. When we reached Brooklyn ferry, the boats had not returned from their last trip, but they very soon appeared and took the whole regiment over to New York, and I think I saw General Washington on the ferry stairs when I stepped into one of the last boats that received the troops. I left my horse tied to a post at the ferry.

The troops having now all safely reached New York, and the fog continuing as thick as ever, I began to think of my favorite horse, and requested leave of volunteers to go with me, and guiding the boat myself, I obtained my horse and got off some distance into the river before the enemy appeared in Brooklyn.

As soon as they reached the ferry we were saluted merrily from their musketry and by their field pieces, but we returned in safety. In the history of warfare, I do not recollect a more fortunate retreat. After all, the Providential appearance of the fog saved a part of our army from being captured and certainly myself; among others who formed the rear guard."

—Benjamin Tallmadge

"THE CAUSES OF FAILURE"

J.T. Headley

"The Battle of Long Island has given rise to much discussion, and various explanations have been covered and excuses rendered of the sad failure. ...The simple truth is the battle should never have been fought, for no precautions could have changed the final result. The enemy were in too strong a force for the American army on the Brooklyn side to resist under the most favorable circumstances that could have been anticipated... There could be no comparison between the military knowledge and ability of the British and American officers...Of the former, of large experiences in many a tedious campaign on the Continent of Europe.

The effect of this defeat on the American army was most disastrous. Despondency and despair took the place of confidence and hope. The militia grew insubordinate, and right in front of the enemy while his strong columns were gathering closer and darker around the city, they began to disband and march away to their homes; nearly whole regiments at a time...heedless of the appeals and threats of their officers. Washington looked around him in dismay, and lost all confidence in his troops...A bombardment was hourly expected, and Washington issued an order for the inhabitants to leave, and soon the roads leading toward Harlem were crowded with fugitives, while hundreds more were seen hurrying across the river to the Jersey shore."

THE MARCH THROUGH NEW YORK CITY

Irving's Narrative continuing:

"Since the retreat from Brooklyn, Washington had narrowly watched the movements of the enemy to discover their further plans. Their whole force except about 4000 men had been transferred from Staten Island to Long Island. 'It is evident,' writes Washington, 'the enemy mean to enclose us on the island of New York by taking post in our rear; while the ships secure the front, and thus by cutting off our communication with the country, oblige us to fight them on their own terms, or surrender.'

General Greene advised that the army should abandon both city and island. Two thirds of the city and suburbs belonged to Tories; there was no great reason therefore to run any considerable risk in its defense. Well might the poor, harassed citizens feel hysterical; threatened as they were by sea and land, and their very defenders debating the policy of burning their houses over their heads. Fortunately for them, Congress had forbidden that any harm be done to New York, trusting that though the enemy might occupy it for a time, it would ultimately be regained.

A resolution of Congress passed the 10th of September, 1776, left the occupation or abandonment of the city entirely at Washington's discretion. The whole of his officers retracted their former opinion and determined that the removal of his army was absolutely necessary.

On the 14th, Washington's baggage was removed to King's bridge; it being clear that the enemy were preparing to encompass him on the island.

Colonel Reed wrote in a letter to his wife in mid-September, 'My country will, I trust, yet be free whatever may be our fate who are cooped up, or are in danger of being so on this tongue of land, where we ought never to have been ...Every night we lie down with the most anxious fears for the fate of tomorrow.'

Three ships of war stood up the Hudson River causing a most tremendous firing; assisted by the cannons of Governor's Island, which firing was returned from the city as well as the scarcity of heavy cannon would allow.

Putnam, on receiving Washington's express, called in his pickets and guards and abandoned the city in all haste, leaving behind him a large quantity of provisions and military stores and most of the heavy cannon. To avoid the enemy, he took the Bloomingdale road, though this exposed him to the enemy's ships anchored in the Hudson. It was a forced march on a sultry day under a burning sun and amid clouds of dust. His army was encumbered with women and children and all kinds of baggage. Many were overcome by fatigue and thirst.

A circumstance which favored Putnam's retreat: Mrs. Murray, of the Society of Friends: The British generals in passing by Murray Hill, made a halt to seek some refreshment. Mrs. Murray set cake and wine before them in abundance. So grateful for these refreshments in the heat of the day, that they lingered over their wine, bantering their patriotic hostess about the ludicrous panic of her countrymen. In the meantime and during that regale, Putnam and his forces had nearly passed by within a mile of them; tradition saying among the American officers that Mrs. Murray saved Putnam's division of the Army.

What were the factors? That mid-September day was an unusually hot day. Had the weather been mild, chances are the British forward march after the Americans would have continued to a dire outcome...

The main body of the army was upon the neck of land several miles long and about a mile wide forming the upper part of Manhattan where It forms a chain of rocky heights and is separated from the mainland by the Harlem River. *Fort Washington* occupied the crest of one of the rocky heights overlooking the Hudson River.

Washington's headquarters continued to be on Harlem Heights for several days, during which time he was continually in the saddle riding about a broken, woody and half-wild country, forming posts and choosing sites for breastworks and redoubts...

In the morning of the 27th of September, the heavy booming of cannon was heard from a distance; seemingly in the direction of *Fort Washington*. Scouts galloped off to gain intelligence. It was the thundering of these cannonades which had reached Washington's camp, then at White Plains, and even startled the highlands of the Hudson..." — W. Irving

New York "So vast a fleet was never before seen together in the port of New York, or perhaps in all of America. The ships are stationed up the East River or Sound as far as Turtle Bay, and near the town. The multitude of masts carries the appearance of a small woods...The Men of War are moored chiefly also up New

York Sound, and make, with the other ships, a very magnificent and formidable appearance." —*Freeman's Journal*

"THE CAPTURE OF FORT WASHINGTON"

"General Howe did not attempt to dislodge Washington from his fastness. He at one time ordered an attack on the rear-guard, but a violent rain prevented it, and for two or three days he remained seemingly inactive...During the night of November 4th, the quiet was interrupted. The enemy were decamping. Long trains were observed crossing the hilly country along the roads leading to Dobbs' Ferry on the Hudson. The movement continued for three successive days until their whole force, British and Hessians, disappeared from White Plains.

On the morning of the 12th of November, 1776, Washington crossed the Hudson River with the remainder of the troops; destined for the Jerseys. Washington struck a direct course for Fort Lee, being anxious about affairs at Fort Washington.

Washington, surrounded by several of his officers, had been an anxious spectator of the battle from the opposite of the Hudson. The action about the lines to the south lay open to him, and could be distinctly seen through a telescope. When he saw...the line broken and troops overpowered by numbers retreating to the fort, he gave up the game as lost. The worse sight of all was to behold his men cut down and bayoneted by the Hessians while begging quarter. It is said so completely to have overcome him that, 'He wept with the tenderness of a child.' The sight of the American flag hauled down, and the British flag waving in its place, told Washington of the surrender." — Irving

The following account of the sufferings of the men was obtained from the prisoners themselves several months later.

"As soon as they were taken, they were robbed of all their baggage, of whatever money they had, of their silver shoe-buckles and knee-buckles, and many were stripped almost naked of their clothes.

After they were taken, they were in the first place put on board the ships and thrust down into the hold, where they nearly suffocated for want of air. They were of a sudden taken out, and put into some of the churches in New York without covering or a spark of fire.

Besides these things, they suffered extremely for want of provisions. What was given for three days was not enough for one day... the water allowed them was so brackish and nasty, they could not drink it, till reduced to extremity. When winter came on, our people suffered extremely for want of fire and clothes. There were no fireplaces in churches...Nor had they a single blanket or any bedding, not even straw allowed them till a little before Christmas.

By these means, and in this way, fifteen hundred brave Americans who had nobly gone forth in defense of their injured oppressed country, but whom the chance of war had cast into the hands of our enemies, died in New York; many of whom were very amiable, promising youths, of good families—the very flower of our land. And of those who lived to come out of prison, the greater part, as far as I can learn, are dead and dying. Their constitutions are broken, the stamina of nature worn out, they cannot recover—they die..." —*Freeman's Journal,* (February 18, 1777)

"TO THE INDEPENDENT SONS OF LIBERTY"

"*By the favor of Providence,* we have reached that political point: Independence. Our work is now plain before us: to persevere to the end in supporting the Declaration we have made to the world. To do this, every consideration urges us; to retreat is death—is slavery; calamities of every name, and all the gloomy horrors of the most odious and execrable tyranny. Before us is all the glory of Freedom, pregnant with every felicity our wishes can grasp, or human nature enjoy. If we continue our exertions with that wisdom and magnanimity with which we began, Liberty will soon triumph, wealth flow in through ten thousand channels, and America become the glory of all lands. Tyranny is now exerting her utmost power, and if resisted a little longer, George, and all his murderers, must bid adieu to America forever; then we shall have the double happiness and honor of subduing the tyrants, and enjoying liberty...If we continue in the way of well-doing, we shall certainly succeed; for unerring wisdom has told us, 'If we trust in the Lord and do good, we shall dwell in the land and be fed.' Therefore, we have nothing to do but to be faithful to God, and our Country, and the blessings we contend for will be the portion to us and our children."

—*New Hampshire Gazette,* November 26, 1776

CHAPTER 9

Crossing New Jersey
By W. Irving

"*The enemy had crossed the Hudson River on a very rainy night in two divisions.* The whole corps, 6000 strong and under command of Cornwallis, were landed with their cannon by ten o'clock; five or six miles above Fort Lee and under that line of lofty cliffs ... the Palisades. The cannon were dragged up a very narrow road for nearly half a mile to the top of a precipice.

Washington was told that the enemy were extending themselves across the country. He at once saw that they intended to form a line from the Hudson to the Hackensack, and hem the whole garrison in between the two rivers. Nothing would save them but a prompt retreat to secure the bridge over the Hackensack. The retreat commenced in all haste. There was a want of horses and wagons; a great quantity of baggage, stores and provisions were abandoned...Even the tents were left standing and camp-kettles left on the fire. With all their speed they did not reach the Hackensack River before the vanguard of the enemy was close upon them. Expecting a brush, the greater part hurried over the bridge, others crossed at the ferry, and some higher up. Some of Cornwallis troops occupied the tents they had abandoned.

At Hackensack the army did not exceed 3000 men, and they were dispirited by ill success and the loss of tents and baggage. They were without entrenching tools in a flat country where there were no natural fastnesses. Washington resolved to avoid any attack from the enemy, though by so doing he must leave a fine and fertile region open to their ravages. A second move was necessary again to avoid the danger of being enclosed between two rivers… He again decamped and threw himself on the west bank of the Passaic, in the neighborhood of Newark.

His army, small as it was, would soon be less. The term of enlistment of those under General Mercer, from 'the flying camp', was nearly expired and it was not probable that; disheartened as they were by defeats and losses, exposed to inclement weather, and unaccustomed to military hardships, they would longer forego the comforts of their homes to drag out the residue of a ruinous campaign.

A letter to Governor Livingston was dispatched describing his hazardous situation, and entreating him to call out a portion of the New Jersey militia. General Mifflin was sent to Philadelphia to implore immediate aid from Congress and the local authorities.

The situation of the little army was daily becoming more perilous…Breaking up his camp once more, he continued his retreat toward New Brunswick, but so close was Cornwallis upon him that his advance entered one end of Newark, just as the American rear-guard had left the other."

A LETTER BY A BRITISH OFFICER TO HIS FRIEND IN LONDON: "The rebel army are in so wretched a condition as to clothing and accoutrements, that I believe no nation ever saw such a set of tatterdemalions. There are few coats among them, but what are out at elbows, and in a whole regiment there is scarce a pair of breeches. Judge then, how they must endure by a winter's campaign. We who are warmly clothed and well-equipped already feel it severely; for it is even now much colder than I ever felt it in England."

IN A LETTER BY WASHINGTON: "The force here...at present is weak, and it has been more owing to the badness of the weather that the enemy's progress has been checked, than any resistance we could make...Their plan is not entirely unfolded, but I shall not be surprised if Philadelphia should turn out to be the object of their movement."

From Brunswick, Washington wrote on the 29th to the Governor of the Jerseys requesting him to have all boats and river craft for 70 miles along the Delaware River removed to the western bank, out of the reach of the enemy, and put under guard.

Washington lingered at Brunswick until the 1st of December, 1776 in the vain hope of being reinforced. The enemy in the meantime, advanced through the country stealing wagons and horses, cattle and sheep, as if for a distant march. At length their vanguard appeared on the opposite side of the Raritan. Washington immediately broke down the end of the bridge next to the village, and after nightfall resumed his retreat. In the meantime, as the river was fordable, Captain Alexander Hamilton planted his field-pieces on high commanding ground, and opened a spirited fire to check any attempt of the enemy to cross...

The people of New Jersey inhabited an open, agricultural country where the sound of war had never been heard...They beheld the Commander-in-Chief retreating through their country with a handful of men who were weary, way-worn, dispirited, without tents, or clothing. Many of them were barefoot; exposed to wintry weather, and driven from post to post by a well-clad, well-fed, triumphant force, tricked out in all the glittering bravery of war.

The harassed army reached Trenton on the 2nd of December. Washington immediately proceeded to remove his baggage and stores across the Delaware River.

'The rear-guard,' says an American account, 'had barely crossed the Delaware River, when Lord Cornwallis came marching down with all the pomp of war, in great expectation of getting boats and immediately pursuing.' Not one was to be had there or elsewhere; for Washington had caused the boats, for an extent of 70 miles up and down the river, to be secured on the right bank. The enemy was effectually brought to a standstill. Cornwallis gave up the pursuit...and stationed his main force at Brunswick, trusting to be able before long to cross the Delaware on ice.

In a letter to his brother Augustine, Washington wrote of the critical state of affairs: 'If every nerve is not strained to recruit the army with all possible expedition, I think the game is pretty nearly up...You can form no idea of the perplexity of my situation. No man I believe ever had a greater choice of evils, and less means to extricate himself from them.'

Congress, prior to their adjourning, had resolved that until they should otherwise order, General Washington should be possessed of all power to order and direct all things relative to the department and to the operations of war. Thus empowered, he proceeded immediately to recruit three battalions of artillery. To those whose terms were expiring, he promised an augmentation of 25 percent upon their pay, and a bounty of ten dollars to the men for six weeks' service...The promise of increased pay and bounties had kept together for a time the dissolving army. The local militia began to turn out freely.

Everything showed careless confidence on the part of the enemy. Howe was in winter quarters at New York. His troops were loosely cantoned about the Jerseys from the Delaware River to Brunswick, so that they could not readily be brought to act in concert on a sudden alarm. The Hessians were in the advance stationed along the Delaware, and facing the American lines, which were along the west bank. Cornwallis, thinking his work accomplished had obtained leave of absence, and was likewise at New York, preparing to embark for England. Washington had now between five and six thousand men fit for service, and these he meditated to cross the river at night at different points, and make simultaneous attacks upon the Hessian advance posts.

He calculated upon the eager support of his troops who were burning to revenge the outrages of their homes and families committed by these foreign mercenaries. They considered the Hessians as mere hirelings; slaves to a petty despot, fighting for sordid pay, and actuated by no sentiment of patriotism or honor. They had rendered themselves the horror of the Jerseys, by rapine, brutality and heartlessness.

A brigade of three Hessian regiments, those of Raul, were stationed at Trenton. Colonel Raul had the command of the post at his own solicitation, and in consequence of the laurels he had gained at White Plains and Fort Washington." —W. Irving

GEORGE WASHINGTON'S
LETTER TO HIS BROTHER

December 18, 1776

"Since that time, of my last letter and a little before, our affairs have taken an adverse turn, but not more than was to be expected from the unfortunate measures, which had been adopted for the establishment of our army. The retreat of the enemy from White Plains led me to think that they would turn their thoughts to the Jerseys, if no farther, and induced me to cross the North River with some of the troops in order, if possible, to oppose them. I expected to have met at least five thousand men of the Flying Camp and militia; instead of which I found less than one half of that number, and no disposition in the inhabitants to afford the least aid. This being perfectly well known to the enemy, they threw over a large body of troops which pushed us from place to place, till we were obliged to cross the Delaware with less than three thousand men fit for duty, owing to the dissolution of our force by short enlistments. The enemy's numbers, from the best accounts, exceeded ten or twelve thousand men...

...We are in a very disaffected part of the province, and between you and me, I think our affairs are in as very bad situation; not so much from the apprehension of General Howe's army, as from the defection of New York, Jerseys and Pennsylvania...

I have no doubt but General Howe will still make an attempt upon Philadelphia this winter. I see nothing to oppose him a fortnight hence, as the time of all the troops, except those of Virginia reduced almost to nothing, and Smallwood's Regiment of Maryland, equally as bad, will expire in less than that time. In a word, my dear

Sir, if every nerve is not strained to recruit the new army with all possible expedition, I think the game is pretty near up, owing in a great measure, to the insidious arts of the enemy, and disaffection of the colonies before mentioned, but principally to the accursed policy of short enlistments, and placing too great a dependence on the militia, the evil consequences of which were foretold fifteen months ago with a spirit almost prophetic. Before this reaches you, you will no doubt have heard of the captivity of General Lee. This is an additional misfortune, and the more vexatious as it was by his own folly and imprudence he was taken; going three miles out of his own camp, and within twenty of the enemy to lodge. A rascally Tory rode in the night to give notice of it to the enemy, who sent a party of Light-Horse that seized and carried him, with every mark of triumph and indignity.

You can form no idea of the perplexity of my situation. No man, I believe, ever had a greater choice of difficulties, and less means to extricate himself from them. However, under a full persuasion of the justice of our cause, I cannot entertain an idea that it will finally sink, though it may remain for some time under a cloud."

PATRICK HENRY, Governor of Virginia, received an anonymous letter saying, "A dreary wilderness is still before us, and unless a Moses or a Joshua are raised up on our behalf, we must perish before we reach the promise land."

"THE AMERICAN CRISIS"

By Thomas Paine, December 23, 1776

"These are the times that try men's souls. The summer soldier and the sunshine patriot will, in this crisis, shrink from the service of his Country, but he that stands it now, deserves the love and thanks of man and woman. Tyranny, like hell, is not easily conquered; yet we have this consolation with us, that the harder the conflict, the more glorious the triumph. What we obtain too cheap, we esteem too lightly: 'tis dearness only that gives everything its value. Heaven knows how to put a proper price upon its goods, and it would be strange indeed, if so celestial an article as *freedom* should not be highly rated. Britain with an army to enforce her tyranny, has declared that they have a right (not only to tax) but 'to bind us in all cases whatsoever,' and if being bound in that manner is not slavery, then is there not such a thing as slavery upon earth.

I have as little superstition in me as any man living, but my secret opinion has ever been, and still is, that God Almighty will not give up a people to military destruction, or leave them unsupported to perish, who have so earnestly and so repeatedly sought to avoid the calamities of war by every decent method which wisdom could invent. Neither have I so much of the infidel in me, as to suppose that He has relinquished the government of the world, and given us up to the care of devils, and as I do not, I cannot see on what grounds the king of Britain can look up to Heaven for help against us: a common murderer, a highwayman, or a housebreaker, has as good a pretense as he...

Howe, in my little opinion, committed a great error in general-ship in not throwing a body of forces off from Staten Island through Amboy, by which means he might have seized all our stores at Brunswick, and intercepted our march into Pennsylvania, but if we believe the power of hell to be limited, we must likewise believe that their agents are under some Providential control.

I shall not now attempt to give all the particulars of our retreat to the Delaware. Suffice it for the present to say, that both officers and men, though greatly harassed and fatigued, frequently without rest, covering or provision; the inevitable consequences of a long retreat, bore it with a manly and martial spirit. All their wishes centered in one, which was, that the country would turn out and help them to drive the enemy back...

I call not upon a few, but upon all; not on this State or that State, but on every State, up and help us. Lay your shoulders to the wheel; better have too much force than too little when so great an object is at stake. Let it be told to the future world, that in the depth of winter, when nothing but hope and virtue could survive, that the city and the country, alarmed at one common danger, came forth to meet and repulse it. Say not that thousands are gone; turn out your tens of thousands; throw not the burden of the day upon Providence, but *show your faith by your works*, that God may bless you. It matters not where you live, or what rank of life you hold, the evil or the blessing will reach you all. The far and the near, the home-counties and the back, the rich and the poor, will suffer or rejoice alike. The heart that feels not now, is dead; the blood of his children will curse his cowardice who shrinks back at a time when a little might have saved the whole, and made them happy.

I thank God that I fear not. I see no real cause for fear. I know our situation well, and can see the way out of it. While our army was collected, Howe dared not risk a battle, and it is no credit to him that he decamped from the White Plains, and waited a mean opportunity to ravage the defenseless Jerseys, but it is great credit to us that, with a handful of men, we sustained an orderly retreat for near an hundred miles; brought off our ammunition, all our field pieces, the greatest part of our stores, and had four rivers to pass. None can say that our retreat was precipitate, for we were near three weeks in performing it, that the country might have time to come in." —Thomas Paine

Thomas Paine's Background

"Thomas Paine was born 1737 in England. His father was a Quaker. He was an avid reader. By stroke of fate, Paine met Benjamin Franklin in London. Franklin, impressed by the 'Ingenious, worthy young man,' gave him letters of introduction to Americans. He emigrated to America, arriving in Philadelphia in 1774. He became caught up in the question of American independence from Great Britain. 'It was the cause of America, that made me an author,' he said.

"Common Sense": [Paine's Book] To those who said that America had flourished under British Rule, Paine answered: 'We may as well assert that because a child has thrived upon milk, that it is never to have meat.' It was a call for independence from Great Britain. 'Everything that is right or reasonable pleads for separation. The blood of the slain, the weeping voice of nature cries, 'Tis Time to Part.' There is no doubt that *Common Sense* was an influence on *The Declaration of Independence*.

Paine joined Washington's army and was with it during the New Jersey retreat in the winter of 1776. 'Writing at every place we stopped.' He composed Number 1 of The *Crisis* papers.

In 1787 he went to France and then to England. After the outbreak of the French Revolution in 1789, he traveled between London and Paris, as a defender of the cause. In 1791 he published *Rights of Man* which was outlawed in England with him. He fled to France and became an honorary French citizen.

He wrote *The Age of Reason* which brought hostility on him for his rejection of orthodox religion. In the first chapter, Paine stated his beliefs: 'I believe in one God, and no more; and I hope for happiness beyond this life. I believe in the equality of man; and I believe that religious duties consist in doing justly, loving mercy and endeavoring to make our fellow creatures happy.'

Paine returned to the United States in 1802 where he spent the last seven years of his life, socially rejected and suffering from poverty and ill health. Time has softened the undeserved hostility. His motto was: *My country is the World, and my religion is to do good.*"—By Saul K. Padover

THE BATTLE OF TRENTON
Described by an Aide to Washington

"DECEMBER 25, 1776: Christmas morning. They make a great deal of Christmas in Germany, and no doubt the Hessians will drink a great deal of beer and have a dance tonight. They will be sleepy tomorrow morning. Washington will set the tone about daybreak. The rations are cooked. New flints and ammunition have been distributed. Colonel Glover's fishermen from Marblehead,

Massachusetts, are to manage the boats just as they did in the retreat from Long Island.

CHRISTMAS, 6 P.M.: The regiments have had their evening parade, but instead of returning to their quarters are marching toward the ferry. It is fearfully cold and raw and a snow-storm is setting in. The wind is northeast and beats in the faces of the men. It will be a terrible night for the soldiers who have no shoes. Some of them have tied old rags around their feet; others are barefoot, but I have not heard a man complain. They are ready to suffer any hardship and die rather than give up their liberty.

DECEMBER 26, 3 A.M.: I am writing in the ferry house. The troops are all over, and the boats have gone back for the artillery. We are three hours behind the set time. Colonel Glover's men have had a hard time to force the boats through the floating ice with the snow drifting in their faces. I never have seen Washington so determined as he is now. He stands on the bank of the river, wrapped in his cape, superintending the landing of his troops. He is calm and collected, but very determined. The storm is changing to sleet, and cuts like a knife. The last cannon is being landed, and we are ready to mount our horses. (Irving: 'The storm had kept everyone indoors, and the snow had deadened the tread of the troops and the rumbling of the artillery.')

DECEMBER 26, NOON: It was nearly four o'clock when we started...A man came with a message to Washington from General Sullivan, that the storm was wetting the muskets and rendering them unfit for service. 'Tell General Sullivan to use the bayonet. I am resolved to take Trenton,' Washington said.

It was just eight o'clock. Looking down the road I saw a Hessian running out of the house. He yelled in Deutsch and swung his arms. Three or four others came out with their guns. Two of them fired at us, but the bullets whistled over our heads.

The next moment we heard drums beat and a bugle sound, and then from the west came the boom of a cannon. General Washington's face lighted up instantly, for he knew that it was one of Sullivan's guns. We could see a great commotion down toward the meetinghouse; men running here and there, officers swinging their swords, artillerymen harnessing their horses. Washington gave the order to advance, and we rushed on to the junction of King and Queen Streets. Forrest wheeled six of his cannon into position to sweep both streets...The Hessians were just ready to open fire with two of their cannon when Captain William Washington and Lieutenant James Monroe with their men rushed forward and captured them. We saw Raul come riding up the street from his headquarters...

His men were frightened and confused, for our men were firing upon them from fences and houses and they were falling fast. Instead of advancing they ran into an apple orchard. The officers tried to rally them, but our men kept advancing and picking off the officers. It was not long before Raul tumbled from his horse and his soldiers threw down their guns and gave themselves up as prisoners.

DECEMBER 26, 3 P.M.: I have been talking with Raul's adjutant, Lieutenant Piel. He says that Raul sat down to a grand dinner at the Trenton Tavern on Christmas Day; that he drank a great deal of wine, and sat up nearly all night playing cards. He had been in bed for a short time when the battle began and was sound asleep. Piel shook him, but found it hard work to wake him up… 'What's the matter?' Raul asked. Piel informed him that a battle was going on…He dressed himself, rushed out, and mounted his horse to be mortally wounded a few minutes later.

We have taken nearly one thousand prisoners, six cannon, more than one thousand muskets, twelve drums and four colors. About forty Hessians were killed or wounded. Our loss is only two killed and three wounded. Two of the latter are Captain Washington and Lieutenant James Monroe who rushed forward very bravely to seize the cannon.

It is a glorious victory. It will rejoice the hearts of our friends everywhere and give new life to our hitherto waning fortunes."

"To Colonel Clement Biddle, Continental Army, to the Committee of Safety: If your Honorable Committee could by any means furnish Shoes & Stockings for our Troops, it will be a great relief." —(signed) Col. John Fitzgerald

THE BATTLE OF PRINCETON

"Washington gave the British another surprise a week later. Alarmed by the capture of the Hessians at Trenton, Howe ordered General Cornwallis to unite the different bodies of troops. Meanwhile Washington, who had first returned to Philadelphia with his prisoners, had crossed the Delaware River again to New Jersey.

On January 2, 1777, Cornwallis thought that he had caught Washington with his back to the Delaware which it would be impossible to re-cross in the presence of a hostile army. Cornwallis exclaimed, 'At last we have run down the old fox, and we will bag him in the morning.' Instead, Washington, leaving his campfires burning to deceive the British, marched around their lines toward Princeton where he put to flight three regiments of British on their way to join Cornwallis, and they took many prisoners.

At daybreak Cornwallis faced an empty camp, while the booming of cannon in the direction of Princeton revealed to him the game *the old fox* had played."

—H. Bourne and E.J. Benton

Newspaper Account by one of the Patriots

"Our fires were built in due season, and were very numerous, and whilst the enemy were amused by these appearances, and preparing for a general attack the ensuing day, our army marched at about one in the morning to Princeton. When our army arrived near the hill, about one mile from the town, they found a body of the enemy formed upon it, and ready to receive them; upon which a spirited attack was made, both with field pieces and musketry, and after an obstinate resistance and losing a considerable number of their men upon the field, those of them who could not make their escape, surrendered prisoners of war. We immediately marched on to the center of town, and there took another party of the enemy near the college...The army is now near Morristown in high spirits...The loss sustained by the enemy was much greater than ours."

—*Pennsylvania Journal* February 5, 1777

"The enemy who had all the Jerseys, are now only in possession of Amboy and Brunswick. This is a great reverse, in the course of a fortnight, to the British power."

> —Letter from Morristown,
> *Freeman's Journal*, January 28, 1777

..."I must do them the justice to add, that they have undergone more fatigue and hardship than I expected militia, especially citizens, would have done at this inclement season. I am just moving to Morristown where I shall endeavor to put them under the best cover I can. Hitherto we have been without any; many of our poor soldiers are quite barefoot and ill clad in other respects."

> —General Washington

"The rest of the winter of 1776-1777, Washington spent with his army undisturbed at Morristown Heights, N.J., near enough to disturb the British line of communications if the latter should make a sudden move on Philadelphia. It was a dark period for the Americans. Washington reorganized his dwindling army, and pledged his own private fortune to sustain his men. Other generals did the same; while Robert Morris, a merchant of Philadelphia raised a subscription of fifty thousand dollars in cash, which he placed with the Commander-in-Chief."

> —Emerson Fite

A Letter from London

"His Majesty intends to open this year's campaign with ninety-thousand Hessians, Tories, Japanese, Moors, Esquimaux, Persian archers, Laplanders, Feejee Islanders and Light horse. With this terrific and horrendous armament, in conjunction with the tremendous and irresistible fleet, he is resolved to terminate this unnatural war the next summer as it will be impossible for the rebels to bring an equal number in the field. His Majesty has also the strongest assurances that France will co-operate with him in humbling his seditions subjects...Fly, fly, oh fly, for protection to the royal standard, or ye will be swept from the face of the earth with the besom of destruction, and cannonaded in a moment into nullities and nonentities, and no mortal can tell into what other kind of quiddities and quoddities."

Freeman's Journal, March 22, 1777

PENNSYLVANIA, JULY 5, 1777: "Yesterday being the first anniversary of the Independence of the United States of America, was celebrated in Philadelphia with demonstrations of joy and festivity. About noon all the armed ships and galleys in the river were drawn up before the city, dressed in the gayest manner with the colors of the United States and streamers displayed. At one o'clock, the yards being properly manned, they began the celebration of the day by a discharge of thirteen cannon from each of the ships, and one from each of the thirteen galleys, in honor of the thirteen United States...

Towards evening several troops of horse, a corps of artillery, and a brigade of North Carolina forces, which was in town on its way to join the grand army, were drawn up in Second Street, and reviewed by Congress and the General Officers. The evening was closed with the ringing of bells, and at night there was a grand exhibition of fire-works which began and concluded with thirteen rockets on the commons, and the city was beautifully illuminated."

—*Pennsylvania Journal*, July 9, 1777

CHAPTER 10

The Battle of Saratoga and the Winter in Valley Forge

E. FITE NARRATIVE

"In the spring of 1777, General Howe set out by water from New York for Chesapeake Bay to attempt the capture of Philadelphia from the south. Washington opposed him at the Brandywine River in southeast Pennsylvania, and at Germantown, a suburb of Philadelphia, but could not prevent him from occupying the city, the then capital of the New United States.

In northern New York, the British were not as successful as around New York City and Philadelphia.

A campaign conceived in London: Col. St. Leger with 2,000 men were to march east from Lake Ontario through the valley of the Mohawk River in the State of New York. General Burgoyne at the head of nine thousand men was to come south from Canada by way of Lake Champlain, and General Howe was to move north from New York City with 18,000 men; the 3 columns were to converge toward a point somewhere in the vicinity of Albany. The design was to gain possession of the Valley of the Hudson River and divide the 'rebellious' colonies into two sections...

St. Leger had in his command British regulars, Tories and Iroquois Indians. He was repulsed by Herkimer in the bloody battle of Oriskany at the headwaters of the Mohawk, and in August, 1777, was finally turned back at Fort Stanwix by Herkimer and Arnold. Howe failed to receive his orders in proper time and went off to the capture of Philadelphia...Burgoyne was left to operate alone against the northern army of the Americans,... now under the command of General Schuyler in the vicinity of Lake Champlain...Schuyler lost Crown Point, and now in 1777 before the oncoming of Burgoyne, was forced to give up Ticonderoga as well as Fort Edward on the Hudson. The way seemed to be opening to the invaders. Burgoyne however, like St. Leger, employed savages whose cruelty aroused the anger of the inhabitants of the surrounding country-side, and contributed greatly to his final undoing. Trees were felled in his path by the zealous patriots; roads and bridges destroyed, and his supplies were cut off.

In desperation, Burgoyne sent a force of Hessians and Indians to overpower the citizen-soldiers at Bennington, Vermont and capture their stores; but the expedition was met and utterly put to rout by hastily gathered volunteers under Colonel Stark. Two hundred of the thousand Germans engaged were killed or wounded and seven hundred captured."

—Emerson Fite

"ACCOUNT BY A GENTLEMAN WHO WAS PRESENT IN THE ACTION"
August 16, 1777, Vermont

... "It seems that General Burgoyne had detached his corps, consisting of about fifteen hundred men to penetrate as far as Bennington, to procure for his army provisions. Colonel Baum had posted his corps within about five miles of Bennington meeting house where they made breastworks for their own security. General Stark, who was at that time Providentially at Bennington, with his brigade of militia from New Hampshire, determined to give him battle and some volunteers from different towns, and Colonel Warner with a part of his own regiment joined him the same day.

The general, it seems wisely laid his plan of operation, and Divine Providence blessing us with good weather, between three and four o'clock he attacked...They fell in upon the enemy with great impetuosity; put them to confusion and flight, pursued them about a mile, taking many prisoners. Two or three brass field-pieces fell into our hands...at this time darkness came upon us, and prevented our swallowing up the whole of this body...

This action, which redounds so much to the glory of the Great Lord of the Heavens, affords the Americans a lasting monument of the Divine power and goodness...This victory is thought by some to equal any that has happened during the present controversy."
—*Pennsylvania Evening Post*, September 4, 1777

BY EMERSON FITE

"Cut off from re-enforcements from St. Leger and Howe and weakened at Bennington, the situation of Burgoyne became critical...The Americans met the desperate British in two engagements on the Hudson near Lake Saratoga. The first proved indecisive, and the second a complete victory for the Americans; a victory which was largely due to General Benedict Arnold's superb leadership. On October 17, 1777, Burgoyne surrendered his entire force of six thousand men.

The victory of Saratoga has been recognized as: "*One of the Decisive Battles of the World*." The French, since their humiliating losses in the French and Indian War, had been burning for revenge on the British...The achievements of Herkimer, Arnold, Schuyler, and Gates and their final victory aroused great enthusiasm in Paris. France concluded a treaty of amity and commerce and another of alliance with the struggling states, which she recognized as a free and independent Nation. The timely intervention proved the turning point of the war for the United States, for it not only greatly encouraged the new Nation, but also secured to them supplies of French guns, ammunition and clothing, and ultimately the assistance of the French army and navy. The success of the negotiations leading up to the French-American treaties was due largely to Benjamin Franklin...Marquis de Lafayette, not yet twenty years of age, had enlisted as a volunteer with Washington before the treaties were concluded, and like him, came the Germans De Kalb and Von Steuben and two Polish nobles; soldiers of fortune in defense of liberty. Before the French supplies arrived, Washington and his men passed the winter of 1777-1778 at Valley Forge, on the Schuylkill River, twenty-four miles above Philadelphia...

Six months in Philadelphia convinced Clinton, who had succeeded Howe in command of the British, that the mere possession of the capital did his cause little good, and learning that a French fleet under Count d'Estaing was crossing the ocean, he marched back to New York in the spring of 1778, undisturbed by Washington save at the Battle of Monmouth. Here the battle was lost to the Americans through the treasonable negligence and disobedience of Charles Lee who was again in the American army by the exchange of prisoners; his treason having been undiscovered, and was in immediate command of the American forces engaged.

Lee was tried by court martial, suspended from command, and later dismissed from the army. After Monmouth, to the end of the war, the only other important battle in the northeast was the capture of *Stony Point* on the Hudson by General Anthony Wayne in 1779. This attack was ordered by Washington in order to draw the British troops away from a marauding expedition into Connecticut." — E. Fite

LAFAYETTE'S LETTER TO HIS WIFE ON ARRIVAL IN THE U.S.

CHARLESTON, S.C. JUNE 19, 1777: "My last letter to you, my dear love, has informed you that I arrived safely in this Country, after having suffered a little from seasickness during the first weeks of the voyage; that I was then, the morning after I landed, at the house of a very kind officer; that I had been nearly two months on the passage, and that I wished to set off immediately. It spoke of everything most interesting to my heart; of my sorrow at parting from you, and of our dear children, and it said, besides, that I was in excellent health. I give you this abstract of it, because the English may possibly amuse themselves by seizing it on its way. I have such confidence in my lucky star, however, that I hope it will reach you. This same star has befriended me, to the astonishment of everybody here...I landed after having sailed several days along a coast, which swarmed with hostile vessels. When I arrived, everybody said that my vessel must inevitably be taken, since two British frigates blockaded the harbor...By a most wonderful good fortune, a gale obliged the frigates to stand out to sea for a short time. My vessel came in at noon-day, without meeting friend or foe...

All with whom I wished to become acquainted here, have shown me the greatest politeness and attention. I wish first to see Congress. I hope to set out for Philadelphia in two days. Our route is more than two hundred and fifty leagues by land. We shall divide ourselves into small parties. I have already purchased horses and light carriages for the journey. Some French and American vessels are here, and are to sail together tomorrow morning, taking advantage of a moment when the frigates are out of sight...

I will now tell you about the Country and its inhabitants. They are as agreeable as my enthusiasm had painted them. Simplicity of manners, kindness, love of country and of liberty, and a delightful equality everywhere prevail. The wealthiest man and the poorest are on a level; and, although there are some large fortunes, I challenge any one to discover the slightest difference between the manners of these two classes respectively toward each other. I am now in the city where everything is very much after the English fashion, except that there is more simplicity, equality, cordiality and courtesy here than in England. The city of Charleston is one of the handsomest and best built, and its inhabitants among the most agreeable, that I have ever seen. The American women are very pretty, simple in their manners, and exhibit a neatness, which is everywhere cultivated...The inns are very different from those of Europe; the host and hostess sit at table with you, and do the honors of a comfortable meal; and, on going away, you pay your bill without higgling.

As to my reception, it has been most agreeable in every quarter. I have just passed five hours at a grand dinner given in honor of me by an individual of this city. Generals Howe and Moultrie, and several officers of my suite, were present. We drank healths, and tried to talk English. I begin to speak it a little.

Considering the pleasant life I lead in this country, my sympathy with the people, which makes me feel as much at ease in their society as if I had known them for twenty years, the similarity between their mode of thinking and my own, and my love of liberty and of glory; one might suppose that I am very happy. But you are not with me; my friends are not with me; and there is no happiness for me far from you and them.

Although I suppose I have drawn upon me the special displeasure of the English by taking the liberty to depart in spite of them, and by landing in their very face; yet I confess they will not be in arrears with me should they capture the vessel, my cherished hope on which I so fondly depend for letters from you...May I say embrace tenderly our children. The father of these poor children is a rover, but a good and honest man at heart; a good father, who loves his family dearly, and a good husband who loves his wife with all his heart." —Adieu, Lafayette

VALLEY FORGE

General Washington and Troops Passed the Winter of 1777-1778 at Valley Forge

Dr. A. Waldo, A Surgeon's Lament

DECEMBER 1777 "The army who have been surprisingly healthy hitherto—now begin to grow sickly from the continued fatigues they have suffered this campaign; yet they still show a spirit of alacrity and contentment not to be expected from troops so young....

I am sick—discontented—out of humor. Poor food—hard lodging—cold weather—fatigue—nasty clothes—nasty cookery—vomit half my time—smoked out of my senses—-the devil's in't—I can't endure it—Why are we sent here to starve and freeze—what sweet felicities have I left at home; —A charming wife—pretty children—good beds—good food—good cookery—all agreeable—all harmonious. Here, all confusion—smoke—cold—hunger and filthiness... Here comes a bowl of beef soup—full of burnt leaves and dirt, sickish enough to make a Hector spew...Your being sick covers your mind with a melancholic gloom, which makes everything about appear gloomy.

See the poor soldier, when healthy—with what cheerfulness he meets his foes and encounters every hardship—if barefoot—he labors through the mud and cold with a song in his mouth extolling War and Washington—if his food be bad he eats it notwithstanding with seeming content—blesses God for a good stomach—and whistle it into digestion. But harkee, patience—a moment—There comes a soldier—his bare feet are seen through his worn out shoes—his legs nearly naked from the tattered remains of an only pair of stockings—his breeches not sufficient to cover his nakedness—his shirt hanging in strings—his hair disheveled—his face meager—his whole appearance pictures a person forsaken and discouraged. He comes, and cries with an air of wretchedness and despair, 'I am sick, my feet lame, my legs are sore, my body covered with this tormenting itch, my clothes are worn out, my constitution is broken, my former activity is exhausted by fatigue, hunger and cold. I fail fast, I shall soon be no more! And all the reward I shall get will be. Poor Will is dead.'

DECEMBER 18TH: Universal Thanksgiving—a roasted pig at night. God be thanked for my health which I have pretty well recovered. How much better should I feel, were I assured my family were in health. But the same good Being who graciously preserves me is able to preserve them—and bring me to the ardently wished for enjoyment of them again...

What have you for our dinners, boys? 'Nothing but fire cake and water, Sir." At night—'Gentlemen, the supper is ready.' What is your supper, Lads? 'Fire cake and water, Sir.'

What have you got for breakfast, lads? 'Fire cake and water, Sir.' The Lord send that our Commissary of Purchases may live on fire cake and water...

Our Division is under marching orders this morning. I am ashamed to say it, but I am tempted to steal fowls if I could find them—or even a whole hog—for I feel as if I could eat one. But the impoverished country about us, affords but little matter to employ a thief—or keep a clever fellow in good humor...

The party that went out last evening has not returned today. This evening an excellent player on the violin in that soft kind of music which is so finely adapted to stir up the tender passions, while he was playing in the next tent to mine these kind soft airs... called up in remembrance all the endearing expressions—the tender sentiments –the sympathetic friendship that has given so much satisfaction and sensible pleasure to me from the first time I gained the heart and affections of the tenderest of the fair.

DECEMBER 24TH: Huts go on slowly—cold and smoke make us fret. But mankind are always fretting, even if they have more than their proportions of the blessing of life. We are never easy—-always repining at the Providence of an all wise and Benevolent Being—blaming our country, or faulting our friends. But I don't know of anything that vexes a man's soul more than hot smoke continually blowing into his eyes, and when he attempts to avoid it, is met by a cold and piercing wind...

DEC. 25TH, CHRISTMAS: We are still in tents; when we ought to be in huts. The poor sick suffer much in tents this cold weather...

DEC. 31ST: Adj. S. taught me how to darn stockings—to make them look like knit work.

1778. JANUARY 1ST NEW YEAR: I am alive. I am well. Huts go on briskly and our camp begins to appear like a spacious city... Bought an embroidered jacket.

SUNDAY, JAN. 4TH: Properly accoutered, I went to work at masonry. Being found with mortar and stone, I almost completed a genteel chimney to my magnificent hut; however, as we had short allowance of food and no grog, my back ached before night.

I was called to relieve a soldier thought to be dying. He expired before I reached the hut. He was an Indian; an excellent soldier, and an obedient good-natured fellow...

8TH: Unexpectedly got a furlough. Set out for home. The very worst of riding—mud and mire."

—Dr. Waldo, was a volunteer surgeon

"The Winter of 1777–1778 at Valley Forge"
By R. Tryon and C. Lingley

"General Washington's headquarters at Valley Forge was twenty miles from the city of Philadelphia. It was at this time that Washington and his small army had the greatest need of courage. Food was lacking, medicines for the sick could not be obtained, and shoes were so scarce that the men could often be followed by the marks of their bleeding feet on the frozen ground. At one time 3000 men had so little to wear that they could not go out on duty.

...However, the one bright spot in the winter at Valley Forge was the valuable assistance given to the Americans by two young Europeans. One of these was the Marquis de Lafayette, a brave Frenchman of whom Washington was very fond; the other was Baron von Steuben, a German officer who reached Valley Forge in the spring of 1778. Steuben knew how to drill an army and could teach the soldiers how to use their weapons to best advantage. His work gave good results in later battles.

The French knew about the kite sent up into the clouds by Benjamin Franklin; also that he had published *Poor Richard's Almanac* of clever and wise sayings. News of Burgoyne's defeat proved that the Americans were making headway in their attempt to defeat England.

The French king therefore, made two treaties with Franklin: The first provided that France should join the United States in the fight against England. The second, the United States and France agreed to trade with each other. Even before Burgoyne's defeat, France had been sending over clothing, ammunition and money to help the American cause. News of the alliance was received at Valley Forge with hurrahs." —Tryon and Lingley

"The armies were likely to suffer for food as soon as they moved far from the waterways. The country was thinly settled and little food could be found in any one region. The roads were poor and there were few wagons. In 1778 a cargo of clothing, sorely needed by the colonial soldiers, reached a port in North Carolina, but it was necessary to send to Pennsylvania for wagons. The next year Philadelphia had more flour than it could sell, while Washington's soldiers in eastern New Jersey and on the Hudson were starving. One difficulty was that the officers in whom Congress put in charge of supplies did not understand how to manage the matter." —Bourne and Benton

"The Hut City and a Run of Shad"

"Twenty odd miles to the west and a little north of Philadelphia, the placid Schuylkill is joined on its eastward course by Valley Creek, flowing from the south. At the junction of the two streams the ground east of the creek rises swiftly to a 250 foot crest, then straightens out into a rolling two-mile plateau. There was little to mark this terrain on a map, just a ford across the Schuylkill, and an old forge on the ravine-like creek that travelers called The Valley Forge.

Winter could not be faced in tents, and on the very first day, orders went out to build huts to a prescribed pattern. Short of tools and nails, weakened men forced themselves into the woods; felled trees, split out boards, and kneaded clay to plug up wall-chinks. Street by street, a hut–city slowly rose, until at last the Commander-in-Chief felt free to quit his own leaky tent and move into the gray field-stone, Isaac Potts' house, close by the junction of the creek and river; a step which he had sternly refused to take as long as his men were under canvas.

Food began to trickle into Valley Forge. The flow dried up; appeared again, stopped in a frightening pattern that was a night-mare for every man in authority...

The food problem was Providentially eased by an unusually early and heavy run of shad up the Schuylkill...With the first warning ripples of crowded fins breaking the surface, men plunged into the river armed with pitchforks, shovels, baskets and broken branches to heave the squirming fish onto the soggy banks. Other detail rushed up barrels and salt to store away the ever-increasing surplus. When it seemed likely that the run would sweep out of reach upstream, Major Henry Lee's Virginia dragoons charged into the river and milled their horses about. The rush was checked, and a long stretch of the Schuylkill became a seething mass of shad, an inexhaustible supply depot."

—*American Heritage Book of the Revolution*

Good News from France

PENNSYLVANIA: "This afternoon, the Commander-in-Chief issued, from head-quarters at Valley Forge, the following after-orders: 'It having pleased the *Almighty Ruler of the Universe,* propitiously to defend the cause of the United American States, and finally, by raising up a powerful friend among the Princes of the Earth, to establish our Liberty and Independence upon lasting foundations— It becomes us to set apart a day for gratefully acknowledging the Divine goodness and celebrating the important event which we owe to His benign interposition...Upon a signal given the whole army will Huzza! Long live the King of France!'"

—*New Jersey Gazette,* May 13, 1778

"One day a Quaker by the name of Potts, was strolling up a creek when he heard, in a secluded spot, the solemn voice of someone apparently engaged in prayer. Stealing quietly forward, he saw Washington's horse tied to a sapling, and a little farther on, in a thicket, the Chief himself, on his knees, and with tears streaming down his cheeks, beseeching Heaven for his country and his army. Before God alone, that strong heart gave way, and poured forth the full tide of its griefs and anxieties. How sublime does he appear, and how good and holy the cause he was engaged in seems."

—Hon. J.T. Headley

"Bride of Spring: The Dogwood Tree."

"Pink flowering dogwood became known to commercial horticulture about eighty-five years ago. Thomas Meehan, a great grower of his day, discovered a branch with lovely rose-blushed petals on a white-flowering tree growing on the hills above Wissahickon Creek (now part of Fairmount Park in Philadelphia). When he saw that it kept on 'coming pink' for several years, he propagated it by grafting it in one of the most magnificent displays of dogwood in the world: at Valley Forge where white drifts of blossoms lie each spring upon the hills. Where those ragged, starving, heroes trod the snows with bleeding feet, the pink boughs mingle with the white. And every Maytime, thousands of Americans make a pilgrimage to this National Shrine to see how immortal glory can be made visible."

—Donald Peattie

CHAPTER 11

George Rogers Clark's Expedition into the Northwest Territory

1778-1779

By Cecil B. Hartley

"The British officers and agents in the northwest were indefatigable in stimulating the Indians to attack the American Colonists in every quarter. They supplied them with arms and ammunition, bribed them with money and encouraged them to attack the young settlements in Kentucky and Tennessee...

Many scouting parties of Indians were scattered about watching all the different settlements in Kentucky and preparing to attack them. In July 1777, a party of immigrants from North Carolina composed of forty-five men arrived into the wilderness at Boonesborough. This caused rejoicing among the settlements; for none of them had been free from attacks by Indians since opening of spring, and one or two small villages had undergone long and regular Indian sieges.

People continued to clear the lands adjacent to the station-fort, and to cultivate crops; some always keeping a vigilant look-out while the others labored. The lives of men, women and children taken by prowling Indians ran into the thousands. In late 1777, Clark approached Patrick Henry, Governor of Virginia, with a plan; which he approved....

Clark and approximately 200 men descended the Ohio River, hid their boats, and marched northward with their provisions on their backs... Rocheblave had been sent to Virginia. On his person were found written instructions from Quebec to incite the Indians to hostilities, and reward them for scalps of the Americans. Hamilton, the British governor of Detroit, bold and tyrannical, was determined with an overwhelming force of British and Indians, to penetrate up the Ohio River to Fort Pitt, and to 'sweep all the principle settlements along the way'. Clark received information that Hamilton who was at Vincennes had weakened his force by sending Indians against the frontiers.

To resolve to attack Hamilton before he could collect the Indians, was the only hope of saving the Country. With a band of hardy comrades, Clark marched across the country. It was February, 1779 when, within nine miles of the enemy, it took five days to cross the flooded lands of the Wabash; having often to wade up to mid-chest in water. Had not the weather been remarkably mild, they might have perished."

"THE CAPTURE OF FORT VINCENNES"
By Colonel George Rogers Clark

"Everything being ready, on the 5th of February after receiving a lecture and absolution from the priest, we crossed the Kaskaskia River with one hundred and seventy men…the weather wet, (but fortunately not cold for the season) and a great part of the plains under water several inches deep, it was difficult and very fatiguing marching.

Crossing a narrow deep lake in the canoes, and marching some distance, we came to a copse of timber called the Warrior's island. We were now in full view of the fort and town; not a shrub between us, at about two miles' distance. Every man now feasted his eyes, and forgot that he had suffered anything.…

Our situation was now truly critical; no possibility of retreating in case of defeat, and in full view of a town that had, at this time, upward of six hundred men in it: troops, inhabitants and Indians… We were now in the situation that I had labored to get ourselves in. The idea of being made prisoner was foreign to almost everyone, as they expected nothing but torture from the savages if they fell into their hands. Our fate was now to be determined, probably in a few hours. We knew that nothing but the most daring conduct would assure success. I knew that a number of the inhabitants wished us well, that many were lukewarm to the interest of either.

The garrison was soon completely surrounded, and the firing continued without intermission…until about nine o'clock the morning of the 24th. I sent a flag with a letter demanding the garrison capitulate.…

We met at the church, about eighty yards from the fort; Lieutenant-governor Hamilton and others. The conference began. Hamilton produced terms of capitulation, signed. After deliberating on every article, I rejected the whole. I told him that I had no other proposition to make than what I had already made; that of his surrendering as prisoners at discretion…I told him I had no objections in giving him my real reasons, which were simply these: that I knew the greater part of the principal Indian partisans of Detroit were with him…that the cries of the widows and the fatherless on the frontiers, which they had occasioned, now required their blood from my hand, and that I did not choose to be so timorous as to disobey the absolute commands of their authority, which I looked upon to be next to Divine. That I would rather lose fifty men than not to empower myself to execute this piece of business with propriety. That, if he chose to risk the massacre of his garrison for their sakes, it was his own pleasure, and that *I might, perhaps take it into my head to send for some of those widows to see it executed.*"

"In the afternoon of the 24th February 1779, the following articles were signed:"
1. Lieutenant-Governor Hamilton engages to deliver up to Colonel Clark: Fort Sackville as it is at present with all the stores…
2. The garrison are to deliver themselves as prisoners of war, and march out with their arms and accouterments.
3. The garrison are to be delivered up at ten o'clock tomorrow… Signed at Post St. Vincent 24th of February, 1779.

GEORGE ROGERS
"CLARK'S VICTORY AT PIQUA, OHIO"

"The year after these victories, [Kaskaskia fell without event] Clark undertook the historic campaign against the Shawnee Indians and their confederates at the Village of Piqua, near Springfield. Clark had learned that the British forces from Detroit planned joining the Indians at this point to attack the Americans, and that British agents in preparation for the attack were at Piqua sharpening the Indians' tomahawks, and getting into shape other war equipment.

On August 8, 1780, with an army of 100 Regulars and 1,000 Kentucky frontiersmen, Clark made an attack on Piqua, completely routing the Indians and burning their village after a hard-fought battle lasting many hours. This victory was as important in the outcome of the American Revolution as was Yorktown in the East. It was the final determining factor with the American commissioners in Paris, in insisting that the boundary line between the British and Americans should be along the Great Lakes and not along the Ohio River.

On the George Rogers Clark monument overlooking the site of the Battle of Piqua, appears the following Inscription:

'Here General George Rogers Clark with his Kentucky soldiers defeated and drove from this region the Shawnee Indians August 8, 1780, and aided to make the Northwest Territory a part of the United States.'"—Ohio Archeologic and Historical Society

CHAPTER 12

The Revolution Continues in the South

APPREHENSION FOR SUCCESS APPARENT IN NEWSPAPER ARTICLES

March 9, 1778

"The Southern States are pursuing the most vigorous measures for strengthening the hands of General Washington during the ensuing campaign. Virginia has drafted two thousand men to recruit her regiments, who are to serve for one year. They have also set on foot an association for raising five thousand volunteers, to serve six months. North Carolina is exerting herself with equal ardor. The Eastern States, who in public concerns always act with a wisdom and vigor that deserves imitation, have already begun to draft, being resolved to fill their regiments completely, and to have them early in the field. If the Middle States take the same resolute steps, the next campaign must be decisive...

We have often thought it strange that America, who could bring three or four hundred thousand men into the field, should so long suffer a paltry banditti to run through her States, and to nestle in her cities. One would be tempted to imagine that we were fond of this destructive war; and yet folly in her highest delirium, would not wish to prolong it.

Every day the war continues our public debts will increase; our necessities will multiply, and our currency depreciate. Britain knows this; she founds her last hopes upon it. She no longer expects to conquer us by the sword, but she flatters herself that our distresses will subdue our minds, break the spirit of opposition, and dissolve in time the glorious confederacy in support of freedom. Hence it will be the policy of her generals to possess themselves of our towns, to destroy our manufactures, to block up our harbors, and to prolong the war. We should change our measures accordingly; bring our thousands into the field; push the enemy with vigor; drive them from our towns; storm them in their strongholds, and never pause till we force them from our shores...These rising States should catch the spirit of the gallant Caesar, and think that 'they have done nothing, while anything remains to do.'"

—*New Jersey Gazette*, March 18, 1778.

PENNSYLVANIA, JUNE 19, 1778 FOR ARNOLD TAKING POSSESSION OF PHILADELPHIA "The British army, early yesterday morning, completed their evacuation of Philadelphia, having before transported their stores and most of their artillery into Jersey where they had thrown up some works, and several of their regiments were encamped...It is supposed they will endeavor to go to New York. A party of the American light horse pursued them very close, and took a great number of prisoners, some of whom were refugees. Soon after the evacuation, the Honorable Major-General Arnold took possession of Philadelphia, with Colonel Jackson's Massachusetts regiment."

—*Pennsylvania Evening Post*, June 20, 1778

Pennsylvania: "Early this afternoon, His Excellency Monsieur Gerard, ambassador from his Most Christian Majesty to the United States, arrived at Philadelphia. He was accompanied from Chester to an elegant apartment provided for him in Market Street by a committee of Congress appointed for that purpose. On his entrance into the city, he was saluted by Colonel Proctor's artillery. It is impossible to describe the joy that appeared in every good man's countenance on this auspicious event. His Excellency came in a frigate, part of a fleet of twelve ships of the line from Toulon, under the Command of Count D'Estaing."

—*Upcott*, V, 139 July 11, 1778

AUGUST 23, 1778: "The French fleet returned to Rhode Island on Thursday last, (20th), but had suffered so considerably in the late storm, together with some slight engagement with the enemy, that they judged it necessary to retire in order to re-fit; in consequence of which resolution, the whole fleet sailed for Boston yesterday."

—*New York Gazette* and *Weekly Mercury*, September 21

MASSACHUSETTS, AUGUST 29, 1778: "Yesterday, the fleet of his Most Christian Majesty, commanded by Admiral Count D'Estaing arrived safe in Nantucket Road, and this morning three of his frigates anchored off Boston. The fleet has received considerable damage in the late storm; the Count's ship, (the Languedoe, of ninety guns) is particularly much damaged, her masts and bowsprits being carried away, and her rudder injured. In this condition she was attacked by a British ship of fifty guns, when to her mortification, she could bring but five or six of her guns to bear upon the enemy. After firing four hours upon the Languedoe, the British man of war left her, having made very little addition to the damage she sustained in the storm, and killed only one man and wounded two or three. The damaged ships are repairing with the utmost expedition, and in all probability will soon be in a condition to give the dastardly Britons a drubbing, should they have the effrontery to attempt to stand before them.

This afternoon the Count D'Estaing, with his suite, came up to Boston in his barge. He was saluted on his landing by the cannon of the American fortresses and ships in the harbor, and all respects were paid him that time and circumstances would allow. The Count and his officers, General Heath, the Marquis de Lafayette, the principal officers of the American Marine, and other gentlemen, dined with General Hancock."

—*New Hampshire Gazette*, September 8, 1778

RHODE ISLAND "This morning The American army pitched their tents on the front of Butt's Hill on Rhode Island, when a heavy cannonade commenced, and has continued through the whole day. At seven this evening, a picket was posted in advance of the first line, and a chain of sentinels formed from the east to the west river. In consequence of authentic intelligence received, that Lord Howe with his fleet had sailed from Sandy Hook, and that from the best information, one hundred and fifty sail of transports were in the

Western Sound with five thousand troops bound to Newport, a council was called, who were unanimously of the opinion…that the island should be evacuated, which has been completed in perfect order and safety, not leaving behind the smallest article of provision, camp equipage, or military stores."

—*New Hampshire Gazette*, September 15, 1778

GEORGIA, NOVEMBER 25, 1778: "A correspondent in Charleston, South Carolina, says, 'A body of armed men, supposed to be about five hundred; chiefly on horseback, with four pieces of artillery from St. Augustine in Florida, have made a very sudden and rapid incursion into the neighboring State of Georgia, burning all the houses, and destroying everything in their way. It does not appear that they were discovered before last Friday; yet by Sunday they had advanced to within four miles of Sunbury, and burnt every house on the other side of Newport Ferry, but not without receiving some check from a body of militia collected under Colonel Screven, together with the continentals of the third and fourth battalions; who had retreated in order to receive reinforcements, to Midway meeting house where they were entrenching to make a stand, but having disputed every inch of ground against a superior enemy, they lost a few men, and had some of their most valuable officers wounded.' We since learn that the militia have everywhere turned out with the greatest alacrity, and that such vigorous measures are pursuing as, with the co-operation of South Carolina, will probably not only disappoint the designs of the enemy, but also cut off their retreat."

—*Rivington's Gazette*, January 20, 1779

1779

NEW YORK, FEBRUARY 4, 1779: "It is painful to repeat the indubitable accounts we are continually receiving, of the cruel and inhuman treatment of the subjects of these States from the Britons in New York and other places. They who hear our countrymen who have been so unfortunate as to fall into the hands of these unrelenting tyrants, relate the sad story of their captivity, the insults they have received, and the slow, cool, systematic manner in which great numbers of those who could not be prevailed on to enter their service, have been murdered; must have hearts of stone not to melt with pity for the sufferers, and burn with indignation at their tormentors. As we have daily fresh instances to prove the truth of such a representation, public justice requires that repeated public mention should be made of them. A cartel vessel lately carried about one hundred and thirty American prisoners from the prison ships in New York to New London in Connecticut...emaciated...enfeebled; and many who continue alive, are never likely to receive their former health...Upwards of three hundred American prisoners were confined at a time on board this ship...It requires no great sagacity to know, that crowding people together without fresh air, and feeding, or rather starving them in such a manner as the prisoners have been, must unavoidably produce a contagion... Some of them, no doubt, thought they acted in all this with the true spirit of the British Parliament, who began hostilities against America by shutting up the port of Boston, interdicting the fishery and those branches of trade that were deemed necessary to our subsistence. ...'Starvation, starvation to the rebels—starvation is the only thing that will bring them to their senses!' In short, the inhumanity of the Britons, from the beginning of this War, and through every stage of it, is without a parallel in the annals of any civilized nation.

These things ought never to be forgotten, though some would fain wink them out of sight. ...We are not, indeed, to resolve never to make peace with our enemies, but never to make a peace that will leave it in their power to act ever again their intolerable oppressions and cruelties. We can never secure ourselves against this, but by maintaining at all adventures, the sovereignty and independence of these States."

—*New Hampshire Gazette*, February 8, 1779

NEW JERSEY, FEBRUARY 26, 1779: "Yesterday morning a body of the British consisting of the 42d and 33d regiments, and the light infantry of the guards, in number about a thousand, commanded by Lt. Colonel Stirling, attempted to surprise the troops and inhabitants of Elizabethtown. They embarked at Long Island the evening before about seven o'clock, and landed on the Salt Meadows, better than a mile to the left of Crane's ferry; between two and three in the morning...

The guard at Crane's ferry having discovered their landing, immediately dispatched the intelligence to town where the alarm being sounded, the troops were afforded an opportunity to collect. The number and movements of the enemy remaining doubtful by reason of the darkness, the troops were marched to the rear of the town.

Finding themselves completely disappointed in every expectation, the British made their visit in town very short. However, during their small halt, they set fire to the barracks, the schoolhouse, and a blacksmith's shop. So soon as they began their retreat to their boats, General Maxwell marched such of his troops, as were yet in reserve against their rear; the number of these however, was small...

About half way between the town and ferry, the enemy; perceiving their rear in danger for the sudden advance of our troops, and the assembling of the militia; faced about and paraded as if for action. A few well-directed shot from our artillery induced them to renew their retreat, leaving two dead on the field. Perceiving an embarkation at the ferry would be attended with considerable hazard, their boats were moved better than a mile up Newark Bay, while the troops marched along the meadow's edge; in many places up to their middles in mud and mire. A galley and two or three gunboats covered their retreat at this place...

They had collected a considerable number of horned cattle and horses, but their retreat was so precipitate, that they were obliged to leave them behind."

—*New Jersey Gazette*, March 3, 1779

NEW YORK, MARCH 18, 1779: "Yesterday, the anniversary of Saint Patrick, the tutelary Saint of Ireland, was celebrated in New York by the natives of that kingdom, with their accustomed hilarity. The volunteers of Ireland, preceded by their band of music, marched into the city, and formed before the house of their Colonel, Lord Rawdon who put himself at their head, and, after paying compliments to his Excellency General Knyphausen, and to General Jones, accompanied them to the Bowery, where dinner was provided. ...The soldierly appearance of the men, their order of march hand in hand being all natives of Ireland, had a striking effect.

…Such men are naturally gallant and loyal; crowned with ardor to stand forth in the cause of their King, of their Country, and of real, honest, general liberty, whenever an opportunity offers."
—*New York Gazette* and *Weekly Mercury*, March 22, 1799

NEW HAMPSHIRE: "Should America continue firmly to oppose the tyranny of Britain," says a correspondent, "may not the promise of the present day sanctify a conjecture, that in a few years the rising grandeur of this New World will invite every man from Europe who is not attached to it by landed property or other similar cause. There is a field opening for every species of manufacture, art and science, trade, and commerce. Finely situated for the encouragement and cultivation of business, every artificer will fly here and transplant with him the art he possesses. Secure from tyrannical burdens, he will apply himself assiduously in the prospect of reaping what he sowed, and will assist in rearing this new Republic to a pitch of grandeur, superior perhaps to any state now existing."
—*New Hampshire Gazette*, June 29, 1779

NEW YORK, JULY 16, 1779: "This morning, **General Wayne**, with the light infantry consisting of about twelve hundred men drawn from the whole of the American army on each side of the North River, surprised the British garrison consisting of five hundred men commanded by a Colonel Johnson in their works at *Stony Point* on the west side of King's Ferry, and made the whole prisoners, with the loss of four Americans killed and General Wayne slightly wounded.

Nothing can exceed the spirit and intrepidity of our brave countrymen in storming and carrying the British fortress at Stony Point. It demonstrates that the Americans have soldiers equal to any in the world, and that they can attack and vanquish the Britons in their strongest works. No action during the war performed by the British military, has equaled this coup de main."

—*New Hampshire Gazette*, July 27, 1779

A British ship on Lake Erie.

CHAPTER 13

The Fall of Charleston, South Carolina

NEW YORK: *"The very remarkable and long-continued severity of the weather at New York, (the* like not having been known, as we are informed, by the oldest man living.) has stopped all the venues of intelligence, and almost cut off all social intercourse between people of the same neighborhood. The incessant intenseness of the cold, the great depth and quantity of the snows following in quick secession one on the back of another, attended with violent tempests of wind; which for several days made the roads utterly impassable, has put a stop to business of all kinds, except such as each family could do within itself. And as many were slenderly provided with necessaries for subsistence, we have reason to apprehend that we shall shortly hear many melancholy accounts of private distress in the country, and that from the sea-coasts and vessels at sea, the accounts will be dreadful."

—*Pennsylvania Packet,* January 27, 1780

NEW YORK FEBRUARY 1, 1780: "The Sound between Long Island and Connecticut, is almost frozen over in the widest part, and some persons have passed over from Long island to Norwalk, and other parts in Connecticut on the ice. Wood is brought from Long Island to New York on sleighs. It is almost passible from Powle's Hook to New York."

—*Rivington's Gazette*, February 16, 1780

SOUTH CAROLINA, FEBRUARY 15, 1780

"The following sketch of *the present situation of affairs in Charleston, South Carolina,* is communicated by Colonel John Laurens. 'The British army, said to be under the command of Sir Henry Clinton, are distributed on Port Royal Island, John's Island, Stono Ferry, and a detachment last night landed upon James' Island. The headquarters are at Fenwick's house, on John's Island. Four of their galleys have been seen between John and James' Island...About twelve deserters from the fleet and army have come into Charleston, and as many prisoners are taken by our light horse. Different deserters from the fleet and army agree in reporting very heavy losses at sea. Three ships floundered, many dismasted, one brig, two ships are taken, and brought into Charleston; a brig is carried into North Carolina. One of the deserters informs, that thirteen sail were left on the rocks of Bermuda. There is undoubtedly some grand impediment to the enemy's progress. Their horses perished at sea, and much of their furniture was captured. Three days ago, passed by Charleston bar in a hard gale of wind, a sixty-four gunship, a frigate, and some transports. These may be gone to New York for further supplies, but all is conjecture. Near the bar of Charleston, daily appears a frigate and other ships of war, reconnoitering and blocking up the harbor. We have four Continental frigates, two French armed ships, two State armed ships, six other armed vessels; some of them carrying very heavy cannon. The enemy's delay has afforded an opportunity for strengthening the lines of Charleston, which will be in pretty good order tomorrow. The number of men within the lines uncertain; but by far too few for defending works of near three miles in circumference, especially considering many of them to be citizens, and unaccustomed to the fatigues of a besieged garrison, and many of the Continental troops half naked.

Reinforcements are expected—General Hogan is within a few miles. The Virginia troops are somewhere! Assistance from that sister state has been expected these eighteen months. General Moultrie is forming a camp at Bacon Bridge, where he has about five hundred horse belonging to South Carolina—Baylor's and Bland's regiments of Virginia. General Williamson is encamped at Augusta—a thousand men are expected from his brigade. General Richardson and Colonel Carlen are raising the militia at and about Camden. At this moment the escape of the Americans depends on further delay on the enemy's part; two or three weeks more will make this garrison strong. The inhabitants in general are in good spirits; competent judges say that Sir Henry Clinton will then have cause to repent his enterprise. This affords encouragement, but events in war are uncertain, and if we do not receive assistance, the next intelligence may be quite contrary.'"

—*Maryland Journal* March 21, 1780

"THE SIEGE OF CHARLESTON
BEGINS: THE TIMELINE"

MAY 12, 1780: "This morning the garrison of Charleston, after sustaining a siege of over a month's duration, surrendered prisoners of war to the combined fleet and army of Great Britain. The *following is a journal* of the siege, from the day previous to the British fleet's crossing the bar, to the present hour:"

MARCH 19, 1780: "The British under Gen. Clinton, now encamped on James Island, seem to wait for the shipping which lay off *the bar*, and have been disappointed at the last springs by southwest winds, which kept down the tides so that they cannot get over. This day the springs are at the highest, but the weather so hazy that they will scarcely attempt it, and will probably clear up with unfavorable winds. We begin to hope that Providence has interposed a second time to prevent their getting over until we are ready.

If they should get over either now or hereafter, there will probably be the hottest contest that has happened this war, just off Fort Moultrie....The British ships destined to come in are said to be the *Renown*, fifty guns; *Roebuck*, forty-four; *Blond,* thirty-two...These are to force their way past the town, and cut off the communication between Charleston and the country. To oppose their passing the fort, the Americans have thrown a boom of cables across the channel at the fort and stationed the *Providence*, of thirty-two guns; *Boston*, twenty-eight; *Bricole,* twenty-eight; *Adventure*, twenty; French vessel, twenty; Queen of France, eighteen...

The enemy's chance of success depends entirely on getting up their shipping, and the American hopes of defending the town greatly depend on preventing it."

MARCH 20: "This morning the British got their ships over the bar. They consist of ten vessels of force; from twenty guns to a sixty-four, as some say, others at fifty. However, ours appeared so inadequate to oppose them by Fort Moultrie; that they were all ordered up to town...Our lines round the whole town are nearly completed, except by Gadsden's wharf...Our people are hard at work there now, as we dread the enemy's shipping on that quarter. We have on the Ashley River, or south side of the town, six batteries—some ten guns, some six, some four, none less, so that no vessel can lay before them."

—*Pennsylvania Packet*, April 25 and May 2

MARCH 30: "Yesterday a large body of British grenadiers and infantry crossed Ashley River, and today they appeared before the American lines where they are now encamped. As the enemy approached, Colonel Laurens with a small party had a brush with the advance body in which Captain Bowman of the North Carolina forces fell, much lamented. Major Herne and two privates were wounded...The enemy's loss is reported to be from twelve to sixteen killed."

—Letter from Charleston, South Carolina:
Pennsylvania Packet, April 25

APRIL: "This afternoon between three and five o'clock, the British fleet passed Fort Moultrie in a heavy gale, and anchored between Fort Johnson and Charleston; just out of reach of the guns from the town, where they now continue. They were so covered with the thunder storm as to be invisible near half the time of their passing. One of their frigates had a fore-topmast shot away by a cannon at the fort, and a store ship was so injured in the rudder as to be incapable of working, and the gale being fresh, she went on shore under the guns of our half-moon battery; on the point of the island which obliged them to burn it to prevent it falling into our hands. After burning awhile, it blew up. We had not a man hurt at the fort, though they kept up a brisk fire as they passed.

Our garrison is in good health and high spirits; the town well-fortified and defended by a numerous artillery; Sir Henry approaching very slowly, and our men longing for the hour in which he may afford them the opportunity of teaching the temerity of the present expedition."

—*Pennsylvania Packet*, May 2

APRIL 12: "Day before yesterday, the British, having completed their first parallel, summoned the town to surrender, of which General Lincoln took no notice, and today Clinton opened his batteries which are answered by the Americans with spirit, but not with the effect that will insure success; the enemy's fire being far superior to ours..."

—*Clift's Diary Gordon*, III, 47

APRIL 18: "The cannonading on both sides still continues. General Clinton received a reinforcement from New York yesterday, and it is probable he will make a further advance on us soon. He is very cautious, and moves with all the care and deliberation of an old Roman, which he certainly is not. Our men are in good spirits, although it seems to be the general opinion that we must at last succumb; not without a hard fight, however."

—*Elliot Manuscript*

APRIL 21: "The British have completed their second parallel, which is within three hundred yards of the American lines. A council of war held this morning, decided that offers of capitulation should be made to the British commander, which may admit of the army's withdrawing, and afford security to the persons and property of the inhabitants."

APRIL 24: "Sir Henry Clinton rejects the American offers of capitulation, and is actively pushing forward his third parallel... This morning Lieutenant-Colonel Henderson led out a party of Americans, and attacked the advance working party of the British, killed several; took eleven prisoners."

—*Clift's Diary Gordon*, III, 48

MAY 6: "This afternoon, the garrison at Fort Moultrie was summoned to surrender by Captain Hudson, commander of his Majesty's ship *Richmond*."

—*Rivington's Gazette*, May 31

MAY 12: "Yesterday the British advanced within thirty yards of the American lines, and commenced preparations for a combined assault by sea and land. The reduced state of the garrison, the urgent solicitations of the inhabitants, and the clamors of the soldiery, compelled General Lincoln to renew negotiations with the British commanders, and today the 'Articles of Capitulation' have been signed. It is stipulated that the Continental troops and sailors shall remain prisoners of war until exchanged, and be supplied with good and wholesome provisions, in such quantity as is served out to the British troops. The militia are to return home as prisoners on parole, which, as long as they observe, is to secure them from being molested in their property by British troops. The officers of the army and navy are to keep their swords, pistols, and baggage, which are not to be searched, and are to retain their servants.

The garrison, at an appointed hour, is to march out of the town, to the ground between the works and the canal, where they are to deposit their arms. The drums are not to beat a British march, nor the colors to be uncased. All civil officers and citizens who have borne arms during the siege, are to be prisoners on parole, and with respect to their property within the city, they are to have the same terms as the militia. All persons in the town, not described in any article, are, notwithstanding, to be prisoners on parole... The French consul, the subjects of France and Spain, with their houses, papers and other movable property, are to be protected and untouched; but they are to consider themselves as prisoners on parole."

—*Clift's Diary Gordon*, III, 49

MAY 20, 1780 MASSACHUSETTS: "Yesterday we were visited by a most unusual and uncomfortable phenomenon. As early as ten o'clock in the morning, a thick darkness came over the face of the country, so that it was impossible to move about the house without the assistance of a candle... Many persons were much frightened at the sudden darkness, and some thought that Judgment-Day had come... In the dark, frogs peeped; in short, there was the appearance of midnight at noon-day. The cloud of darkness in one writer's opinion, was sent by God as a sign of his anger."

—*Viator, Boston Country Journal,*
May 29; *New Jersey Gazette*, June 21

"The DARK DAY of MAY 19, 1780"

"All nature stands, when He commands,
    Or changes in its course;
His mighty hand rules sea and land—
    He is the Lord of Host.
Nineteenth of May, a gloomy day,
    When darkness veil'd the sky
The sun's decline may be a sign
    Some great event is nigh…"

—Isaiah Thomas

"VOLUNTEERS MADE SHIRTS, B. ROSS MADE BANNERS, STATUE YIELDED MUSKET BALLS"

By Elizabeth Ellet

"On May 12, 1780, Charleston, South Carolina was conquered by the British. This was a bitter defeat for the Patriots. They suffered from lack of clothing, ammunition and weapons. The army was in need of more soldiers to replace the too exhausted or enlisted time up. Reed decided to start a nationwide fund drive, wanting to give money to each soldier to show them their dedication to the cause, and show their sacrifices were genuinely appreciated. Fund collectors and volunteers believed a sum of money would boost the Patriots' spirits and prove that Colonists were not as divided as British leaders thought…Volunteers in Philadelphia raised more than $300,000 in continental money which was highly inflated and worth only about $7,000 in gold. The drive was a success. Other groups were organized in at least seven other Colonies.

170

Washington requested they provide much needed clothing. They began making plans for the manufacture of linen shirts for the soldiers. Sarah Franklin Bache set aside a room in her house and volunteers made 2,200 shirts. Each shirt was signed by the one who made it.

Betsy Ross made regimental banners. Two were taught how to make and repair guns. Women held scrap drives to collect old pewter dishes that could be melted down and made into bullets. When the leaden statue of George 111 was pulled down, a group of women helped to break it into pieces, melt the lead and pour the molten metal into bullet molds, producing 40,000 musket balls."

—*Women of the Revolution*

BY J.T. HEADLEY: "General Washington remained comparatively inactive during the summer, awaiting the arrival of the French fleet and army. Nothing could be done with his feeble force, unsustained by a fleet, except to hold the country around New York. In the meantime, his heart was filled with the deepest solicitude for the fate of Charleston and the army under Lincoln, which occupied it. Hemmed in by the enemy, whose shot and shells fell with an incessant rash into the dwellings of the inhabitants, this intrepid commander, Lincoln, who had held out long after hope had abandoned every heart, was at last compelled with his three thousand troops to surrender.

In the meantime, the French fleet arrived July 10, 1780 at Newport. Then came news of successive defeats in the South. The fall of Charleston in May was followed in August by the complete overthrow of Gates, at Camden; the loss of many noble troops and the death of Baron De Kalb."

CHAPTER 14

Toward Victory

"THE GAZETTE OF TODAY: SENTIMENTS OF A LADY IN NEW JERSEY."

"The War carried on by the British Nation against my native Country, cannot fail to excite in the humane and virtuous mind, sentiments very unfavorable to the authors and instruments of such a variety of complicated evils and misfortunes as we have suffered in the course of it.

The contest began on their part without principle—has been prosecuted without humanity. Devoid of those sentiments and that conduct which do so much honor to the civilized nations of Europe, even in the time of war, they have thrown off all restraint, and fully displayed in their military operations in this part of the world, the true characteristic of their country—a fierce and barbarous spirit...

As if it were not enough unjustly to spill the blood of our countrymen, to lay waste the fields, to destroy our dwellings, and even the houses consecrated and set apart for the worship of the Supreme Being, they have desolated the aged and unprotected, and waged war against our sex. Who that has heard of the burning of Charlestown, in New England—of the wanton destruction of Norfolk and Falmouth—of their wasting the fine improvements in the environs of Philadelphia—of the tragic death of Miss M'Crea, torn from her house, murdered and scalped by a band of savages hired and set on by British emissaries.

These feelings and these sentiments have been particularly manifested by the ladies of Philadelphia in their liberal contributions of money towards rendering the situation of the soldiery of the Continental army more convenient and comfortable. It is to this class of men we more immediately owe our defense and protection; they have borne the weight of the war, and met danger in every quarter, and what is higher praise, they have with Roman courage and perseverance, suffered the extremes of heat and cold, the attacks of hunger, and the pain of long and fatiguing marches through parts before unexplored by armies, and which had scarcely ever before borne the print of human feet.

It was enough for these brave men to reflect they were engaged in the best and most glorious of all causes—that of defending the rights and liberties of their Country—to induce them to behave with so much resolution and fortitude. Their many sufferings so cheerfully undergone, highly merit our gratitude and sincere thanks, and claim all the assistance we can afford their distresses. If we have it not in our power to do from the double motive of religion and a love of liberty what some ladies of the highest rank in the Court of France every day perform from motives of religion only, in the hospitals of the sick and diseased, let us animate one another to contribute from our purses in proportion to our circumstances towards the support and comfort of the brave men who are fighting and suffering for us on the field. We ought to do this if we desire to keep the enemy from our borders—if we wish that there may not be occasion to call forth our husbands, our children, and our dearest friends, to risk their lives again in our defense. I can truly say that I have experienced the most heart-rending anxieties when my friends and relations have been called upon as free citizens to march against the enemy." —*New Jersey Gazette*, July 12, 1780

AUGUST 1, 1780: "Britain has long seen that the conquest of America by force alone is impractical. She has therefore had recourse to stratagems, by which she hopes to gain an accommodation, if not a victory; an accommodation that will give such power to neutrals and Tories as will gain a slower, but not less certain, nor less fatal, victory in the end. To accomplish this, she has too well succeeded in depreciating our money by her emissaries, both without and within our councils. But she can never accomplish her design unless our zeal and vigor are depreciated with our money...From Lord North downward, they are all declaring they do not mean to injure America, but to watch the favorable movement of the war to give the Americans peace and order. That all their barbarity in the field, the destruction of our property, and the far more cruelly slow murders of thousands in their prisons, is only designed for our good, and to prepare us for the olive branch...

The death of our paper currency and the fall of Charleston happening near together, flushed the hopes of the British, and in their opinions, gained them the point which Lord North deemed proper for extending the olive branch...

Our dwelling-houses and temples in flames before our eyes. The aged, the widow, the fatherless; insulted, beaten, and plundered without pity, are arguments we understand and feel...

If they could conquer this country for the present, they could not hold the conquest without crushing us.

In these circumstances, *Divine Providence* is rousing to action by the most favorable prospects. Our allies are gaining the superiority by sea in the different quarters of the globe, and at the same time have sent a very powerful *Aid* to us. The remains of this campaign are big with important events...

Let affection, strengthened by suffering; fears roused by dangers, and fortitude supported by the greatest prospects, unite and invigorate the grand struggle that we may soon be in full liberty and peace; each enjoying all that is contained in the character of *A Citizen*."

—New Jersey Journal, August 2, 1780

THE FOLLOWING IS FROM
"HISTORY OF THE UNITED STATES."
by E.D. Fite

"The British remained largely on the defensive in the North, secure in the possession of New York City, and of the country north as far as West Point. Their offensive operations were directed against the States in the South, in the hope of penetrating the colonies there; summoning the Loyalists to their standard, and working northward. In 1778 they took Savannah and reinstated the royal governor in Georgia. In 1780 they took Charleston, which was defended by General Lincoln with three thousand Continentals, and the Brits over-ran the whole of the State of South Carolina. At first the chief resistance came from small isolated bands of patriots fighting in guerrilla warfare under the brave southerners: Pickens, Marion and Sumter. Small re-enforcements arrived from the North before the surrender of Charleston, and afterward came more northern troops and General Gates to succeed General Lincoln in command. At Camden in South Carolina, the new commander met with humiliating defeat and great losses at the hands of Cornwallis.

Pushing on from this victory to the invasion of North Carolina, Cornwallis sent a division of one thousand Tories under Major Ferguson to scour the highlands for more Tory recruits. The backwoodsmen there however, proved more devoted to the Patriot cause than was expected, and to the number of one thousand came together at the first warning under Sevier and other pioneer leaders, to resist the invasion.

It was similar to the gathering of the *Minutemen* at Concord and Lexington and the *citizen- soldiers* at Bennington in the Saratoga Battle, and with similar results, for Ferguson's entire force of twelve hundred men was entrapped at King's Mountain, just over the line in North Carolina in October 1780 and killed, wounded, or captured to the last man.

'Marion was called *the old swamp fox* because he could escape by paths across the Carolina swamps…The men camped in the woods and mountains where it was difficult to find them, and dashed out to fight wherever they could find small English forces,' (wrote one historian).

Reinforcements from the patriots poured in from the North. The chief command of the southern army was taken from General Gates and given to General Greene…

By a rapid march to the north, Green contrived to decoy Cornwallis across the entire State of North Carolina to the Virginia line, far from his base of supplies at Charleston, South Carolina. A drawn battle was fought at Guilford Court House in North Carolina where the Americans again availed themselves of Cavalry; after which Cornwallis...withdrew into Virginia to join the British forces harassing that State. Greene wisely refused to follow the enemy farther, but returned southward...

After some maneuvering against Lafayette, who was in command of the Americans in Virginia, Cornwallis settled down at Yorktown, Virginia. He chose a position near the coast on the narrow peninsula between the York River and the James River, with water on three sides."

—E.D. Fite

NEW YORK, SEPTEMBER 26, 1780: "*Treason* of the blackest dye was yesterday discovered. General Arnold, who commanded at West Point, lost to every sentiment of honor, of public and private obligation, was about to deliver up that important fort into the hands of the enemy. Such an event must have given the American cause a deadly wound if not a fatal stab. Happily, the scheme was timely discovered to prevent the fatal misfortune. The Providential train of circumstances which led to it, affords the most convincing proof that the liberties of America are the object of Divine protection.

Arnold the traitor has made his escape to the enemy, but Mr. Andre, Adjutant-General to the British army, who came out as a spy to negotiate the business, is our prisoner.

His Excellency the Commander-in-chief has arrived at West Point, from Hartford, and is now doubtless taking proper steps to unravel fully so hellish a plot."

—*Pennsylvania Packet*, October 10, 1780

CHAPTER 15

1781 Cornwallis Surrenders
Yorktown: October, 18, 1781

SOUTH CAROLINA, MAY, 1781

A British Soldier's Letter to a Friend in London

"The retrograde progress of our arms in the country, you have seen in your newspapers, if they dare tell you the truth...

Our victories have been dearly bought, for the rebels seem to grow stronger by every defeat, like Antaeus, of whom it was fabled, that being the son of the goddess Tellus, or the earth; every fall which he received from Hercules gave him more strength, so that the hero was forced to strangle him in his arms, at last.

I wish our ministry could send us a Hercules to conquer these obstinate Americans, whose aversion to the cause of Britain grows stronger every day.

If you go into company with any of them occasionally, they are barely civil, and that is, as Jack Falstaff says, *by compulsion.* They are in general sullen, silent, and thoughtful. The King's health they dare not refuse, but they drink it in such a manner as if they expected it would choke them.

The assemblies which the officers have opened, in hopes to give an air of gayety and cheerfulness to themselves and the inhabitants, are but dull and gloomy meetings; the men play at cards, indeed, to avoid talking, but the women are seldom or never to be persuaded to dance. Even in their dresses the females seem to bid us defiance. The gay toys which are imported here they despise; they wear their own homespun manufactures, and take care to have in their breasts-knots, and even on their shoes something that resembles their flag of the thirteen stripes. An officer told Lord Cornwallis not long ago, that he believed if he had destroyed all the men in North America, we should have enough to do to conquer the women. I am heartily tired of this country, and wish myself at home.'"

—*Pennsylvania Packet*, December 11, 1780

PENNSYLVANIA, JUNE 28, 1781: "The United States of America have at this moment, a fair prospect of establishing their peace and independence, which may soon be realized, if the Americans be not wanting to themselves. The Britons, by turning their arms to the southern States, have experienced what the wise and sagacious predicted from this measure; they have greatly exhausted and dissipated their army, and found it easier with a collected force covered by a superior navy to penetrate into a thinly settled country, then to spread themselves over it, and maintain their conquests.

The climate, and the brave persevering efforts of the patriots in that quarter, have almost ruined the army of Cornwallis, which having been drawn from New York, must have greatly weakened that important post. The Spaniards have greatly distressed the British settlements in the Floridas, and have taken Pensacola. A great part of Georgia is recovered from the British, and almost the whole of South Carolina is at this hour in the possession of the United States. Virginia, under particular disadvantages at its first invasion, is now collecting its whole force to co-operate with the assistance it has received and to which it is entitled, and the prospect there is far from being discouraging.

Britain has received an unexpected and terrible shock in the late account from the East Indies, where the loss of a large share of their settlements and the tottering state of the rest, threatens the total ruin of her finances. At the same time, she cannot but look with anguish on the good condition of the finances of France, where not a single new tax has been levied during the war, but the whole charge of it defrayed by the mere savings of economy...

The present then, is the critical day for America. Dissentions languor in our councils or conduct, would revive the hopes of Briton, and might be an irreparable injury to the Americans and their latest posterity. Union and vigor through the present campaign, may lay a stable foundation of liberty and happiness to these States. Having expended already so much blood and treasure in their glorious cause, it should be a first principle in the mind of every free citizen, that the only way to reap the fruits of all, and to make a safe and honorable peace, is to conduct the remainder of the war with vigor. This, and this alone, will make it short. A good army in the field, and well-provided, is absolutely necessary to give the finishing stroke to the establishment of America's invaluable rights."

—*Pennsylvania Packet*, July 14, 1781

VIRGINIA, JULY 8: "Cornwallis having encamped near Jamestown in Virginia, the Marquis de Lafayette sent General Wayne with the Pennsylvania line to take their station within a small distance of the British army, and watch their motions. About three hundred riflemen occupied the ground between General Wayne and Lord Cornwallis. They were directed to scatter themselves in the woods, without order, and annoy the enemy's camp...At length the whole of General Wayne's division were engaged...They drove the advance detachment back to their lines and without stopping there, attacked the whole British army drawn up in order of battle, and charged them with their bayonets.

The disproportion of numbers was too great. The Marquis arrived, in person, time enough to order a retreat, and to bring off the Pennsylvania troops before they were surrounded, which the enemy were endeavoring to effect being able greatly to outflank them. Cornwallis did not pursue them more than half a mile in the retreat, apprehending that the rest of the Americans were near enough to support them, and not choosing to risk a *general engagement...*" *(Letter from a Soldier from Holt's Forge, July 11), New Jersey Gazette, August 8, 1781*

PENNSYLVANIA, AUGUST 31: "Yesterday at one o'clock in the afternoon, his Excellency the Commander-in-Chief of the American armies, accompanied by the General's Rochambeau and Chastellux with their respective suites, arrived in Philadelphia. The general was received by the militia light horse in the suburbs, and escorted into the town. He stopped at the city tavern, and received the visits of several gentlemen, from thence he proceeded to the house of the Superintendent of Finances, where he now has head-quarters.

About three o'clock he went up to the State House, and paid his respects to Congress. He then returned to the superintendent's where…General Knox, General Moultrie, and several other gentlemen, had the pleasure of dining with him.

After dinner, some vessels belonging to the port, lying in the stream, fired salutes to the different toasts which were drunk. In the evening the city was illuminated, and his Excellency walked through some of the principle streets, attended by a numerous concourse of people, eagerly pressing to see their beloved general."
—*Pennsylvania Packet*, September 1, 1781

VIRGINIA, SEPTEMBER 7, 1781: "The light infantry are advanced to Williamsburg; the Pennsylvanians lay near us, and it is the talk of the camp that the French troops will take their position tomorrow in its vicinity. The French ships lay in James River to prevent a retreat in York River, and at the capes…We have a brave army to contend against, furnished in provisions with all the necessaries for a gallant resistance, and in number fully sufficient for the defense of their post, but we shall do very well, for to the common motives of our profession will be joined an emulation arising from the fighting by the side of our allies.

The British are entrenching at York with great industry. Everything is landed from their shipping, and dispositions made for their destruction…"

—*Pennsylvania Packet*, September 18

VIRGINIA, SEPTEMBER 27, 1781 "The American army and their allies near Williamsburg, in Virginia, formed the line of battle today. Tomorrow morning, they expect to march to a position near

York, to commence a siege. They make a brilliant appearance as to numbers, and are fifteen thousand strong, not including the Virginia militia. General Wayne was wounded in the thigh the 2nd instant by a sentinel, who conceived him to be an enemy, but has since recovered. We congratulate our friends upon the prospect of reducing his lordship, and restoring peace and liberty to our country." Letter from camp.. *New York Gazette and Weekly Mercury*, October 22

VIRGINIA, OCTOBER 9, 1781: "The British in Yorktown and Gloucester, in Virginia, are now completely invested by land and water. The allied army, under his Excellency General Washington's command, commenced operations against the enemy in those towns, on Thursday, the 27th ultimo, and we are assured that the French and American batteries were playing successfully against the enemy, on that and three following days."

—*New York Gazette and Weekly Mercury*, Oct 22

VIRGINIA, OCTOBER 19, 1781 "Be it remembered, that on the seventeenth of October, 1781, Lieutenant–General Earl Cornwallis, with above five thousand British troops, surrendered prisoners of war to his Excellency General George Washington, Commander-in-Chief of the allied forces of France and America! Laus Deo!"

—*New York Packet*, October 25

A Letter from Cornwallis to Clinton on His Misfortune

VIRGINIA, OCTOBER 20, 1781 "This morning, Cornwallis in a letter to Sir Henry Clinton, gives the following account of the siege which ended yesterday in his surrender to the allied forces."

"I never saw Yorktown in any favorable light, but when I found I was to be attacked in it in so unprepared a state, by so powerful an army and artillery, nothing but the hopes of relief would have induced me to attempt its defense, for I would either have endeavored to escape to New York by rapid marches from the Gloucester side immediately on the arrival of General Washington's troops at Williamsburg, or I would, notwithstanding the disparity of numbers, have attacked them in the open field.

The enemy broke ground on the 30th of September, and constructed on that night, and the two following days and nights, two redoubts...On the night of the 6th of October they made their first parallel...Having perfected this parallel, their batteries opened on the evening of the 9th against our left...The fire continued incessant from heavy cannon, and from mortars and howitzers, throwing shells from eight to sixteen inches, until our guns on the left were silenced, our works much damaged and our loss of men considerable. On the night of the 11th, they began their second parallel, about three hundred yards nearer to us...I did everything in my power to interrupt their work, by opening new embrasures for guns, and keeping a constant fire with all the howitzers and small mortars that we could man.

On the evening of the 14th they assaulted and carried two redoubts that had been advanced about three hundred yards...

At this time, we knew that there was no part of the whole front attacked in which we could show a single gun, and our shells were nearly expended. I had therefore only to choose between preparing to surrender the next day; or in endeavoring to get off with the greatest part of the troops, and I determined to attempt the latter reflecting that though it should prove unsuccessful in its object, it might at least delay the enemy in the prosecution of further enterprises.

Sixteen large boats were prepared, and upon other pretexts were ordered to be in readiness to receive troops precisely at ten o'clock. With those I hoped to pass the infantry during the night, abandoning our baggage, and leaving a detachment to capitulate for the town's people, and for the sick and wounded, on which subject a letter was ready to be delivered to General Washington. After making my arrangements with the utmost secrecy, the light infantry, the greatest part of the guards, and part of the 23rd regiment, embarked at the hour appointed, and most of them landed at Gloucester, but at the critical moment, the weather, from being moderate and calm, changed to a most violent storm of wind and rain, and drove all the boats, some of which had troops on board, down the river.

It was soon evident that the intended passage was impracticable, and the absence of the boats rendered it equally impossible to bring back the troops that had passed, which I had ordered about two o'clock in the morning. In this situation, with my little force divided, the enemy's batteries opened at daybreak. The passage between this place and Gloucester was much exposed, but the boats having now returned, they were ordered to bring back the troops that had passed during the night, and they joined us in the forenoon without much loss. Our works in the meantime were going to ruin...which the enemy's artillery were demolishing whenever they fired...I therefore proposed to capitulate."

—*Rivington's Gazette*, November 24

YORKTOWN

BY COLONEL AZOY "The end came at ten o'clock on the morning of October 17, 1781. An English officer appeared waving a white handkerchief. He was blindfolded and conducted to Washington. Washington would give Cornwallis two hours in which to submit his proposals in writing to terms of capitulation.

All ranks of the English army and navy at Yorktown and Gloucester were to be prisoners of war. All English arms, ammunition, stores and ships were to be given up; all officers were to keep their side-arms and personal servants; General officers and staff officers were to be given paroles; Yorktown and Gloucester were to be delivered over to the allies. The British troops were to quit their camps with colors cased and music playing either a German or English march.

At noon the French and American Flags went up on the Yorktown ramparts and two hours later the head of the English column appeared. Cornwallis said he was ill, and could not attend the ceremony...The regimental bands played, *The world turned upside down.*

The neighborhood night watchman in Philadelphia heard the news, and went crying through the silent streets: 'Past three o'clock, and Cornwallis taken! All is well!'"

Procession of Congress to Church

BY M.E. THALHEIMER: "Early in the morning, Congress went in solemn procession to church to render thanks to God for the deliverance of the Nation. In England as well as in America, it was felt that the question of Independence was decided. The House of Commons voted, March 4, 1782, that whoever should advise a continuance of the war was an enemy to the King and country."

The Formal Surrender at Yorktown on October 19, 1781

"At about twelve o'clock, the combined army was arranged and drawn up in two lines extending more than a mile in length. The Americans were drawn up in a line on the right side of the road, and the French occupied the left. At the head of the former, the great American commander mounted on his noble courser, took his station, attended by his aides. At the head of the latter was posted the excellent Count Rochambeau and his suite. The French troops in complete uniform, displayed a martial and noble appearance; their band of music, of which the timbre formed a part, is a delightful novelty, and produced while marching, a most enchanting effect. The Americans, though not all in uniform; nor their dress so neat, yet exhibited an erect soldierly air, and every countenance beamed with satisfaction and joy. The concourse of spectators from the country was prodigious in point of numbers; probably equal in the military, but universal silence and order prevailed...After having grounded their arms and divested themselves of their accoutrements, the captive troops were conducted back to Yorktown and guarded by our troops till they could be removed to the place of their destination."

—By James Thacher

GRATITUDE TO FRANCE

"The well-concerted and animated support of the Count de Grasse, was essentially conducive to the completion of this glorious event, and deserves the warmest thanks of his own Country, and the grateful plaudits of every American.

The exertions of the Count de Rochambeau, and all the officers and soldiers of the French army, can never be excelled, and only equaled by their American friends, who glowed with the laudable ambition of imitating the achievement of the finest body of men in the world."

—*New York Journal*, November 12, 1781

"GENERAL WASHINGTON'S REPORT TO CONGRESS OCTOBER 19, 1781"

"I should be wanting in the feelings of gratitude, did I not mention on this occasion, with the warmest sense of acknowledgment, the very cheerful and able assistance which I have received in the course of our operation from his Excellency the Count de Rochambeau and all his officers of every rank in their respective capacities...

I wish it was in my power to express to Congress how much I feel myself indebted to the Count de Grasse and the officers of the fleet under his command, for the distinguished aid and support which has been afforded by them."

GENERAL WASHINGTON COMMENDS HIS MILITIA: "The generous task for which we first flew to arms being accomplished, the liberties of our Country being fully acknowledged and firmly secured, and the characters of those who have persevered through every extremity of hardship, suffering and danger, are hereby immortalized by the illustrious appellation of: *THE PATRIOT ARMY.*

..."May ample justice be done them here, and may the choicest of Heaven's favors, both here and hereafter, attend those, who, under the Divine auspices, have secured innumerable blessings for others. With these wishes and this benediction, the Commander-in-Chief is about to retire from service. The curtain of separation will soon be drawn, and the military scene to him will be closed forever."

"Liberty is the basis, and whoever would dare to sap the foundation, or overturn the structure, under whatever specious pretext he may attempt it, will merit the bitterest execration and the severest punishment which can be inflicted by his injured country." —General George Washington

"THE ANNIVERSARY OF AMERICAN INDEPENDENCE JULY 4, 1799"

"It becomes us on this anniversary, to offer to the Supreme Being our most fervent and devout acknowledgments.

I presume I am speaking to an audience which consists of such persons as believe in a Universal Providence; or that God has the disposal of all events. The Sacred Scriptures teach us with great explicitness, that the agency of God is concerned in the rise and fall of Nations. Moses, when speaking of the deliverance of the Israelites from Egyptian bondage and their being made an independent Nation, ascribes it to the agency of God.

The disposing hand of God *is as visible*, in taking the United States, "from the midst of another nation," and raising them to a state of independence, as it was in the case of the Israelites! … The hand of God was as visible in the American Revolution, as in the other case. No human calculations could have ascertained the result of the conflict between Great Britain and the Colonies which now compose the United States. These observations might be illustrated by having recourse to many facts which are now fresh in the memories of the elder part of this audience, but omitting them, we are taught from the Sacred Scriptures to view such events as the effect of God's Providential government. We ought, therefore, by solemn and religious manner, to acknowledge God, and ascribe the glory of all our deliverances to Him…

My fellow-citizens, since so fair an inheritance is given us by the beneficent Ruler of the Universe, after making due acknowledgments to Him, let us resolve to defend it—to be good subjects and good citizens."

—Cyprian Strong, 1799

A TRIBUTE TO THE MARQUIS DE LAFAYETTE

"General Persing in France"
By Floyd Gibbon

"We landed that day at Boulogne, June 13, 1917. Military bands massed on the quay, blared out the American National Anthem as the ship was warped alongside the dock. Other ships in the busy harbor began blowing whistles and ringing bells. Loaded troop and hospital ships lying near by burst forth into cheering.

Rank upon rank of French marines, and sailors with their flat hats with red tassels, stood at attention awaiting inspection. The docks and train sheds were decorated with French and American flags and yards and yards of the mutually-owned red, white and blue. General Pershing, as a guest of the city of Boulogne, took a motor ride through the streets of this busy port city. He was quickly returned to the station where he and his staff boarded a special train for Paris. I went with them...

His party stopped in front of two marble slabs that lay side by side at the foot of a granite monument. From the General's party a Frenchman stepped forward and, removing his high silk hat, he addressed the small group in quiet, simple tones and well-chosen English words. He was the Marquis de Chambrun.

He said, 'The principles of liberty, justice and independence are the glorious links between our Nations...Today when, after nearly a century and a half, America and France are engaged in a conflict for the same cause upon which their early friendship was based, we are filled with hope and confidence.

We know that our great Nations are, together with our Allies, invincible, and we rejoice to think that the United States and France are reunited in the fight for liberty, and will re-consecrate, in a new victory, their everlasting friendship of which your presence today at this grave is an exquisite and touching token.'

General Pershing advanced to the tomb, and placed upon the marble slab an enormous wreath of pink and white roses. Then he stepped back. He removed his cap and held it in both hands in front of him. The bright sunlight shone down on his silvery grey hair. Looking down at the grave, he spoke in a quiet impressive tone, four simple, all-meaning words:" *Lafayette, we are here.*

PART 2

The Northwest Territory

"When we see the land cleared of those enormous trees, and the cliffs and quarries converted into materials for building, we cannot help dwelliing upon the industry and art of man which by dint of toil and perseverace can change the desert into a fruitful field and shape the rough rock to use and elegance.

When the solitary waste is peopled and convenient habitations arise amidst the former retreats of wild beasts; when the silence of nature is succeeded by the buzz of employment, the congratulations of society, and the voice of joy, in fine, when we behold competence and plenty springng from the bosom of dreary forests, what a lesson is afforded of the benevolent intentions of Providence!"

—THADDEUS HARRIS' 1803 JOURNAL

CHAPTER 16

The Northwest Territory

"TO COMPRISE THE STATES OF OHIO, INDIANA, ILLINOIS, MICHIGAN, AND WISCONSIN"

By J.W. Mackinnon

"When the Congress of the American Colonies on July 2, 1776, passed a resolution declaring *'That These United Colonies are, and of Right Ought to be Free and Independent States,* and that all political connection between them and the state of Great Britain is, and ought to be totally dissolved,' the first important step was taken toward the making of a new Nation in the New World....

To declare themselves free and independent was one thing for them to do; but to compel Great Britain to acknowledge it, and give up her claims was quite a different thing. To accomplish this, the Colonies all realized that they must work together, and that some sort of a central government must be formed, and maintained. The work was new and strange for them and necessarily slow...In

1777 the *Articles of Confederation* were adopted by Congress and submitted to the States for their approval.

...The first step in the establishment of a real nationality depended upon this, our *Northwest Territory.* Territorial expansion—the erection and addition of new States—appears as the first important factor in determining the beginning, the continuing of our Nation.

Congress did not care for the control of this territory, with which it did not know what to do, but it was forced to assume authority because of the determination of the smaller States that the larger ones should not do so. The wise men of this time had little faith in the future of this interior country, and had doubts about its final settlement. Many of them could hardly believe that any considerable number of people would venture so far away into the *far west* in search of homes. But when a number of men in Massachusetts, whose fortunes had been shattered by the ravages of war, and who were consequently compelled to look about for some way of starting anew in life, they organized "The Ohio Company," and presented a petition to Congress for a grant of land out here in the western wilderness. That petition was heard with delight. Such a request made the doubters think that this [portion of the] country was not a hopeless waste, and that it might amount to something after all...For a year and a half it was delayed by various difficulties, until October 1787, when a contract was closed with representatives of *The Ohio Company* for a tract of five million acres of land on the Ohio River near the mouth of the Muskingum River, at sixty-six and two-thirds cents an acre, to be paid for in United States certificates of debt; worth then about twelve cents on the dollar, and making the actual cost of the land about eight cents an acre.

This law we know as *"The Ordinance of 1787,"* and still further know it as *the most notable law ever enacted by the representatives of the American people.* It marks the beginning of one of the most remarkable growths ever known in territorial expansion, and it has furnished the bases for the Constitutions of several States...

"THE ORDINANCE OF 1787"

"It is hereby ordained and declared by the authority aforesaid (United States), that the following articles shall be considered as articles of compact between the original States and the people and States in the said territory and forever remain unalterable, unless by common consent. In Brief:

ARTICLE I provides that no one should ever be molested on account of his religious belief or mode of worship so long as he conducts himself in a peaceable and orderly manner.

ARTICLE II secures protection for person and property for everyone in the territory. It guarantees the right of Habeas Corpus, which gives every person imprisoned upon any charge, the right to demand a hearing at once, and thus secure his release unless it can be shown that there is reasonably good ground for his arrest and detention.

ARTICLE III states religion, morality, and knowledge being necessary to good government and the happiness of mankind, schools and the means of education shall forever be encouraged.

ARTICLE IV carries in it a very plain though indirect declaration against the right of secession, when it provides against the possibility of this territory, or any States that might afterward be formed from it, ever seceding from the Union, by saying that they, 'shall forever remain a part of the confederacy of the United States.'

ARTICLE V provides for the formation of three or five States from this territory as Congress might deem expedient, and it fixes the boundary lines in every respect, and provides that when any of these sections so bounded shall have sixty-thousand free inhabitants, such section shall be admitted into Congress on an equal footing with the original States in all respects whatsoever, and shall be at liberty to form a permanent constitution and state government; provided such constitution and government shall be republican and in conformity to these articles of this ordinance.

ARTICLE VI prohibits every form of human slavery except such as might be imposed as a punishment for crime, for which the party had to be duly convicted."

"DANIEL WEBSTER SAID OF THE ORDINANCE OF 1787: 'No single law of any lawgiver, ancient or modern, has produced effects of more distinct, marked and lasting character than this Ordinance.'"

"MARIETTA: THE EARLIEST SETTLEMENT IN OHIO"

Recollections of a Founder
By Joseph Barker (1765-1843)

"A meeting commenced in August, 1787 by officers and soldiers who formed an association named The Ohio Company. Resolved that they would send out to the Muskingum River, four surveyors and 22 men; 6 boat builders, 4 carpenters, 1 blacksmith and 9 workmen. That the boat builders and men with the surveyors be proprietors of the Company. That their tools; one ax and one hoe to each man, and 30 lbs. weight of baggage be carried in the company wagons and their subsistence on their Journey be furnished by the Company.

That each man furnish himself with a good small arm, bayonet, flints, a powder horn and pouch, priming wire and brush, half lb. powder, one-pound balls and one lb. buckshot.

When the men and material were collected, Putnam moved on for the Muskingum. When near the mountains, he sent one forward to Sumrill's Ferry 30 miles above Pittsburgh on the Youghiogheny River with some boat builders to procure timber and commence building a boat. Devol, who had been a ship builder in Rhode Island, took charge of constructing a boat 45 feet long and 12 feet wide; bow curved, covered with a roof like a house...

'All of March was consumed in the building of boats, and on the 1st of April the united company, embarking upon a little flotilla consisting of three log canoes, a flat-boat, and a galley of fifty tons burden called the *Adventure Galley*, but afterward renamed the

Mayflower, left Sumrill's Ferry on the Youghiogheny, and floating down that stream to the Monongahela, guided their way onward to the Ohio River.' —A. F. Matthews

> The surveyors commenced their work. Colonel R.J. Meigs took the meanders of the Muskingum. The others surveyed the small lots; examined and reported the best situations for settlements along the two streams: the Muskingum and the Ohio."

Barker's narrative continues in earnest:
"On the first of November, 1789, the day I arrived, 90 families had landed and associations to 250 settlers had been formed...All hands had been busily employed during the summer of 1788 and most of the winter in the employ of the surveyors in building log cabins, sawing plank and putting up the block houses in Campus Martius for the Ohio Company, and in building a large heavy bridge over Tibe Creek where the stone bridge now stands. By May, 1790 there were very few lots in Belpre and Newberry without a settler...

In case of an alarm on Sundays, that part of the congregation who were armed, rushed out of Meeting to meet any danger and pursue the Indians which several times happened.

Colonel Sproat was considered Commander-in-Chief of the military, and his aid was solicited to procure arms for the citizens who were deficient. He sent immediately to Pittsburgh to the commanding officer of the U.S. old fort, who sent down about 30 old soldiers' muskets which had been thrown by as unfit for use and very rusty and damaged. The blacksmiths were set to repair them, which were then distributed where the service most required.

Powder and lead were furnished and cartridges fixed to suit each caliber, and placed in the blockhouses for distribution on the first emergency. In '92, received 25 new muskets from the factory, dealt to soldiers and inhabitants. The county was now well-armed; many rifles. Those who were good marksmen were selected as sentries and were always ready to start upon any discovery or pursue an Indian trail...

I cleared and fenced two and a half acres of land and set out 50 apple trees...Word that land was to be given for settlement on the Muskingum had spread through the upper country and many persons came into the settlement.

Capt. Rogers was a brave and humane old soldier. He was an officer in the *rifle core,* and the taking of Burgoyne. Having served honorably through the Revolution, he resided some time with his friends, but having cast his bread upon the waters of the Revolution, he with many an old soldier, marched towards the setting sun in hopes to find it in the West...

When the Ohio Company first came out, every person found in this region was a woodsman; a hunter of game and Indians. They knew their customs and habits of warfare, and were always ready and proud of imparting information to whoever would listen to their teaching.

Maple sugar in the first settlement formed a valuable constituent. In many families where solid food was scarce and dear, and in fact not to be had; in particular where there was no money, sugar was a substitute for many things.

We had a good sled road over the Muskingum on which we hauled walnut logs to Putnam's Mill for two or three weeks as there were no roads. In 1799 we had a similar winter—the cold set in and the snow fell in January, and we had good sledding across all the waters until 23rd of February, 1800. On the 22nd Governor Meigs delivered an oration on the death of General Washington who died the December before, and nearly all the people along the river from Waterford down, passed up and down, and across the river on sleds and sleighs.

While residing in Belpre, Captain Devol, in company with another, built the first floating mill to be operating upon, and put in action by the natural current of the Ohio River…This mill was placed upon two boats of unequal size; the waterwheel running between them and the machinery, and stones for grinding were placed in the larger which likewise received the grain and the tenders and customers. This mill was anchored in the quickest water and a communication with the shore was kept up by means of canoes and boats which were the only traveling carriages incident to a country where there were neither roads nor bridges, but only the navigable streams. This Mill, although but a make shift, supplied the garrisons and scattered inhabitants for 20-30 miles up and down the Ohio…

These Patriots of the Revolution did not forget that they were the recipients of the gifts of a protecting Providence, and did not neglect to meet on the Holy Sabbath, and offer up their prayers and adoration to our Gracious and Merciful Father; their constant and bountiful benefactor, and with thankfulness and gratitude for the present and past, implore His protecting care for their Country and themselves in time to come…

Many of our Revolutionary settlers had been practiced to watchfulness and inured to danger, and disciplined to use sword and gun; who were not familiar with the plow and the scythe and the sickle, but by the example of those better skilled they soon became good farmers…

It was easier, cheaper and more expeditious traveling by water than on land. Here were no bridges, no roads, no taverns, and but few cabins, but in a canoe or pirogue, one could carry his kitchen, his dormitory and his magazine, and could shift sides of the river to avoid danger. In '92 a mail route was established from Pittsburgh to Cincinnati. Mr. M. who now resides in Gallia County was employed to carry the mail from Marietta to Gallipolis once a week in a skiff or canoe…

There was kindness of feeling and friendship which had been created by an association in peril and toils and dangers, and which were renewed and strengthened by a reunion in the toils and watch-fulness in subduing and cultivating a wilderness and repelling the dangers which threatened their peace and security from a crafty and vindictive enemy, while securing a second independence—a permanent competency for themselves and families.

There were but few merchants, and those with limited capital; no one came here with property who could do better with it somewhere else.

Sugar, we made ourselves. Sugar trees were plenty, but metal to boil in was scarce and dear, so that many settlers labored under the want of kettles who otherwise might have gone far towards supporting their families. Lady Washington sent out a Keg of Loaf made from maple sugar to be distributed among the ladies of the officers of the Revolutionary Army residing in the Ohio Company purchase…

To the circumstance of the Indians destroying nearly all the game in the neighborhood combined with that of a severe frost in early September 1789, may be attributed the very great scarcity of bread and meat in spring and summer of '90. Many families were destitute of cows; there were few yoke of oxen which could be spared from the clearing and the plow…People got along until the season brought relief of squashes, beans, then potatoes, then green corn. Then wheat harvest, and the hand mill was considered a luxury…

In January 1790, the company were taking their mill stones up in a small keel boat. Through carelessness of the hands, the water rose in the night and took the boat off, which was taken up by Captain Stone next morning at Belpre.

We had a large pirogue and 650 bushels of principally corn…A four-ox team took our grain to the mill. We landed within half a mile of the mill at 10, and we had all ground and started for Marietta at two; arriving at Marietta before sundown. I saw a bushel of corn ground at that mill in two minutes by a watch.

In 1792, a demand for corn for all that could be spared was to supply the commissaries dept. at Fort Washington, Cincinnati preparatory to Wayne's march against the Indians. As the people worked in large parties and kept a sentinel, and had escaped attack, they felt themselves tolerably secure from surprise, and almost every man had more or less of a cornfield for which he could get any kind of goods on credit, or money by waiting till the return of the corn delivery.

By 1793, the travel up and down the river added to the emigration into the settlement; furnished a ready market and demand for all the surplus produce that could be spared from home consumption.

Belpre was the most thriving settlement. There was a greater proportion of Revolutionary officers whose military education, mature judgment, industry, and perseverance gave them a decided superiority of success over less fortunate contemporaries.

The rough Journey over the Mountains & wear & tare incident to a new settlement, the old clothes were getting threadbare. Captain Dana of N. Hampshire, in spring 1790 sowed flax, pulled it in the blossom in June; into the swamp near the bank, dressed, had it spun & wove by Dana and made up into shirts and trousers and worn on the fourth of July at a meeting for the Celebration.

While the spies were looking out for the whole by making large circuits around the settlements, by which it was difficult for the Indians to come in without leaving a trail or sign, there were few instances the savages were not discovered before they made an attempt at mischief...In spring 1792, Goodale was clearing and preparing some ground for planting. With his team he was moving some timber for clearing and fencing near the edge of unlearned land. He had been there but a short time when the oxen were observed standing still, but he was not to be. Moccasin tracts were discovered. No other information on the manner of his capture or direction.

On the conclusion of Wayne's treaty, signed the 3rd of August, 1795, the Indian war closed, and brought that security of person and property which had been so long withheld and kept the settlement of the County dormant for nearly four years.

A general joy was the first effect, then a general anxiety to locate and make a permanent settlement. Each individual bid adieu to the garrison like the Tenants of the Ark, and went in search of a resting place from the confinement and watching incident to a four-year Indian war."

"The Miami Valley Settlements & Pioneers Mothers"
By Charles Cist, 1844

"It is hardly possible for those who are now living in Cincinnati, in the enjoyment of every comfort or luxury which money can procure, to form any notion of the privations which were suffered by the hardy settlers of the west—the pioneers of the Miami Valleys among others. 55 years ago, the condition of the great thoroughfares to the West—of the route across the Allegheny Mountains especially—was such as to forbid taking by the emigrants any articles but those of indispensable necessity. When the pioneer westward had reached Redstone or Wheeling, the difficulties of transportation were not much lessened. There were no wagon roads through the intermediate country if the hostility of the implacable savage *had* permitted traversing the route by land in safety. The family boats which carried the settlers down river, were so encumbered with wagons, horses, cows, pigs, &c., as to have little room for anything else but a few articles of family housekeeping of the first necessity.

On reaching their destinations, cabins had to be erected; the land cleared and cultivated in the presence, as it were, of the relentless Indian who watched ever opportunity of destroying the lives of the settlers, and breaking up the lodgments as fast as they were made. In the meantime, supplies of food not yet raised on the improvement, had to be obtained in the woods from hunting, which in most cases was a constant exposure of life to their enemies.

Under these circumstances, some general idea may be conceived of the sufferings and privations which those endured, who formed the vanguard of civilization, and prepared the way for the present generation to enjoy the fruit of past labors and sufferings.''

EARLY RECORDS OF CINCINNATI

''I copy the following memoranda book of old field notes kept by John Dunlop, who appears to have been engaged in the surveys of Symmes' purchase, as early as January 8, 1789.

'On the 12th December a young man, son of John Hilliers of North Bend, going out in the morning to bring home the cows; about a half a mile from the garrison, the Indians came upon him. They tomahawked him.

On the 17th following, two young men...went on a hunting excursion across the river. When they encamped at night, and had made a fire, they were surprised by Indians and fell a sacrifice into the hands of the savages, being killed by their first fire...

December 29th General Harmar arrived at Cincinnati, and was received with joy. They fired fourteen cannon at the garrison on his landing. January 1, 1790—Governor St. Clair arrived. On his arrival they fired fourteen guns...As soon as he landed, they sent express for Judge Symmes who went the next day to see him, and appoint civil and military officers for the service and protection of the settlement.'''

A Boy's Reminiscences

''OLIVER M. SPENCER, then a boy, was at Columbia as early as 1790. In 1792 he was taken prisoner by the Indians. In his *Reminiscences* he has left this description of the life of the first settlers:

'It is perhaps unknown to many that the broad and extensive plain stretching along the Ohio from the Crawfish to the mouth and for three miles up the Little Miami River, and now divided into farms, highly cultivated, was the ancient site of Columbia...

This plain on our arrival, we found scattered about fifty cabins flanked by a small stockade nearly half a mile below the mouth of the Miami, together with a few block-houses for the protection of the inhabitants at suitable distances along the bank of the Ohio.

Fresh in my remembrance is the rude log-house; the first humble sanctuary of the first settlers of Columbia, standing amidst the tall forest trees on the beautiful knoll where now, 1834 is a graveyard, and the ruins of a Baptist meeting-house of later years. There on the holy Sabbath we were wont to assemble to hear the word of life, but our fathers met with their muskets and rifles prepared for action, and ready to repel any attack of the enemy...The sentinels without at a few rods distance, with measured step were now pacing their walks, and now standing and with strained eyes, endeavoring to pierce through the distance; carefully scanning every object that seemed to have life or motion.

I well recollect that in 1791, so scarce and dear was flour that the little that could be afforded in families was laid by to be used only in sickness, or for the entertainment of friends, and although corn was abundant, there was but one mill, a floating mill on the Little Miami. It was built in a small flat boat tied to the bank, its wheel turning slowly with the natural current running between the flat and a small pirogue anchored in the stream, and on which one end of the shaft rested. It was barely sufficient to supply meal for the inhabitants of Columbia, and the neighboring families...

The men generally worked in companies exchanging labor, or in adjoining fields with their firearms near them, that in case of an attack they might be ready to unite for their common defense.'"

—History of Hamilton County

The Surveyors Hard Times

"He notes that his surveyors were having a hard time of it, at work as they were in midwinter with snow deep, the cold severe, and supplies short. One of them who lived in Losantiville, but was formerly of Westfield, New Jersey had lost his life by drowning during a freshet in the Licking River.

Under the new arrangement, fifty of the small lots were to be given to the first applicants on condition they should build a house and agree to reside three years in the city. They were rapidly taken up. As applications continued to be made, further surveys were extended up and down the Ohio River until over one hundred acre lots were laid out, giving the place a front on the Ohio River of about one and a half miles…Judge Symmes remained for six weeks in the rude shelter he had built upon first landing, then to a more comfortable log cabin enclosed and roofed.

…By the middle of May following the landing of the colony, about forty of the lots had each a comfortable cabin erected upon it covered with shingles or clapboards. The place was known as Symmes' City. It continued to be popularly called North Bend…In 1791 it was deemed worthy of a garrison of eighty soldiers…who had a great deal to do with the prosperity of the settlement, and when withdrawn, the people rapidly followed them to Cincinnati…After St. Clair's defeat, there was a perfect stampede to the back country."

—S.B. Nelson

When Cincinnati was, *Three Little Cabins*

"My father, mother and seven children landed at Cincinnati on the eighth of February, 1789. There were three little cabins here when we landed where the surveyors and chain carriers lived. They had no floors in these cabins…Mr. Ludlow came down to our boat and invited my father and mother up to stay in their cabin until we could get one built, but my mother thought they could remain more comfortable with their small children in their boat. So we lived in our boat until the ice began to run, and then we were forced to contrive some other way to live.

What few men that were here, got together and took apart our boat and built us a camp. We lived in our camp six weeks. Then my father built us a large cabin…Father intended to have built our house on the corner of Walnut and Water Streets, but not knowing exactly where the streets were, he built our house right in the middle of Water Street. The streets were laid out but the woods were so very thick, and the streets were not opened, so it was impossible to tell where the streets would be. By May first, the population increased to eleven families and twenty-four unmarried men. The number of log cabins was now twenty, and nearly all the large trees had been cut down between Water Street and Broadway."

The Centinel of the Northwestern Territory
"Open to all parties—but influenced by none."

1793: On sailing from Cincinnati to Pittsburgh

SATURDAY, NOVEMBER 9, 1793: "This country is in its infancy and we are daily exposed to an enemy who is not content with taking away the lives of men in the field, have swept away whole families, and burnt their habitations. We are well aware that the want of a regular and certain trade down the Mississippi, deprives this country in a great measure of money at the present time. There are discouragements."

NOVEMBER 16TH, 1793, *THE CENTINEL:* "Two Boats for the present will set out from Cincinnati for Pittsburgh, and return to Cincinnati in the following manner:

First boat will leave Cincinnati this morning at eight o'clock, and return to Cincinnati so as to be ready to sail again in four weeks from this date...and so regularly, each boat performing the voyage to and from Cincinnati to Pittsburgh once in every four weeks.

No danger need be apprehended from the enemy, as every person on board will be under cover, made proof against rifle or musket balls, and convenient port holes for firing out of. Each of the boats are armed with six-piece good muskets, and amply supplied with plenty of ammunition; strongly manned with choice hands, and the masters of approved knowledge.

A separate cabin from that designed for the men is partitioned off in each boat for accommodating ladies on their passage.

Conveniences are constructed on board each boat, so as to render landing unnecessary, as it might, at times, be attended with danger.

A table of the exact time for the arrival and departure to and from the different places on the Ohio River between Cincinnati and Pittsburgh, may be seen on board each boat."

—Jacob Myers

*The 1794 Wayne's Battle of Fallen Timbers brought an end
to Indian incursions into settlements for a score of years.*

"The census of 1795 showed five hundred persons in the village
sheltered in ninety-four log cabins and ten frame houses. 14,900
settlers came by flatboat and overland trails during the next five
years. The Germans fleeing religious persecution began a mass
migration there.

The city's fame as a prosperous place where work could be
found, spread through Europe...Immigrants who could not speak
English managed somehow to have themselves routed straight
through to, 'That new city on the Ohio River.'"

—*The Ohio Guide*

CHAPTER 17

War and Peace with the Indians

"CAUSES FOR THE WAR"

By Henry Knox, The Secretary for the Department of War

"Although partial treaties or conventions were formed with some of the northern and western tribes in the years 1775 and 1776, yet those treaties were too feeble to resist the powerful impulses of a contrary nature…Accordingly various Indian nations lying on our frontiers from Georgia to Canada, armed against us.

It is yet too recent to have been forgotten, that great numbers of inoffensive men, women and children fell a sacrifice to the barbarous warfare practiced by the Indians, and that many others were dragged into a deplorable captivity. Notwithstanding that these aggressions were entirely unprovoked, and yet as soon as the war ceased with Great Britain, the United States, instead of indulging any resentments against the Indian nations, sought only how to establish a liberal peace with all the tribes throughout their limits.

Early measures were accordingly taken for this purpose. A treaty was held, and a peace concluded in the year 1784 with the hostile part of the northern Indians, or Six Nations, at Fort Stanwix.

In January 1785, another treaty was formed with part of the western tribes at fort M'intosh, on the Ohio, to wit, with the Wyandots, Delawares, Ottawas and Chippewas.

In January 1786, a treaty was formed with the Shawanese at the confluence of the Great Miami with the Ohio River.

On the 2nd day of July, 1788, Congress appropriated the sum of twenty thousand dollars, in addition to fourteen thousand dollars before appropriated, for defraying the expenses of the treaties which had been ordered or which might be ordered to be held in the then present year with the several Indian tribes in the Northern Department. and for extinguishing the Indian claims…to the lands they had already ceded to the United States…

Accordingly, new treaties were held at Fort Harmar the latter part of the year 1788, and concluded on the 9th day of January, 1789.…By these treaties, the same early boundaries were recognized and established by a principle of purchase, as had been stipulated by the former treaties of Fort Stanwix and Fort M'Intosh.

Thus careful and attentive was the Government of the United States to settle a boundary with the Indians on the basis of fair treaty…

At the council of the tribes convened in 1788 at the Miami River, the Miami and Wabash Indians were pressed to repair to the treaty with great earnestness *by the chiefs of the Wyandots and Delawares.* The Wyandot chiefs particularly presented them with a large belt of wampum…which was refused. The Wyandots then laid it on the shoulders of a principal chief; recommending to him to be at peace with the Americans, but without making any answer, he leaned himself and let the wampum fall to the ground. This so displeased the Wyandots, that they immediately left the council house.

In the meantime, the frontier settlements were disquieted by frequent depredations and murders, and the complaints of their inhabitants... were loud, repeated, and distressing; their calls for protection incessant—till at length they appeared determined by their own efforts to endeavor to retaliate the injuries they were continually receiving, and which had become intolerable.

In this state of things, it was indispensable for the government to make some decisive exertion for the peace and security of the frontier.

Accordingly, in April 1790, Anthony Gamelin, an inhabitant of Post Vincennes, and a man of good character, was dispatched to all the tribes and villages of the Wabash River and to the Indians of the Miami village, with a message encouraging them to a general peace and treating them with perfect humanity and kindness, and at the same time warning them to abstain from further depredations.

The Indians in some of the villages on the lower part of the Wabash appeared to listen to him. Others manifested a different disposition; others confessed their inability to restrain their young warriors...They promised an answer that was never received. A chief informed him that a party of seventy warriors from the more distant Indians had arrived, and were gone against the settlements.

In three days after his departure from the Miami village, a prisoner there was burned to death. In the course of the three months immediately after the last-mentioned invitation, upwards of one hundred persons were killed, wounded and taken prisoners upon the Ohio, and in the district of Kentucky.

It is to be remarked, that previous to the last invitation, the people of Kentucky who, in consequence of their injuries, were meditating a blow against the hostile Indians; were restrained by the president of the United States from crossing the Ohio until the effect of the friendly overture intended to be made should be known.

It is also to be observed, that the Wyandots and Delawares, after having frequently and fruitlessly endeavored to influence the Miami and Wabash Indians to peace; upon mature conviction, finally declared that *force only* could affect the object.

As an evidence that the conduct of the hostile Indians has been occasioned by other motives than a claim relatively to boundaries— It is to be observed, that their depredations have been principally upon the district of Kentucky, and the counties of [W.] Virginia, lying along the south side of the Ohio River: a country to which they have no claim.

It appears by respectable evidence, that from the year 1783, and until the month of October, 1790, the time the United States commenced offensive operations against the said Indians, that on the Ohio, and the frontiers on the south side thereof, they killed, wounded and took prisoners, about one thousand five hundred men, women and children; besides carrying off upwards of two thousand horses, and other property to the amount of fifty thousand dollars.

The particulars of the barbarities exercised upon many of their prisoners, of different ages and sexes, although supported by indisputable evidence, are of too shocking a nature to be presented to the public. It is sufficient upon this head to observe, that the tomahawk and scalping-knife have been the mildest instruments of death: that in some cases torture by fire and other execrable means have been used.

But the outrages which were committed upon the frontier inhabitants were not the only injuries that were sustained: Repeated attacks upon detachments of the troops of the United States were, at different times made. The following from its peculiar enormity deserves recital—In April, 1790, Major Doughty was ordered to the friendly Chickasaws on public business. He performed this duty in a boat, having with him Ensign Sedam, and a party of fifteen men. While ascending the Tennessee River, he was met by a party of forty Indians in four canoes, consisting principally of the aforesaid banditti of Shawanese and outcast Cherokees. They approached under a white flag, the well-known emblem of peace. They came on board the Major's boat, received his presents, continued with him nearly one hour, and then departed in the most friendly manner. But they had scarcely cleared his oars, before they poured in a fire upon his crew, which was returned as soon as circumstances would permit, and a most unequal combat was sustained for several hours when they abandoned their design, but not until they had killed and wounded eleven out of fifteen of the boat's crew. This perfidious conduct, in any age, would have demanded exemplary punishment.

All overtures of peace failing, and the depredations still continuing, an attempt at coercion became indispensable. Accordingly, the expedition under Brigadier General Harmar, in the month of October, 1790, was directed. The event is known.

The different measures which have been recited must evince, that notwithstanding the highly culpable conduct of the Indians in question, the government of the United States, uninfluenced by resentment, or any false principles which might arise from a consciousness of superiority, adopted every proper expedient to terminate the Indian hostilities, without having recourse to the last extremity; and after being compelled to resort to it, has still kept steadily in view the re-establishment of peace as its primary and sole object.

To obtain protection against lawless violence, was a main object for which the present government was instituted. It is indeed, a main object of all government. A frontier citizen possesses a strong claim to protection as any other citizen. The frontiers are the vulnerable parts of every country; and the obligation of the government of the United States to afford the requisite protection, cannot be less sacred in reference to the inhabitants of their Western, than to those of their Atlantic Frontier.

A perseverance in exertions to make the refractory Indians at last sensible that they cannot continue their enormous outrages with impunity, appears to be as indispensable, in the existing posture of things, as it will be advisable whenever they shall manifest symptoms of a more amicable disposition, to convince them by decisive proofs, that nothing is so much desired by the United States as to be at liberty to treat them with kindness and beneficence."

—H. Knox, Secretary of War
War Department, Jan. 26, 1792, Philadelphia

"CENTENNIAL ANNIVERSARY OF GENERAL WAYNE'S TREATY OF GREENVILLE"

August 3, 1895

Speech by Governor William McKinley

"It is pleasant not only to meet on this historic ground and occasion, but both a privilege and a pleasure to have the opportunity to attest my respect and veneration for the brave men and women who were the pioneer settlers of Ohio and of the great Northwest. Seldom has a great community been established under circumstance more adverse, nor with greater cost in blood and suffering, privation and toil, than attended the erection of the State of Ohio in what was then a savage and unbroken wilderness from the Ohio River to Lake Erie...

If we may judge events by their subsequent results, we can heartily agree with the historians that the signing of the treaty of peace at Greenville on August 3, 1795, was the most important event necessary to permanent settlement and occupation in the existence of the whole Northwest Territory...The power of the savages to stop the onward march of civilization was broken, and the soil of Ohio was practically free from Indian outbreaks and outrages, from which the struggling settlements had severely suffered for more than seven years. It is, my countrymen at this remote period, difficult to conceive the unprotected state of the frontiersmen a century ago. We too little appreciate their sacrifices. From the first settlement at Marietta until Wayne's great victory there was not a day and scarce an hour when the few white inhabitants over a wide region of the wilderness were not in constant danger of massacre by the Indians. They intercepted almost every boat that passed up the Ohio River. They picked off the few farmers who ventured to attempt to level the forests or cultivate the soil beyond the close proximity of the block house, and emboldened by their success, frequently attacked the garrisons themselves. They were constantly inspired to attack the Americans, not only by the Indians themselves and their principal chiefs, but by almost equally cruel and vindictive British and Canadian officers of Detroit and other lake posts still occupied by them. So numerous were these affrays and massacres and murders that it is assumed by one writer that twenty-thousand men, women and children were killed by the Indians before they finally abandoned the attempt to prevent the occupation of Ohio by the white people...A reign of terror possessed all the settlements.

In September, 1790, General Harmar, then chief lieutenant of the United States Army, made a raid into the Indian country, as the whole territory northwest of the Ohio River was then properly called. This expedition was unsuccessful and also resulted in the annihilation of his command.

...President Washington had in person, witnessed all the horrors of savage warfare, and persuaded Congress in 1791 to authorize him to raise a regiment of regulars and two of volunteers for a campaign of six months against the Indians. The command of this army was entrusted to General Arthur St. Clair. He advanced with a large force upon the principal villages upon the Miami and Wabash Rivers...His unit was surprised by a large body of Indians and routed; more than half the army was killed or captured. ...It is said that the Indians were so emboldened by their great victory that they even ventured by night into the streets of Cincinnati to spy out the exposure of the town, and the best points from which to make an attack upon Fort Washington...So disheartened was the Country that it was even proposed by a few timid members of Congress to abandon the whole of the Northwest Territory and make the Ohio River the northern bounds of the United States.

On April 17, 1792, General Anthony Wayne was appointed by Washington to command the third expedition. He was then the Commander-in-chief of all the armies of the United States.

One of his biographers happily describes him as a *born soldier*. The ill-fated expedition to Canada in 1776, and although wounded, effected the retreat that saved the American army both from capture and serious loss...His capture of *Stony Point* in 1779 wherein he was struck on the head by a musket ball and sank to the ground. Instantly recovering, he arose and exclaimed, 'March on! Carry me into the fort. I will die at the head of this column.'

Instead of proceeding precipitately into this disturbed territory, he spent nearly a year in collecting and drilling his men. Meanwhile the commissioners of the government exhausted every effort for peace, but all such efforts were unavailing. In September, 1793, General Wayne had so organized his army, that by rapid marches he advanced up the valley of the Great Miami to Fort Jefferson, and thence proceeded to establish a strongly fortified camp for the winter headquarters, and called the place *Greenville*. From that point he advanced to the scene of St. Clair's defeat and there built another stockade, which he named *Fort Recovery*. He pushed on through the wilderness during the following summer, driving the Indians before him to the junction of the Auglaize and Maumee Rivers. Here he constructed, in the very heart of the Indian country, a very strong and scientifically arranged work which he styled, in intrepidity, *Fort Defiance*. The Indians had entirely failed to surprise him, and did not dare to stand before his brave and well-disciplined troops. They vainly assailed Fort Recovery on June 30, 1794 with great loss. They realized they must at last fight one who, they were clear to see, deserved their own titles, 'The Wind,' 'The Tornado,' and 'The Warrior who never sleeps.'

Having finished Fort Defiance, Wayne again pressed forward to what are called *rapids* of the Miami and here built Fort Wayne. The army consisted now of 2,000 regulars and 1100 riflemen under command of General Scott. On August 13th he sent a pacific message to the Indians urging them to come into camp, and enter a permanent and lasting peace with the United States. They did not come. Encouraged by assurances of assistance from the British, the Indians, contrary to the advice of their chieftain, declined all these overtures. General Wayne immediately prepared for battle and on August 20th, attacked the savages almost within the range of the guns of the British forts. The Indian forces amounted to fully 2,000 braves; the resistance was stubborn, but they were at length completely routed and driven more than two miles through the woods with great slaughter until within pistol shot of the British garrison.

Their houses, corn, and personal effects were completely destroyed throughout the whole country, on both sides of the Miami, for a distance of fifty miles. General Wayne in his official report to the President said, 'The horde of savages abandoned themselves to flight, dispersing with terror and shame, leaving our victorious army in full and quiet possession of the field.'

...Early in January, 1795, measures were taken to assemble all the tribes of the Northwest to Greenville, and the following June the council began between General Wayne, acting for the United States, and some 1100 chiefs representing the twelve principal tribes of the West. After six weeks of deliberation, the treaty was signed. The Indians relinquished practically all control of the soil of Ohio, with certain small and unimportant reservations along the Auglaize, St. Mary's, Sandusky and Miami Rivers.

There could not have been a more gratifying or spontaneous outburst of public admiration than was shown to General Wayne after the signing of *The Treaty of Greenville* one hundred years ago. On every hand, Wayne was greeted as a public benefactor and a hero, by people and government, of the important services he had rendered to his country.

Besides putting an end to a brutal and bloody war, waged without respect for age or sex throughout our western territory, his success had the effect of quieting Indian disturbances both north and south; of opening to the civilized population the fertile region which had been the theatre of the late hostilities, and eventually added much greater territory, equally inviting to settlement and culture."

"I read a letter now from the British commander to General Wayne on August 21, 1794, He says:

'Sir: The army of the United States of America said to be under your command have taken post on the banks of the Miami for upwards of the last twenty-four hours, almost within the reach of the guns of this fort, which being a post belonging to his Majesty, the King of Great Britain, occupied by his Majesty's troops, and which I have the honor to command, it becomes my duty to inform myself as speedily as possible in what light I am to view your making such near approach to this British garrison.' *Signed, William Campbell, commanding a British post on the banks of the Miami.*

To that letter General Wayne replied, 'I have received your letter of this day requiring from me the motives which have moved the army under my command to the position they at present command. Without questioning the authority or the propriety, sir, of your interrogatory, I think I may without breach of decorum observe to you that, were you entitled to an answer, the most full and satisfactory one was announced to you from the muzzle of my gun yesterday.

I have the honor to be, sir, yours with great respect,

Anthony Wayne, Major-General,

Commander-in-chief of the Armies of the United States.'"

"CONQUERING THE WILDERNESS"
By Colonel Frank Triplett

"I have read nearly every book bearing upon the Indian subject, and have been forced to the conclusion that it is an absolute impossibility for the man who has not mingled with them, to place himself *en rapport* with them…

…To understand him, you must have fought him, hunted and trapped with him, slept in his lodge, and joined in his forays. Then his secret thoughts become yours, and you learn to appreciate at his true worth, or want of it, this tawny robber and stoic murderer. Until then he is a sealed book, or a riddle to which the key has been lost. Of course, there are some exceptions to the opinions herein expressed...and I am only too glad to admit it—would they were more frequent.

It has long been my intention to endeavor to correct in some measure, the erroneous ideas so generally prevalent...From the hand that has wielded rifle and trap upon the plains, and pole-pick and gold-pan in the mountains, may not flow the honied graces of the *sentimental scribblers* who paint ideal Indians and benevolent Indian-agents, but it will honestly record the life of plains and mountains, as seen in the lodge of the Indian, the tent of the prospector, and the camp of the trapper.

Pouring across the Allegheny Mountains in a flood, at first insignificant, the tide of immigration may not be inaptly compared to a leak in one of the dykes of Holland. At first a few drops trickle slowly through the mighty barrier, but as the hours go by, these tiny drops become a flowing stream.

In the settlement of Kentucky, we find first Findley, then Boone, Harrod, Kenton, Clark—the multitude...their tales led on their comrades. The solitary camp grew into the block-house, the block-house into the larger post, the post into the fort with proper walls and bastions. These in turn were replaced by villages, and later these last gave way to the towns and cities. All the while the Indian fought stubbornly against his manifest destiny, and did not fail to add torture to death, in order to preserve his hunting grounds...

...The handwriting was plain upon the wall, but the savage could not, or would not read it. His purposeless warfare of hatred and revenge was as the battling of children against giants, and its end was decreed ages before the arrival of the white man upon his shores. His destiny had been accomplished; he lingered superfluous upon the scene, and now he must make way for the superior race, and his barbarism must go down before the grand forces of civilization. Is it possible that anyone can regret the result?

The fertile valleys, which could at best supply the game for a few hundreds of wandering savages were to teem with thousands of husbandmen, and the miserable wigwams and lodges of the Indians were to be displaced by happy homes where peace was the theme and love the motive, instead of hate and war. Where the savage, in his indolence, paid no heed to the passing hours, there were to spring up industries that would benefit the world, and where his superstition made him the prey of gloomy prejudices and of horrible sacrifices, there was to arise the pure and noble fabric of the Christians' creed...

...The harsh measures being necessary to substitute for the evils of barbarism: the benefits of civilization. No moral suasion would force the Indian to honor *as sacred* his solemn treaties. No regard for truth to keep him to the line of honesty in his dealings with the white man. Commiseration he repaid with treachery, and forbearance with midnight murder. His virtues, as well as his vices, were those of a child grown to a man's stature.

He could never comprehend that any being could or would rely on aught save brute force, in his dealings with others weaker than himself. He could never learn truth and honor, either as a policy or a principle, and ever regarded theft as a legitimate acquisition of property.

His bravery was not the steady, enduring courage of the Caucasian, but the fierce, sudden ebullition of the beast, that makes its mad rush and, if it does not carry all before it, retires to make another spring at some future time. Unlike every other nation, he spared neither infancy, sex nor age, in his cruel warfare, and utterly without magnanimity, made horrid tortures the prelude to the death of his prisoners.

In vain we search for any virtues to counterbalance the hideousness of his crimes, for if we except his love of offspring—it is shared in common with the fiercest of brutes.

...If we take Boone as the type of the Kentucky pioneers, we find in him united the philosophy of the firm purpose of the statesman, and the humanity of the Christian. Confident of his mission from the Almighty to colonize Kentucky, no hardships could daunt him, no dangers turn him from his path.

Boone stands forth a true representative of his people and his class.

...That such men have left their imprint not only on their own time, but have transmitted to their posterity their traits and their peculiarities, is not to be doubted. Everywhere we find their descendants, men and women free of heart and noble of soul. Hospitality with them is a duty, and readiness to assist anyone in distress as natural to their heart...Brave even to recklessness, and somewhat too ready to avenge an insult, they are yet kind and chivalrous to all, and to such men much of rashness may easily be forgiven.

...And nobly do these people continue the purposes of their fathers. Without them today, we would have no broad and boundless West—the grandest empire the world ever saw. Without their spirit to have planned and pushed our conquest, the close of the Revolutionary War would have found the United States comprised within the bounds east of the Appalachia Range, and all the rest of our broad territory in possession of the English, French and Spaniards.

Had not Kentucky, first, then Illinois and Ohio been wrenched from the grasp of the Indians and their British allies by the adventurous spirit of the pioneers, the Americans would have been cooped up in the narrow territory lying along the Atlantic seaboard, and within our present bounds we should now have witnessed the establishment of three, if not four, nations.

The unity of our nationality is due to the aggressive and adventurous spirit of these pioneers, whom no dangers could deter, no numbers appall, and before whom not only the savage Indian, but the imperious Briton, the haughty Spaniard and the gallant Frenchman were forced to retire.

Thus, are we indebted to these noble pioneers, not only for the grandeur of our territory, but also for the inherited love of liberty that has made us freemen, and will keep us free."

—Col. Frank Triplett

"LITTLE TURTLE"
By William D. Howells

"Little Turtle of the Miamis lived for thirty years after signing the treaty, and then died of gout at Fort Wayne. He traveled through the Eastern States the first years of the peace. He struck all who met him as a man of intelligence and wit. He got the habit of high living and bore himself like the gentlemen whose company he loved to frequent...

His business in the East was to interest people in the civilization of his tribe, but he had no purpose of living among the whites. In Philadelphia, he said, 'When I walk through the streets, I see every person in his shop employed about something: one makes

228

shoes, another pots, a third sells cloth. I say to myself, which of these things can you do? Not one. I can make a bow or an arrow, catch fish, kill game, and go to war, but none of these things is of any use here. To learn what is done here would require a long time. Old age comes on. I should be a useless piece of furniture, useless to my nation, useless to myself. I must go back to my own country.'

This was what he did, and as long as he lived, he was steadfast for peace, for he remembered that it would be foolish for the Indians to fight the Americans.

After the *Battle of the Fallen Timbers*, he urged his people to treat with Wayne rather than fight. 'We have beaten the enemy twice under separate commanders,' he said referring to Harmar and St. Clair. 'The Americans are now led by a chief who never sleeps. The night and the day are alike to him; think well of it. There is something which whispers to me that it will be prudent to listen to his offers of peace.'"

CHAPTER 18

Westward the Course of Empire

ZANE'S TRACE

"A Virginian by birth, Zane had moved into Pennsylvania when he was 21. From Brownsville he migrated westward, arriving at the mouth of Wheeling Creek in Virginia in 1778. He knew that this was the place of his destiny. The Ohio River, great and broad and deep, ran placidly within yards of his cabin.

...Wheeling was a river port where overland travelers frequently sold their oxen and wagons, and turned to boats. Emigrants timidly trusted themselves to the Ohio River only because no road led from Wheeling through Ohio by land."

—Philip Jordan

By Norris Schneider and Claire Stebbins:
"In order to obtain from Congress, the right to establish a road through Ohio, Colonel Zane...drew up a petition which set forth the need for an overland route between Wheeling and Maysville,

Kentucky which, he claimed, would save 300 miles on a trip between Philadelphia and Frankfort, Kentucky.

The contract stipulated that Zane was required to operate a ferry at each of the river crossings at the opening of his Trace: The Muskingum River in Zanesville, the Hocking River in Lancaster and the Scioto River at Chillicothe. Zane opened his roadway in 1797...

Col. Zane made use of old paths when they suited his purpose. The completed *Trace* was a narrow trail for mail carriers on horseback, but not wide enough for wagons...

New settlers packed their household goods on horses and cattle and walked with them from the East into Ohio. Before the Trace was wide enough for wagons, some families came up the rivers by canoe. Levi Moore and his party from Maryland floated with their goods down the Ohio River, and then paddled and poled up the Hocking River to their farm near Lancaster. In the summer of 1800, John McIntire's family brought their household goods down the Ohio River and up the Muskingum River to Zanesville in a flatboat...

On the old maps the road was called Wheeling. Each of the three towns of Lancaster, Zanesville and Cambridge named a Wheeling Street for the route by which the road left the town for Wheeling...

The covered wagons with westward moving emigrants, and stagecoaches carried mail and passengers between Wheeling and Aberdeen, Ohio. Lumbering wagons crept westward with merchandise from Baltimore and Philadelphia.

Taverns appeared along the Trace at an average of four miles apart. Tired travelers were glad to see the light of the inn where the stagecoach stopped for the night.

Chillicothe became the first capital of Ohio when Ohio was organized in 1803. The Trace opened a vast fertile section of the United States for development." (Schneider and Stebbins)

"Emmitt of Chillicothe, became a teamster at six dollars a month. He drove a six-horse team, drawing an immense Conestoga wagon between Portsmouth, Chillicothe, Lancaster, and Zanesville. Everything in the way of [Eastern] merchandise in those days arrived by Ohio River steamboats at Portsmouth, and from that point distributed to all sections of the 'up Country.' The bulk of it was made up of dry goods, groceries and imported brandies."

—James Emmitt

"Aberdeen, Ohio was the Ohio River terminus of Zane's Trace. For more than a century people and goods were ferried over to Limestone; later Maysville, Kentucky, the gateway into the Bluegrass Country. The unused ferry is still tied to the deserted wharf."

—Ohio Guide, 1940

"MAYSVILLE has always made honest, solid things, like ploughs, coaches and wagons, and furniture—things you could load on steamboats and carry to other towns on the inland waters."

—Mason County Museum, Maysville, Kentucky

"THE UNITED STATES IN 1800"

By Henry Adams

"According to the census of 1800, the United States of America contained 5,308,483 persons. In the same year, the British Islands contained upwards of fifteen million.

Even after two centuries of struggle, the land was still untamed; forest covered every portion except here and there a strip of cultivated soil. The minerals lay undisturbed in their rocky beds, and more than two-thirds of the people clung to the seaboard within fifty miles of tide-water, where alone the wants of civilized life could be supplied...The interior was little more civilized than in 1750, and was not much easier to penetrate than when LaSalle and Hennepin found their way to the Mississippi more than a century before.

A great exception broke this rule. Two wagon-roads crossed the Alleghany Mountains in Pennsylvania; one leading from Philadelphia to Pittsburg; one from the Potomac to the Monongahela...At Pittsburg and on the Monongahela existed a society already old, numbering seventy or eighty thousand persons, while south of the Ohio River the settlements had grown to an importance. In the territory north of the Ohio, less progress had been made. A New England colony existed at Marietta; some fifteen thousand people were gathered at Cincinnati. Half way between the two, a small town had grown up at Chillicothe, and other villages or straggling cabins were to be found elsewhere, but the whole Ohio Territory contained only forty-five thousand inhabitants...the germ of an independent empire which was to find its outlet, not through the Alleghany Mountains to the seaboard, but by the Mississippi River to the Gulf.

Nowhere did eastern settlements touch the western. At least one hundred miles of mountainous country held the two regions everywhere apart...Even western New York remained a wilderness: Buffalo was not laid out...Albany was still a Dutch city with some five thousand inhabitants, and the tide of immigration flowed slowly through it into the valley of the Mohawk.

America, so far as concerned physical problems, had changed little in fifty years. The same bad roads and difficult rivers connecting the same small towns, as when the armies of Braddock and Amherst pierced the western and northern wilderness; except that these roads extended a few miles farther from the seacoast. Nature was rather man's master than his servant, and the five million Americans struggling with the untamed continent seemed hardly more competent to their task than the beavers and buffalo which had for countless generations made bridges and roads of their own.

The voyage to Europe was comparatively more comfortable and more regular than the voyage from New York to Albany, or through Long Island Sound to Providence. No regular packet plied between New York and Albany. Passengers waited till a sloop was advertised to sail. They provided their own bedding and supplies.

While little improvement had been made in water-travel, every increase of distance added to the difficulties of the westward journey. The settler who, after buying wagon and horses, hauled his family and goods across the mountains, might buy or build a broad flat-bottomed ark to float with him and his fortunes down the Ohio, in constant peril of upsetting or of being sunk, but only light boats with strong oars could mount the stream...The Cuyahoga and Muskingum were the first highways from the Lake to the Ohio; the Ohio itself, with its great tributaries, the Cumberland and the Tennessee, marked the lines of western migration, and every stream which could at high water float a boat, was thought likely to become a path for commerce...The Americans of 1800 were prepared to risk life and property on any streamlet that fell foaming down either flank of the Alleghenies. The experience of mankind proved trade to be dependent on water communications.

Nature had decided that the experiment of a single republican government must meet extreme difficulties. Physical contact alone could make one country of these isolated empires, but to the patriotic American of 1800, struggling for the continued existence of an embryo nation with machinery so inadequate; the idea of ever bringing the Mississippi River either by land or water into close contact with New England, must have seemed wild. By water, an Erie Canal was already foreseen. By land, centuries of labor could alone conquer those obstacles which Nature permitted to be overcome.

Even the lightly equipped traveler found a short journey no slight effort. Between Boston and New York was a tolerable highway along which thrice a week, light stage-coaches carried passengers and the mail in three days. From New York, a stage-coach started every week-day for Philadelphia, consuming the greater part of two days in the journey...Between Baltimore and the new city of Washington, the road meandered through forests; the driver chose the track which seemed least dangerous, and rejoiced if in wet seasons he reached Washington without miring or upsetting his wagon...South of Petersburg even the mails were carried on horseback.

The stage-coach was itself a rude conveyance; of a kind still familiar to experienced travelers. Twelve persons crowded into one wagon were jolted over rough road; their bags and parcels thrust inside cramping their legs, while they were protected from the heat and dust of mid-summer and the intense cold and driving snow of winter only by leather flaps buttoned to the roof and sides…When spring rains drew the frost from the ground, the roads became nearly impassable, and in winter when the rivers froze, a serious peril was added; for the Susquehanna or the North River at Paulus Hook must be crossed in an open boat, an affair of hours at best, sometimes leading to fatal accidents. The public as a rule, grumbled less than might have been expected…

Throughout the land the eighteen hundreds ruled supreme. Only within a few years had the New Englander begun to abandon his struggle with a barren soil among granite hills, to learn the comforts of easier existence in the valleys of the Mohawk River and the Ohio River.

For several years after the Revolution, Boston numbered less than twenty thousand, but in 1800 the census showed twenty-five thousand inhabitants. In appearance, Boston resembled an English market-town, of a kind even then old-fashioned. The footways or sidewalks were paved like the crooked and narrow streets, with round cobblestones, and were divided from the carriage way only by posts and a drain-way. The streets were almost unlighted at night, a few oil lamps rendering the darkness more visible and the rough pavement rougher…

New York was still a frontier State…travelers needed to go few miles from the Hudson in order to find a wilderness like that of

Ohio and Tennessee...If Boston resembled an old fashion English market-town, New York was like a foreign seaport...

The city of New York was so small as to make extravagance difficult. The Battery was a fashionable walk, Broadway a country drive, and Wall Street an uptown residence...John J. Astor was a fur merchant, and had not yet begun those purchases of real estate which secured his fortune. Cornelius Vanderbilt was a boy six years old, playing about his father's ferry-boat at Staten Island. New York City itself was what it had been for a hundred years past; a local market.

'Philadelphia,' wrote the Duc de Liancourt, 'is not only the finest city in the United States, but may be deemed one of the most beautiful cities in the world.' ...The city, well-paved and partly drained, was supplied with water in wooden pipes, and was the best lighted town in America...Philadelphia held the seat of government until July, 1800.

The city of Washington, rising in a solitude on the banks of the Potomac, was a symbol of American nationality in the Southern States...When in the summer of 1800, the government was transferred to what was regarded by most persons as a fever stricken morass, the half-finished White House stood in a naked field overlooking the Potomac, with two awkward Department buildings near it, a single row of brick houses and a few isolated dwellings within sight, and nothing more until across a swamp a mile and a half away; the shapeless, unfinished Capitol was seen, two wings without a body...The conception proved that the United States understood the vastness of the task, and were willing to stake something of their faith on it.

Among the numerous difficulties with which the Union was to struggle, and which were to form the interest of American history, the disproportion between the physical obstacles and the material means for overcoming them was one of the most striking.

The true American was active and industrious. No immigrant came to America for ease or idleness. If an English farmer bought land near New York, Philadelphia, or Baltimore, and made the most of his small capital, he found that while he could earn more money than in Surrey of Devonshire, he worked harder and suffered greater discomforts. The climate was trying; fever was common; the crops ran new risks from strange insects, drought, and violent weather. The weeds were annoying, the flies and mosquitoes tormented them and their cattle...

New settlers suffered many of the ills that would have afflicted an army marching and fighting in a country of dense forest and swamp; with one sore misery besides—that whatever trials the men endured, the burden bore most heavily upon the women and children.

Few laborers of the Old world endured a harder lot, coarser fare, or anxieties and responsibilities greater than those of the western emigrant."

—Henry Adams

ABIGAIL ADAM'S LETTER TO HER DAUGHTER

from The White House, 21 November, 1800

My Dear Child,

"I arrived here on Sunday last, and without meeting with any accident worth noticing except losing ourselves when we left Baltimore, and going eight or nine miles on the Frederick Road; by which means we were obliged to go the other eight through woods, where we wandered two hours without finding a guide or the path. Fortunately, a straggling black man came up with us, and we engaged him as a guide to extricate us out of our difficulty, but woods are all you see from Baltimore until you reach the city which is only so in name. Here and there is a small cottage without a glass window, interspersed amongst the forests, through which you travel miles without seeing any human being. In the city there are buildings enough if they were compact and finished, to accommodate Congress and those attached to it, but as they are, and scattered as they are, I see no great comfort for them. The river, which runs up to Alexandria, is in full view of my window, and I see the vessels as they pass and re-pass. The house is upon a grand and superb scale requiring about thirty servants to attend and keep the apartments in proper order, and perform the ordinary business of the house and stables; an establishment very well proportioned to the President's salary. The lighting in the apartments, from the kitchen to parlors and chambers, is a tax indeed; and the fires we are obliged to keep to secure us from daily agues is another very cheering comfort. To assist us in this great castle, and render less attendance necessary, bells are wholly wanting, not one single one being hung through the whole house, and promises are all you can obtain. This is so great an inconvenience that I know not what to do, or how to do.

The ladies from Georgetown and in the city have many of them visited me. Yesterday I returned fifteen visits, but such a place as Georgetown appears; why, our Milton is beautiful, but no comparison. If they will put me up some bells and let me have wood enough to keep fires, I design to be pleased. I could content myself almost anywhere three months, but surrounded with forests, can you believe that wood is not to be had because people cannot be found to cut and cart it! Mr. B. entered into a contract with a man to supply him with wood. A small part, a few cords only, has he been able to get. Most of that was expended to dry the walls of the house before we came in, and yesterday the man told him it was impossible for him to procure it to be cut and carted. He has had recourse to coal, but we cannot get grates made and set. We have, indeed, come into a new Country...

The house is made habitable, but there is not a single apartment finished... We have not the least fence, yard, or other convenience without, and the great unfinished audience-room I made a drying-room of, to hang up the clothes in. The principal stairs are not up, and will not be this winter... Upstairs there is the oval room which is designed for the drawing-room, and has the crimson furniture in it... Since I sat down to write, I have been called down to a servant from Mount Vernon with a billet from Major Custis and a haunch of venison, and a kind, congratulatory letter from Mrs. Lewis upon my arrival in the city; with Mrs. Washington's love, inviting me to Mount Vernon, where health permitting, I will go before I leave this place."

—Abigail Adams

"AN EARLY SETTLER'S JOURNEY TO NORTHERN OHIO"

By R. Taylor

"In the spring of 1807, my father determined to remove to Ohio, (from Middlefield, Massachusetts), and on the eighth of May, our family with relatives and neighbors, numbering in all thirty-six persons started on our journey. We pursued our way to Reading, Harrisburg and Pittsburgh, Pennsylvania, where we remained one day and two nights to rest our teams, and procure provisions for our journey through the wilderness to Aurora, Portage County, Ohio.

At that time Pittsburgh was a very small village with only a few hundred inhabitants. The only attractive feature of the place, was the little stockade fort covering about one acre of ground in what is now called 'the Diamond,' with a flagstaff in the center.

Our next place of destination was the Beaver crossing, as it was then called, where Robert D. kept a store and tavern, and from thence we made our way to... Youngstown and Warren, where we remained one day to give our ax-men time to cut out the timber and bridge the marshes and swamps so that our teams and wagons could pass along safely.

We were four days on the road from Warren to Aurora, a distance of less than thirty miles, where our journey of forty-five days terminated, June 22, 1807.

When we built our first log cabin, the nearest neighbor on the north was thirty miles away; on the west, sixty miles... and on the south of Aurora about ten or eleven miles to a house...

At that time northern Ohio was a vast wilderness with but few inhabitants except the Indians, who outnumbered the whites two or three to one; but the forests were filled with deer, bear, wolves, elk, raccoon, wildcats, turkeys and various other kinds of wild animals, including a good supply of serpents of several varieties. During the night-time we had serenades from the hooting of owls... or the more enlivening howl of the wolf...

Those persons who came to this part of Ohio after the War of 1812, can have no just conception of the hardships and privations endured by those who were here before and during that struggle...It would be egotism in me to speak of myself, or what I have done since that time."

Very respectfully,
R. Taylor

"A JOURNEY TO WARREN, OHIO IN 1810"
By Margaret Van Horn Dwight

To Elizabeth, (home-town friend in Connecticut)

"We are four miles from Strasberg and the mountains...We are not as blessed as the Israelites were, for our shoes wax old and our clothes wear out...I don't know that mine will last till I get there...The first mountain is 3 1/2 miles over—better road than we expected, but bad enough to tire the horses almost to death. We met and were overtaken by a number of people. We all walked the whole distance over...When we had nearly reached the foot of it, we heard some music in the valley below, and not one of us could imagine from what it proceeded, but soon found it was from the bells of a waggoner—He had twelve bells on the collars of his horses, and they made a great variety of sounds which were really musical at a distance. I have walked about eight miles today and feel as much fatigue as I have almost ever been in my life.

...We had a good night's rest, but I am so lame I can scarcely walk this morning. I have a mountain to walk over, notwithstanding...The weather looks stormy and where we shall get to, and what we shall do, I cannot imagine.

...All this afternoon we have been walking over young mountains...I could not ride—the road was so bad, it was worse than walking. It rained a very little all day, but just at night it began to rain very fast, and I expected we should all catch our death walking through mud and mire with no umbrella, or but one that would not cover us all. Oh, had I the wings of a dove, so soon would I meet you again. One waggoner very civilly offered to take Susan or me on to Pittsburg in his wagon if we were not likely to get there till spring. One wagon in crossing the creek this afternoon, got turned over and very much injured. We have concluded the reason few are willing to return from the western country, is not that the country is so good, but because the journey is so bad...

I hope tomorrow's Sun will deign to smile upon us—it is long since we have seen it.

We left the Inn this morning in the hope of getting a little piece on our way, but have only reached the baker's half mile from where we set out. The creek is so high we cannot cross it yet.

The stream runs so fast, that we did not dare cross it alone, as there was nothing but a log to cross on, so the waggoners and our own party were obliged to lead and pilot us over the stream, and through a most shocking place as I ever saw. The men were all very civil...they are waiting with their wagons, like the rest of us. We fair worse and worse and still Mr. W. and his wife tell us this is nothing to what will come. I do not fully believe them, for we cannot endure much more and live.

We are not able to get beds here at an inn, and are to sleep on the floor tonight. There is another family here with several little children…They say there has been a heap of people moving this fall. I don't know exactly how many a heap is, or a sight either, which is another way of measuring people…I have such an enormous appetite the whole time that I have been in some fear of starving. Food of every kind is scarce with us. Money will not procure it…

We have gone 8 ½ miles on our journey today and now it rains again. If I could describe to you our troubles from roads, waggoners and creeks, I would, but it is impossible…there is another impassable creek ahead, and a hundred wagons waiting to cross it…

We are now at the tavern half a mile from the top of the Alleghany Mt. This mountain is 14 miles over—at the highest part of it is a most beautiful prospect of mountains….

After a comfortable night's rest, we set out on foot to reach the height of the mountain. It rained fast for a long time, and at length began snowing. We found the roads bad past description— Large stones and deep mud holes every step of the way. We were obliged to walk as much as we possibly could, as the horses could scarcely stir the wagon—the mud was so deep and the stones so large…From what I have seen and heard, I think the State of Ohio will be well-filled before winter, wagons without number every day go on—One went on containing forty people…We almost every day see them with 18 or 20…

We are on the top of Laurel Hill, the 6th mountain…We women and girls have walked between five and six miles this morning. We left the wagons getting along very slowly, and came on to a house to warm us. It is a log hut and full of children, as is every one we come to. The wind whistles about us, and it looks very much like snow. This is a little hut, one window in front, but it is neat and comfortable inside, and we were all quietly seated round the fire. We are now 41 miles from Pittsburg.

I have not spent so pleasant an evening this long time as this last...Will you believe me, when I tell you we heard some waggoners conversing upon religious subjects...instead of swearing and cursing?...One is an Irish waggoner, and appears to be a sensible, well-informed man and what is more has read his Bible... 2 clever waggoners! I think I shall never condemn a whole race again.

One misfortune follows another, and I fear we shall never reach our journey's end...After coming down an awful hill, we were obliged to cross a creek. The horses got mired and we expected every moment one of them would die, but E. held his head out of water, while Mr. W. was attempting to unharness them, and Mrs. W. and Susan were on the bank calling for help...Mr. W. waded through the water and then 2 men with 3 horses came over. I had sadly expected to see the horse breathe his last...

We got into the Slough of Despond yesterday and are now at the foot of the hill Difficulty which is half a mile long...One wagon is already fast in the mud on it. 10 miles as usual has been our day's ride...I have not walked my nine miles, but I walked as much as I could. We are in a comfortable house before an excellent fire. It is snowing very fast.

We set out early with the hope of getting to Youngstown at night, but four miles from Y. horses were so tired they would not stir, so we stopped at a private house for the night an hour before sundown. I soon saw Mr. Edwards and two horses...I was never so happy, I think. I ran out to meet him. He came and sat a while and just at dark we started for Youngstown...We reached cousin J's about the middle of the eve. They got us a good supper and gave us a bed...They live in a very comfortable log house, pleasantly situated. I would give more for one in this country, than for 20 in old Connecticut. We set out for Warren soon after breakfast...

Cousin Louisa was as happy as I could wish, and I think, I shall be very happy and contented. The town is pleasanter than I expected...Mrs. Waldo is just going to Connecticut, and lest I should not have another opportunity, I intend sending this by them, without even time to read it over and correct it. I am asham'd of it my dear Elizabeth, and were it not for my promise to you, I don't know that I should dare to send it. Let no one else see this but your own family."

Most affectly, yours—MVD

CHAPTER 19

The War of 1812

AN OVERVIEW OF THE MAIN EVENTS

"As the British controlled the Ocean and Napoleon the Continent of Europe, certain decrees meant the destruction of the American carrying trade. With Great Britain moreover, the United States had another cause of grievance—the controversy over *impressment*... British naval captains began stopping American vessels on the high seas, and taking seamen for service in the British navy...As the war progressed, the British practically blockaded the more important American ports, and removed seamen from outgoing vessels before they had even lost sight of land. The American government denied the right of foreign cruisers to stop American vessels on the high seas for any purpose whatsoever except to ascertain their nationality."

—Edward Channing

"Feeling against Great Britain was increased in the West by the belief that British emissaries were instigating outbreaks of the Indians. The Indians in the Northwest Territory, after their defeat by General Wayne in 1794, had remained quiet for almost a score of years, when suddenly a new Indian leader arose in the person of *Tecumseh,* who formed the ambitious plan of uniting the Indians in one grand assault against the whites.

William Henry Harrison, Governor of Indiana Territory, correctly scented the Indian unrest, and in 1811 engaged them in battle at Tippecanoe on the Wabash River in northern Indiana. Though Harrison allowed himself to be surprised, he retrieved himself and won a victory."

—Emerson D. Fite

"While the **Battle of Tippecanoe** was being fought, Tecumseh and his brother were traveling throughout the northwest and southwest. While *standing in the flickering light of council fires* they encouraged Indian tribes to form a confederation that would systematically wage war against white settlements: [His battle-cry for driving them out]: "Back! Back! Aye Into the great waters whose curs'ed waves brought them to our shores!"

General Hull had been dispatched through the woods of northwestern Ohio and southern Michigan to Detroit. Most of the way, he was obliged to cut a road for his troops. It was difficult to feed his soldiers, for few settlers lived on the southern and western shores of Lake Erie. The single boat which the Americans had on the lake was soon captured by the British…The difficulty was increased by the hostility of the Indians, who had not been crushed by their defeat at Tippecanoe the year before. Indeed, Tecumseh rallied them to the aid of the English all through the Northwest Territory...General Hull surrendered in August 1812 and was disgraced for having done so."

—Bourne and Benton

FEARFUL OHIOANS

"The *War of 1812* was in progress and Hull's surrender at Detroit left the isolated settlements open to the assaults of not only the British, but their merciless Indian allies.

The dispersed and exposed white families of Ohio, therefore for a time, were in abject terror. Settlers from Delaware, Worthington, Dublin and the surrounding country hurried to Franklinton for a place of refuge and safety. Stockades were begun in the vicinity of the Court House, but the panic subsiding, they were never completed. Then it was that Franklinton became a place of gathering for troops, and a base of supplies for the Western Army. Troops from Virginia, Pennsylvania, Kentucky, and Tennessee came marching into the village where they were rested and supplied, and then marched on to the Maumee."

—*Franklinton, Ohio:* An Historical Address

"By autumn of 1812, Great Britain had control of Lake Erie, and their navy sailed the Lake defiantly. Detroit had surrendered to British troops. Fort Dearborn where Chicago now stands, capitulated, and its inhabitants were massacred. Both the United States and Great Britain realized that possession of the Old Northwest Territory depended on control of Lake Erie.

General Harrison, now in command, built Fort Meigs where he was besieged by British General Proctor and Tecumseh on the first day of May, 1813. General Clay, however came to the rescue with 1,200 Kentuckians, and after a sharp conflict succeeded in raising the siege.

The Indians acted with their customary ferocity toward the unfortunate men who fell into their hands. On one occasion Tecumseh saved a prisoner from Indian brutality. Tecumseh thereafter rebuked General Proctor for his inaction; complaining that he could not restrain the young warriors. Tecumseh stated bitterly: 'Go put on petticoats. You are not fit to command men!'"

—Everit Brown

"After the loss of Detroit, the United States was anxious to destroy the British fleet on Lake Erie. Captain Oliver Hazard Perry was entrusted with the endeavor, but it was necessary to build ships before the operation could begin.

Timber was at hand along the Erie shore, and workmen were brought in from Philadelphia. Iron was gathered from farm buildings and shops, and every available source. Sails, ropes, guns, and ammunition had to be carried overland from Philadelphia and Pittsburgh to Erie, Pennsylvania.

The ships were finally ready, and on September 13, 1813, Perry encountered the British squadron in battle near Put-in-Bay."

—*Bourne and Benton*

The Niagara

"THE BATTLE OF LAKE ERIE"
By Commodore Oliver H. Perry

September 13, 1813

Sir,

"In my last letter, I informed you that we had captured the enemy's fleet on this lake. I have now the honour to give you the most important particulars of the action. On the morning of the 10th instant, at sunrise, they were discovered from Put-In-Bay, where I lay at anchor with the squadron under my command. We got under way, the wind light at S.W. and stood for them. *At 10 A.M. the wind hauled to S.E. and brought us to windward; formed the line and bore up*. At 15 minutes before 12, the enemy commenced firing; at 5 minutes before 12, the action commenced on our part. Finding their fire very destructive, owing to their long guns, and its being mostly directed at the *Lawrence*, I made sail and directed the other vessels to follow for the purpose of closing with the enemy. Every brace and bow-line being shot away, she became unmanageable, notwithstanding the great exertions of the sailing master. In this situation she sustained the action upwards of 2 hours within canister distance, until every gun was rendered useless, and the greater part of her crew either killed or wounded. Finding she could no longer annoy the enemy, I left her in charge of Lieut. Yarnall…At half past two, *the wind springing up*, Capt. Elliott *was enabled to bring his vessel the Niagara, gallantly into close action*. I immediately went on board, when he anticipated my wish by volunteering *to bring the schooners which had been kept astern by the lightness of the wind, into close action*. It was with unspeakable pain, that I saw soon after I got onboard the *Niagara*, the flag of the Lawrence come down, although I was perfectly sensible that she had been defended to the last, and that to have continued to make a show of resistance would have been a wanton sacrifice of the remains of her brave crew. But the enemy was not able to take possession, and circumstances soon permitted her flag again to be hoisted.

At 45 minutes past 2, the signal was made for 'close action.' The *Niagara* being very little injured, I determined to pass through the enemy's line, bore up and passed ahead of their two ships and a brig, giving a raking fire to them from the starboard guns, and to a large schooner and sloop from the larboard side at half pistol-shot distance. The smaller vessels that this time having got within grape and canister distance, under the direction of Capt.

Elliott, and keeping up a well-directed fire, the two ships, a brig and a schooner surrendered; a schooner and sloop making a vain attempt to escape...

It has pleased the Almighty to give to the arms of the United States a signal victory over their enemies on this Lake."

Very respectfully, I have the honour to be, Sir, your obedient servant,

O.H. Perry

Hon. William Jones,
Sec'y of the Navy."

The Battle of Lake Erie as told by one of the enemy

"Perry took advantage of the smoke upon the British fleet to go from the *Lawrence* to the *Niagara.* We did not see him till he had nearly effected his purpose, but the wind causing the smoke to lift, I saw the boat and aimed a shot at her and saw the shot strike the boat. I then saw Commodore Perry strip off his coat and plug the hole with it.

Having gained the ship, Perry sent Captain Elliott to bring the schooners into action. Captain Finnis of the Queen Charlotte had intended to pour in one broadside, and then board, but his design was frustrated by the falling of the wind which was blowing firmly just before.

The cutting away of the down haul of one of the sails left the Charlotte at the mercy of the wind which again rose suddenly and she ran afoul of the Detroit and became entangled with her.

The American schooners coming into action in the meantime raked the fore and aft carrying away all the masts of the Detroit and the mizzen of the Charlotte, besides crippling her severely otherwise...The surrender was unconditional."

—John Chapmen of Hudson

Two Citizens on Lake Erie's Shore

"On the day of the Battle, nearly all the men of Euclid were raising a log house within a half-mile of the Lake. When the firing commenced, it was thought to be thunder. The feelings of all soon became so excited that we left our work half done, rushed to the Lake and listened eagerly until the battle was over."

One woman exclaimed, "The night of the 10th was a sleepless one to many; for if the British had gained the victory, we felt that our little village of Cleveland was in great danger. But the next night the news came of Perry's gallant victory, and joy at once took the place of fear."

"THE BATTLE OF THE THAMES RIVER AND OUTRAGEOUS BRITISH ACTS"

M. E. Thalheimer

"The victorious fleet later conveyed an army under General Harrison across Lake Erie to Canada where a fierce land battle was fought against the combined British and Indian forces on the Thames River. The great Tecumseh, who had joined his Indian forces to those of the British as soon as the War was declared, was killed. The British were defeated; Detroit was won back, and the Northwest Territory rendered secure.

The early months of the year 1814 were marked by the overthrow of Napoleon in Europe and the release of thousands of British veterans for service in America. ...The British troops, encouraged by the arrival of re-enforcements from across the Atlantic, embarked on a bold offensive campaign by an invasion of the United States...In August they made a dash up the Chesapeake Bay and the Potomac River. The Capital City of Washington was burned and Baltimore was threatened. President Madison and the cabinet were forced to flee in haste before the invaders to escape capture. The priceless treasures as Stuart's portrait of George Washington, as well as the original draft of The Declaration of Independence were saved by Dolly Madison and someone from the State Department."

FRANCIS SCOTT KEY

"Shortly before the enemy fell back from their attempt on Baltimore, a young American lawyer, Francis Scott Key, was detained on a ship overnight by the British, where he had gone to seek the release of a friend who was being held captive. In the morning, beholding his Country's flag still flying over Fort McHenry, Key wrote a poem destined to become our National Anthem.

[The intermittent light from exploding bombs revealed the American Flag intact and still waving; the event described so well by F. S. Key: *The bombs bursting in air gave proof to the night that our flag was still there."*]

The New England States suffered even more than the Southern, for their commerce and fisheries were broken up by a strict blockade. The light-houses were kept in darkness as they served only as guides to the enemy...The spirit of the Americans rose with difficulty. On the third of July they captured Fort Erie, opposite

Buffalo, and two days later defeated General Riall at Chippewa, after a hard-fought battle.

A naval battle lasted only two hours, but the American victory was complete. The British commodore was killed; his larger vessels were captured. The combat on land was equally severe to the invaders, and it ended in success for the Americans. The British forces marched back into Canada."

THE TREATY OF GHENT

"Peace was signed at Ghent on Christmas Eve, 1814 between the United States and Great Britain, but as ocean steamers and the telegraph were not yet in existence, a needless battle was fought below New Orleans before the news arrived in America...The news of peace was hailed with joy by the whole Nation. Bells rang merrily; bonfires blazed; messengers on fleet horses galloped to inland villages, shouting the glad tidings as they rode.

The Second War of American Independence had commanded the respect of other Nations."

—M.E. Thalheimer

With the end of "The War of 1812," the United States had gained control of Lake Erie. The British abandoned Detroit as well as their forts. The United States, at last was free of foreign intrusion. The Monroe Doctrine would soon seal that very popular decision.

"Only a few weeks after the victory, Washington Irving, in a biographical sketch of Commodore Perry, wrote: "The last roar of cannon that died along Erie's shores was the expiring note of British

domination, and this victory which decided the fate of this Mighty Empire, will stand unrivaled and alone, deriving luster and perpetuity in its singleness. In future times, when the shores of Erie shall hum with busy population; when towns and cities shall brighten where now extend the dark and tangled forests; when ports shall spread their arms, and lofty barks shall ride where now the canoe is fastened to the stake; when the present age shall have grown into venerable antiquity...then will the inhabitants look back to this Battle we record as one of the idyllic and grandest of achievements of the past."

—W. Irving

A VERY EARLY MANUFACTURER
(AFTER THE WAR)

"The Son's Memories"
William C. Howells

"My father emigrated from Brecknockshire in South Wales in 1808, landing at Boston. I was then just one year old. He had acquired a thorough knowledge of the manufacture of woolen goods. In 1812 he was at Waterford, Virginia, having made his way to that point from Boston, when he made the acquaintance of a Quaker, Joseph Steer, who had a large flouring-mill and water-power on Short creek, about eighteen miles from Steubenville and four from Mt. Pleasant. This was a Quaker settlement of considerable importance, and the wealth and influence of that locality were chiefly in their hands; and they were not excelled by any in all useful enterprises that tended to improve the then new and growing Country.

Along the little river of Short Creek, they had built flouring mills, salt-works and a paper-mill of no mean capacity.

Joseph Steer had sought to supply a needed woolen manufactory, and he engaged my father to put it in operation.

In the spring of 1813 as soon as the roads were in proper condition, my father engaged with one of the "Waggoners of the Alleghenies," for our passage from Waterford to Brownsville, Pa., which was the usual place of changing shipments from wagons to boats, on the way to Ohio. The wagons used in the transportation of goods on that route were large and heavy, drawn by teams of four, five, or six horses. They would hold and carry 5,000 to 9,000 pounds and movers took passage in them as they would in boats for themselves and household effects. The wagon in which we travelled was one of the five-horse class, owned and driven by one Thomas who did not drink whisky or swear at his horses, which my mother regarded as virtues of high esteem. ...I very well remember that mother, my sister, brother and myself, were weighed at the time our goods were loaded on and all charged at so much per pound. My father had a pony, which he rode in company with the two wagons that travelled together for mutual help over bad places and steep hills, when they joined teams. The trip was necessarily a slow one, as twenty miles was a long day's drive.

Arriving at Brownsville, we gladly stopped to rest and wait for a boat. We happened upon a new flatboat, which was being floated to Pittsburg in which we found unbounded room after the cramped journey in the wagon. At Pittsburg, we changed to a keel boat and on to Short Creek, then a thriving village, and an important point for building flat boats, and loading them with flour and other produce for the New Orleans market. Three miles up the creek brought us to our destination and we took our position as Ohioans seventy-five years ago.

DIFFICULTIES OF NEW MANUFACTURING ENTERPRISES: The woolen mill was limited machinery adapted to country custom; carding and spinning machine, fulling-mill, etc. in a small way. Though a child, I very well remember that this new business was started under very great difficulties. Many of the parts of the machine had to be made by local mechanics. For the spinning "jenny" a blacksmith forged the spindles, and finished them with grindstone and files; while a tinsmith, a cabinetmaker, a turner and one or two ingenious general workers made the other parts. My father superintended the job; made the drawings etc. and in due time before winter set in, the little factory was in operation.

EARLY MANUFACTURES OF SOUTHEASTERN OHIO: My father moved the family into Steubenville in 1816 when I had just entered upon my tenth year. I was a rather forward boy, and especially interested in manufacturing and mechanical work so that now I have a good recollection of what I then saw. –Say August 1818 and onward for a few years—I am rather surprised at the variety as well as extent, of manufactures in which the people in Southeastern Ohio and the adjacent parts of Virginia and Pennsylvania were engaged. The town of Steubenville, whose inhabitants then numbered about 2,000 was a center of these operations that was typical in its way of the whole. The chief manufacture of the place was woolen cloths carried on by a company formed about 1812; on a more extensive scale than any in the State, west of the Allegheny Mountains at the time.

LOSSES THROUGH IMPROVEMENTS IN MACHINERY: About 1818 another firm was organized...The manager changed the style of the product to a less expensive kind, and made it pay its way for a time. It was successful in the manufacture of great quantities of good cloth, and cheapening the cost to consumers who were largely the people of the State, and making a market for good wool; besides introducing greatly improved brands of sheep...As a profit to those who invested money, it must have been one of the worst of failures. The original cost was necessarily very great; while the introduction of new machinery and new styles of working every year absorbed a great part of the profits.

I well remember when very young, being impressed with the terrible losses that were evident to me, in the discarded machinery that filled every vacant spot of the ground and buildings. This was not the result of dishonesty or very bad management. It seemed to have come of the crowding growth of improvements, which often made it economy to cast aside a machine of real value. To this may be added successive fires, panics, and money depressions following the war of 1812. This factory and its various buildings occupied about ten acres near the west end of Main Street...

On the river bank, a short distance below, there was an iron foundry...Connected with this, a machine shop where much of the machinery of the factory and mills of the vicinity was made or repaired."

—William C. Howells

CHAPTER 20

Pittsburgh

"Pittsburgh grew because *Providence* endowed the area with fabulous riches: Timber in forests, coal in the hills, limestone, sandstone, clay in the soil...Iron ore though not in the immediate neighborhood, was readily available, and timber for charcoal."

EARLY PITTSBURGH

"The Ohio River runs northeast from Pittsburgh for some twenty-five miles, turning into a general southwest direction near the mouth of Beaver River.

The Pioneers reaching Brownsville on the Monongahela River, found that by a short and easy *land* journey of less than fifty miles across this frontier, Wheeling could be reached, and a long dangerous river journey [on the Monongahela around Pittsburgh] could be saved. The Ohio River was always navigable below Wheeling.

[Written of Pittsburgh after the Revolutionary War:] 'Their means of livelihood had been limited to farming and trade in skins and furs. Now however, as very considerable settlements have already been begun farther down the Ohio River which increase constantly and rapidly because of the number of people who are daily moving in that direction, the inhabitants of Pittsburgh derive much profit from trade and the coming and going of travelers. On account of its advantageous situation, Pittsburgh, inconsiderable as the town now is, cannot fail to be in the future an important place for inland trade."

—Archer B. Hulbert, *The Ohio River*

"THADDEUS HARRIS' 1803 JOURNAL"

Pittsburgh "The local situation of this place is so commanding that it has been emphatically called, 'The Key to the Western Territory.'

Dry goods in general are sold here. The merchants here as well as those of the western country purchase their goods from Philadelphia and Baltimore, some from New York. Most of the articles of merchandize are brought in wagons over the mountains in the summer season, and destined for trade down the River, are stored at this place to be ready for embarkation. With this, a great many trading boats are laden which float down the river stopping at the towns on its banks to vend the articles. The trading boats contribute very much to the accommodation of life, bringing necessities from great distances....

At Wheeling we left our carriage and took passage down the River in a keel boat to Cincinnati.

When we see the land cleared of those enormous trees, and the cliffs and quarries converted into materials for building, we cannot help dwelling upon the industry and art of man which by dint of toil and perseverance can change the desert into a fruitful field, and shape the rough rock to use and elegance. When the solitary waste is peopled and convenient habitations arise amidst the former retreats of wild beasts; when the silence of nature is succeeded by the buzz of employment, the congratulations of society, and the voice of joy; in fine, when we behold competence and plenty springing from the bosom of dreary forests, what a lesson is afforded of the benevolent intentions of Providence!"

—T. Harris

"MORRIS BIRKBECK'S 1817 TRIP TO ILLINOIS"

"Steam engines of great efficiency are made here and applied to various purposes…Establishments which are as likely to expand and multiply as the small acorn, planted in a good soil and duly protected, is to become the 'Majestic Oak, that flings his giant arms amid the sky.'

Pittsburgh, has about 7000 inhabitants, and is a place of great trade as an entrepot for the merchandise and manufactures supplied by the Eastern States to the western. The inhabitants of Kentucky, Ohio, Indiana, Illinois, are customers, and are continually increasing in their demands upon the merchants and artisans of Pittsburgh.

…Arks of which hundreds are on the river are procured of a size suitable for the numerous travelers. They are long floating rooms built on a flat bottom with rough boards and arranged within for sleeping and other accommodations. You hire boatmen and lay in provisions and on your arrival at the destined port, sell your vessel as well as you can."

"PITTSBURGH IN 1884"

By Captain Willard Glazier

"The tranquil Monongahela comes up from the south, alive with barges and tug boats. The Ohio River makes its beginning here, and in all but the season of low water the wharves of the city are lined with boats, barges and tugs, destined for points on the Ohio and Mississippi Rivers.

The crowning glory of Pittsburgh is her monster iron and glass works. One-half the glass produced in all the United States comes from Pittsburgh. This important business was first established here in 1787 by A. Gallatin. There are rolling mills, foundries, potteries, oil refineries and factories of machinery. All these works are rendered possible by the coal which abounds in measureless quantities in the immediate neighborhood of the city. All the hills which rise from the river back of Pittsburgh, have a thick stratum of bituminous coal running through them, which can be mined without shafts. All that is to be done is to shovel the coal out of the hill-side, convey it in cars or by means of an inclined plane to the factory or foundry door, and dump it ready for use. In fact, these hills are immense coal cellars ready filled for the convenience of the Pittsburgh manufactures. The 'Great Pittsburgh Coal Seam' is from four to twelve feet thick…it is bituminous coal…It has even been estimated as covering eight and a half millions of acres. Pittsburgh consumes one-third of the coal produced, and a large proportion of the rest is shipped down the Ohio and Mississippi Rivers.

No other city begins to compare with Pittsburgh in the number and variety of factories. Down by the banks of the swift-flowing Allegheny most of the great foundries are to be discovered.

The American Iron Works Company employs 2,500 hands and covers seventeen acres. They have a coal mine at their back door, and an iron mine on Lake Superior, and they make any and every difficult iron thing the country requires. In the nail works, a thousand nails a minute are manufactured...

George F. Thurston, writing of Pittsburgh says, 'It has thirty-five miles of factories in daily operation, twisted up into a compact tangle; all belching forth smoke; all glowing with fire; all swarming with workmen; all echoing with the clank of machinery.'"

A. B. HULBERT'S DESCRIPTION
OF A NIGHT SCENE

"At night when the winds are driving the smoke away, the great City lies in the moonlight like a mighty battleship at anchor; two tides rush silently together at the tip of the dark sharp prow.
The growth of Pittsburgh has been a natural growth...The secret of its success lies in its strategic position, and the nature of the *Monongahela Country* about it. Pittsburgh is preeminently a typical American City. The Mountains and Rivers made the Point the site for a great City."

CHAPTER 21

The Ohio River

"WESTWARD THE COURSE OF EMPIRE MAKES ITS WAY"

By Archer B. Hulbert

"It *was* a course of Empire. The Great Lakes did not become an emigration route until the steamboat had established its reputation in the third decade of the nineteenth century. By that time the entire eastern half of the Mississippi Basin had received a great bulk of population, and the occupation of its western half was merely a matter of time. From the Eastern seaboard there were many river routes into the interior; the St. John, Penobscot, Connecticut, Hudson, Delaware, Potomac, and James were avenues of approach for the race that fell heir to this Continent. But once across the Appalachian range there was but one river, and on the Ohio River and its tributaries, that race spread its marvelous conquest...

The vital question was not whether the Rocky Mountains could be crossed and the Pacific Coast secured, but rather, could the

Appalachian Mountains be crossed and the eastern half of the Mississippi Basin be occupied. The Ohio River was one strategic course of empire to the heart of the continent, and there is no phase of its history that is not of imperishable significance...

Few streams ever played so vital a part in the development of the United States. *Providence* meant this should be so. With a lavish Hand these waters were thrown where they would count magnificently toward the building of a new Republic...The water passing from this area flows in the right direction—Westward.

The Ohio reached far out into the foothills of the Allegheny and Cumberland Mountains, beckoning to the Colonists on the Atlantic Seacoast. With outstretched arms, spread as wide apart as are the sources of the Allegheny on the north and those of the Tennessee on the south, the Ohio River called through the dark forests to the conquerors of the West to come to their own, for their own would receive them gladly."

—A.B. Hulbert

"A RIVER CALLED BEAUTIFUL"
By Harlan Hatcher

"The Ohio River was designed on a rare scale. Its parallel ridges...follow its course and gently restrain its windings without ever showing the hand of authority. The hills are from one to three miles apart, while the River is about a third of a mile wide. There is plenty of room left on both sides for good farms, gardens, and orchards, for houses and barns, for towns and villages, and even for a double tracked-railroad and paved U.S. highways that will run on both sides...It accommodates all its boats without jamming

267

traffic. It has always been friendly to the hundreds of little shanty-boats tied to willow trees, with a plank stretched across the bank and fishing poles dangling over from stern and bow.

...People from almost everywhere were taking a boat at Pittsburgh and passing down the River to a more golden West. This by-gone pageantry of the expanding Republic that once moved down the Ohio takes the place of castles on the Rhine in lending romance to the River.

Fogs rise and cover, blotting out red and green beacon lights on the banks by which the captains steer at night. The sun shines on it; the moon casts a glow over it; rains fall, and one may see the advancing front crossing the river changing its color. Sometimes it freezes and I have heard tell of my grandfather driving his horse and buggy over it from Coal Grove to Ashland one winter back in the 1880s. I have seen it almost full of rafts in the spring. Before the bridges were built in the boom of the 1920s, ferries scurried across at every town. The ferry boats and wharf-boats were end-lessly entertaining...

The demand for boats made of every town between West Newton, Pittsburgh and Louisville a busy dockyard. Pittsburgh was most thriving. Hundreds of families with household goods piled on the river bank, awaited transportation or completion of their boats...Pittsburgh built fine boats including the first steamboat on the Ohio. Steamboats were constructed chiefly at Pittsburgh and Cincinnati, but the little settlements built flatboats by the hundreds to float produce to market."

"THE CINCINNATI LANDING"
By Alexander Lewis

"Traveler Burnet says that in 1817 a number of arks with emigrants and their families bound to various parts of the western country were generally near the landing. He counted seven Kentucky boats with coal, iron and dry goods from Pittsburgh. There were four barges or keel boats, one with two masts, which traded up and down the river between Pittsburgh and New Orleans, and four large flats or scows with stone for building and salt from Kanawha 'works.'

Six arks were loaded with emigrants and their household furniture. The emigrants who came down the Ohio River usually stopped at Cincinnati to purchase provisions and collect information.

Soon afterward, steamboating became a common industry and boat building here became quite active and profitable in Cincinnati. Between 1817 and 1819, nearly one fourth of the steamboats built for the Western waters were constructed in Cincinnati...The woodwork was superior. Black locust, not found even at Pittsburgh, was considerably used for boats and vessels. Upon these waters there had been 233 steamboats by 1826. ...Older readers will recall the scenes of excitement attendant on the arrival at the wharf of these magnificent floating palaces, as they were called, and the pride with which they were regarded by their owners and the people. There were 23 lumber yards in 1840. These boats plied between Pittsburgh, St. Louis and New Orleans, and did a large transportation business in freight and passengers.

Ohio packet boats of Cincinnati and New Orleans trade, brought up cotton from Natchez, sugar, coffee, rice, hides, wines, rum and dry goods of all kinds then in demand, and carried back the produce of the Miami Country."

"HOWELL'S RECOLLECTION OF LIFE IN OHIO"
By William Dean Howells

"Families were constantly leaving for the countries down the river, and they made these rafts available as the means of moving. Indeed, for the purpose, nothing could be more convenient; for the movers could build themselves a comfortable shanty of the loose lumber, a shed for their horses or cows, if they wanted to take them along, and be quite at home during a journey that would often occupy three or four weeks. I have seen the shanties of two or three families, with wagons, horses, cows and even poultry, all snugly situated, with room for the children to play outside. Often, I have seen the women washing, and a clothes line hung with the linen, as if the door yard they had left...To the young children it must have had an incomparable charm. I know I often watched them from the bank of the river with longing envy."

"THE GOVERNMENT LAND OFFICE (FOR NEW SETTLERS)"
By Walter Havighurst

"The land office was a square bare room with a rough table and an open ledger beside the surveyors' plots of the public lands. Steubenville, Marietta, Chillicothe and Cincinnati had the first offices. In all these places a familiar ritual was repeated, day after day; year after year, till the public lands were private homesteads...

The emigrant pays and signs the ledger. The wagon leaves the town, and makes its way through the woods. A new family soon arrives on their land."

"FAMILIES AND FLATBOATS"
By Frank Gregg

"As an experienced river man of an early day warned: 'No man should undertake by himself the charge of a family flatboat down the river.' Great numbers of emigrants, who are utterly ignorant of the first principles of navigation undertake the management of those awkward boats. They generally loaded their boats down to the gunwales and go wherever the stream carries them, calling out to persons ashore for direction whenever they perceive an island or a ripple.

The trick of the river was to keep the flatboats in the channel where there was deep water, and in the current where there was the most power; a matter of skill and experience.

A time came when so many people wanted to travel the river that there were not enough professional flatboatmen to meet the demand. Many emigrants lost their lives on the Ohio because of their ignorance of its pitfalls. A Pittsburgh citizen, Zodac Cramer arose to the situation by preparing a manual called, *The Navigator* which gave in detail the location of channels, sand bars, islands, ripples and creeks...*The Navigator* immediately became America's best seller; holding first position during the entire flatboat era of more than 60 years."

"TRAVELS IN THE UNITED STATES AMERICA IN 1806"

By John Melish

"Down the Ohio River from Marietta to Cincinnati: We had got well accustomed to traveling by water, and found it easy and agreeable. Our boatman, Peter, answered our purpose remarkably well, and could row about three miles an hour. The water was low, and we found the current assisted us very little. In order to relieve the boatman, and to give ourselves exercise, we frequently took a turn at the oars, and we generally made from 30 to 36 miles a day.

Our general rule was to look out for a settlement at sunset, and stop at the first we came to thereafter, and it was hardly ever necessary to make a second call. As soon as we had engaged lodgings, we ordered supper... The boatman got supper along with us, and then returned to the skiff, where he slept all night. I always found the people with whom we stopped very obliging, and ready to answer all my inquiries, so that it gave me real pleasure to travel on this delightful River, and to converse with the friendly settlers on its banks. In the morning we carried some bread, cheese and milk into the skiff.

We met up with an Irishman and his wife traveling by a skiff for Kentucky. The woman had kindled a fire on the beach to cook some eggs, and the man had gone up to a settlement to get some milk. A shower of rain, and we took shelter in a small log cabin where the landlord told us he was a native of Ireland, and had come out to fight for America during the war. He was an excellent musician, and amused us with some tunes on the violin. The afternoon clear, and we made good progress to Letart Falls...Letart Falls are only a swift current which the keel boats ascend upwards. In the course of the day we passed several families moving down the river to Kentucky. We also passed a floating store."

Gallipolis on the Ohio River

CHAPTER 22

Rough, Brave; Yet Loyal Boatmen

"A FLATBOAT TRIP IN THE MID-1800S"

By Uriah Quillen

"It was March, 1847 that I was asked by a man to accompany him on a trip to New Orleans. He had two large boats, each which was loaded with 2,400 barrels of flour which was a very large load. The wages paid to flatboatmen in those days were not very enticing, being but 30 cents a day, but being a young man anxious to see a little of the country, I decided to go. An older brother also decided to go, so it was not lonesome for me. With the provisions and the crew which were 10 men and the captain, we began the trip.

The two boats were lashed together, having on each side two oars 45 feet long with which we might keep the boats in the channel. This was not very hard to do as there was a good stage of water.

The boats were very heavy, and having square ends in them, were hard to handle. There would be five men on a watch and sometimes it would take two hours to straighten the boats around when the wind would be blowing and the current running rapidly. We had plenty of time to see the country and to take hunts. The river front was then nothing but a mass of timber and underbrush; there being but few towns to change the monotony of the scenery. Here and there you could see a house or barn peeping through the trees. Now and then an eagle would fly over your head, and a deer seen at the water's edge. Sometimes we would take the small boat, row to shore and with our guns, secure a mess of squirrels. Then we would row after the boats and have a mess of fresh meat for supper. This would be a great treat and change from the regular bill of fare which consisted of bread, beans, pork, potatoes and coffee.

We had several severe storms on the Ohio which delayed us. One beautiful moonlight April night, we were floating along on the Mississippi in the shadows of the willows and everything was wrapped in silence save the muffled oar of the pilot. Presently a gentle breeze began to blow, and soon this increased until it came in gusts. The boats began to rock and swerve from their course. The wind increased. The lashed boats were separated. Then all of us were kept busy keeping the boats apart. Finally, a lull and we were able to get to shore. It took four days to repair the boats.

A few days after, there was the hardest storm on the Mississippi that was ever known, but we got landed before it began. Hundreds of boats were sunk in this. Produce boats could be seen standing on end, and in some places, leaning against trees. Coal boats were sunk by the score, and thousands of bushels of coal were lost. A man said that he had just lost 1000 cords of wood the last night by the bank caving off. We stayed on the boats at New Orleans for about three weeks, and then took passage for home. From

Cincinnati, I came home to Syracuse on the old Messenger, the fare being 50 cents."

"LIFE ON THE MISSISSIPPI"
They floated, sailed, or poled up stream.
By Mark Twain

"The River's earliest commerce was in great barges: keelboats and broadhorns. They floated and sailed from the upper Rivers to New Orleans; changed cargoes there, and were tediously warped and poled back by hand. A voyage down and back sometimes occupied nine months. In time, this commerce increased until it gave employment to hordes of rough and hardy men: rude, uneducated, brave; suffering terrific hardships with sailor-like stoicism, heavy drinkers, coarse frolickers...Like the Natchez-under-the-hill of that day, reckless fellows, everyone...Prodigious braggarts; yet, in the main, honest, trustworthy, faithful to promises and duty, and often picturesquely magnanimous.

By and by the Steamboat intruded. Then, for fifteen or twenty years, these men continued to run their keelboats downstream, and the steamers did all of the upstream business; the keelboat men selling their boats in New Orleans, and returning home as deck passengers on the steamers.

But after a while, the steamboats so increased in number and in speed that they were able to absorb the entire commerce; and then keelboating died a permanent death. The keelboatman became a deck hand or a mate, or a pilot of the steamer.

When steamer berths were not open to him, he took a berth on a Pittsburgh coal flat, or on a pine raft constructed in the forests up toward the sources of the Mississippi.

I remember the annual procession of mighty rafts that used to glide by Hannibal when I was a boy. An acre or so of white, sweet smelling boards in each raft; a crew of two dozen men or more, three or four wigwams scattered about the raft's vast level, spaced for storm quarters...We used to swim out a quarter or a third of a mile and get on these rafts and have a ride."

"THE KEELBOATMEN"
By James Hall

"The keelboat was longer than the barge, had less depth, and was better fitted to run in narrow and shallow channels.

In his calling as master of a boat, Mike Fink...was faithful; a quality which seems to have belonged to most of his class, for it is a singular fact that lawless and wild as these men were, the valuable cargoes of merchandise committed in their care, and secured by no other bond than their integrity, were always carried safely to their destination.

In the earlier periods of this navigation, the boats employed in it were liable to attacks from the Indians, who devised a variety of artifice to decoy the crews into their power. Sometimes a single individual, disguised in the apparel of some unhappy white man, who had fallen into the Indians' hands, appeared on the shore making signals of distress, and mimicking the motions of a wounded man. The crew, supposing him to be one of their countrymen who had escaped from the Indians, would draw near the shore for the purpose of taking him on board; nor would they discover the deception until, on touching the bank, a fierce band of painted warriors would rush upon them from an artfully contrived ambuscade. Sometimes the savages crawled to the water's edge, wrapped in the skins of bears, and thus allured the boatmen, who were ever ready to exchange the oar for the rifle into their power. But the red warriors often found it difficult to accomplish their devices against men as expert in border warfare, as themselves unless their numbers were sufficiently numerous.

A month was usually consumed in the passage from Pittsburgh to New Orleans, while the return voyage was not effected in less than four months, nor without a degree of toil and exposure to which nothing but the hardiest frames, and the most indomitable spirits, would have been equal. The heavily laden boats were propelled against the strong current by poles, or where the stream was too deep to admit the use of those, drawn *by ropes*. The former process required the exertion of great strength and activity, but the latter was even more difficult and discouraging; as the boatman, obliged by the heat of the climate to throw aside his clothing and exposed to the sun's rays, was forced to wade through mire, to climb precipitous banks, to push his way through brush, and often to tread along the undermined shore..."

"THE BOATMAN'S HORN"
By *Willian O. Butler*

"O, Boatman! Wind that horn again,
For never did the listening air
Upon its lambent bosom bear
So wild, so soft, so sweet a strain!
What, though thy notes are sad and few,
By every simple boatman blown,
Yet is each pulse to nature true,
And melody in every tone.
How oft in boyhood's joyous days,
Unmindful of the lapsing hours,
I've loitered on my homeward way
By wild Ohio's banks of flowers;
While some lone boatman from the deck
Poured his soft numbers to the tide,
As if to charm from storm and wreck
The boat where all his fortunes ride!
Delighted Nature drank the sound,
Enchanted echo bore it round
In whispers soft and softer still
From hill to plain and plain to hill
Till e'en the thoughtless, frolic boy...
Feels something new pervade his breast...
Bends over the river his eager ear
To catch the sounds far off, yet dear;
Drinks the sweet draft, but knows not why
The tear of rapture fills his eye."

CHAPTER 23

The Steamboat

By James Hall

"In a population so active as ours, and spread over so wide an expanse of territory; with lands so prolific, a climate so diversified, productions so varied, mineral treasures so vast and facilities for interior navigation so great, the pursuit of commerce must form a prominent occupation.

The application of steam power to the purposes of navigation forms the brightest era in the history of this Country. It is that which has contributed more than any other event or cause to the rapid growth of our population, and the almost miraculous development of our resources. We need not pause to inquire whether the honor of the invention be due to Fitch, to Rumsey or to Fulton—for that inquiry is not involved in the discussion in which we are now engaged. But if we seek for the efficient patron of this all powerful agent in the West; for the power that adopted, fostered, improved and developed it—from an unpromising beginning, through discouragement, failure, disappointment—through peril of life, vast expenditure of money, and ruinous loss, to the most complete and brilliant success; we are again referred to the liberal spirit of commercial enterprise.

Science pointed the way, but did no more. It was the wealth of the western merchant and the skill of the western mechanic that wrought out the experiment to a success. The first fruits for the enterprise were far from encouraging. Failure after failure attested the numerous and embarrassing difficulties by which it was surrounded. For although all the early boats were capable of being propelled through the water, and although the last was usually better than those which preceded, it was long a doubtful question whether the invention could be made practical and useful upon our western rivers, and it was not until five years of experiment, and the building of nine expensive steamboats, that the public mind was convinced by the brilliant exploit of the *Washington* which made the trip from Louisville to New Orleans and back in forty-five days.

The improvements in this mode of navigation since then have been surprising. The voyage from New Orleans to Louisville has been made in less than six days. The trip from Cincinnati to New Orleans and back is made easily in two weeks. During the high water in the spring of 1846, the trip from Pittsburgh to Cincinnati was made in twenty-seven hours, and the packet boats between these places have now regular days and hours of departure.

Explosions and other destructive casualties have become rare, and the navigation is now safe, except only from obstructions existing in the channels of the rivers. All that skill, enterprise, and public spirit could do to bring this navigation to perfection, has been done by the liberal proprietors of steamboats. The wealth of individuals has been freely contributed while that of the government has been withheld with a degree of injustice which has scarcely a parallel in the annals of civilized legislation.

The history of man does not exhibit a spectacle of such rapid advancement in population, wealth, industry and refinement; such energy, perseverance, and enlightened public spirit on the part of individuals as is exhibited in the progress of the western people.

By our own unaided exertions, we have now actively employed, in the transportation of passengers and merchandise, more than five hundred steamboats, worth ten millions of dollars; having the capacity of one hundred thousand tons, and plying a connected chain of river navigation of twelve thousand miles in extent.

The value of the exports and imports floating on the western waters annually, has been estimated at two hundred and twenty millions of dollars, consisting of the products of our soil and manufactures on the one hand, and on the fabrics of foreign countries on the other; all bought with the money of our merchants, and by them thrown into the channels of trade.

If the mercantile class had rendered no other service to our Country, than that of introducing and fostering the agency of Steam, in navigation and manufactures, they would have entitled themselves to more lasting gratitude and honor, than the most illustrious statesman or hero has ever earned from the justice and the enthusiasm of his Country." —J. Hall

"THE CLERMONT'S MAIDEN VOYAGE TO ALBANY IN 1807"

By Robert Fulton

"My steamboat voyage to Albany and back has turned out rather more favorably than I had calculated. The distance from New York to Albany is one hundred and fifty miles. I ran it up in thirty-two hours, and down in thirty. I had a light breeze against me the whole way, both going and coming; and the voyage has been performed wholly by the power of the steam-engine. I overtook many sloops and schooners beating to windward, and parted with them.

The power of propelling boats by steam is now fully proven. The morning I left New York, there were not perhaps thirty persons in the city who believed that the boat would ever move one mile an hour or be of the least utility, and while we were putting off from the wharf, which was crowded with spectators, I heard a number of sarcastic remarks. This is the way in which ignorant men compliment what they call philosophers and projectors. Having employed much time, money and zeal in accomplishing this work, it gives me, as it will you, great pleasure to see it answer my expectations. It will give a cheap and quick conveyance to the merchandise on the Mississippi, Missouri and other great rivers, which are now laying open their treasures to the enterprise of our countrymen, and although the prospect of personal emolument has been some inducement to me, yet I feel infinitely more pleasure in reflecting on the immense advantage my Country will derive."

"PROPELLED BY THE POWER UNDISCOVERABLE"

By Walter Havighurst

"Cramer wrote in *The Navigator*: 'There is now on foot a new method of navigating our western waters, particularly the Ohio and Mississippi Rivers. This is with boats propelled by the power of steam. It will be a novel sight, and as pleasing as novel to see a huge boat working its way up the windings of the Ohio without the appearance of sail, oar, pole or any manual labor about it—moving within the secrets of her own wonderful mechanism and propelled by the power undiscoverable. This plan, if it succeeds, must open to view flattering prospects to an immense country, an interior of not less than 2,000 miles of as fine a soil and climate as the world can produce, and to a people worthy of all the advantages that nature and art can give them. The numerous sources of trade and wealth opening to the enterprising and industrious citizens, are a reflection that must rally the most disinterested.'"

"A STEAMBOAT CAPTAIN RECALLS 'THE WATER-WITCH'"

By Captain Wilson Daniels

"I will give a brief description of the steamer *Water Witch*. She was a single engine, side-wheel boat. The engine was a rotary four feet stroke, twenty inches in diameter, slide valve with three small boilers, single flues, very low between decks. Full length cabin open, no state rooms, bunks all curtained, no skylights in the cabin. Had a bowsprit same as a sea-going vessel. The pilot wheel was very small and beautifully inlaid with silver and ivory; with a twisted linked chain for tiller rope to guard against fire. This heavy chain made it very hard on the pilot. It took a great deal of power to turn the wheel with the length of chain required for a boat with such a small wheel, and very little leverage besides. It kept up a continuous squeaking and rattling noise that prevented the guests from sleep. This chain was so heavy, it was killing to a pilot to handle the wheel.

The pilot house on the *Water Witch* was quite small and low. No glass, canvas curtains instead, and no stove to keep you warm. Consequently, the pilot was at the mercy of wind, and rain, especially at night when very dark. He must keep the curtains rolled up so as to see his side and after-marks to enable him to guide the boat and keep it in proper course.

Consequently, he must get the full benefit of the rain and wind. There was no way to evade it; had to stand and take the weather as it came. Many is the time I have gone to my bunk without a dry piece of clothing on my person, turn in without removing anything but shoes.

I merely describe those old-time steamboats in a brief way so that the readers may see the progress that has been made in the construction of boats in the short space of sixty years. We have at this time boats that can be described as floating palaces with all modern improvements that vie with the finest hotels in the world for comfort and culinary arrangements.

The *Water Witch* was constructed very much like Fulton's first boats. When I reflect and bring back to memory the old Water Witch; her looks, her oddly constructed engines and boilers, her cabin without staterooms, the little dark pilot house and small pilot wheel, I can't see for my life how we got along so nicely with so few casualties…No bells to ring for stopping or starting the engines. Instead of bells there were speaking tubes that led from the pilot house to the engine room, and the engine was handled by word of mouth. Notwithstanding all those rude inconveniences, there were very few serious disasters."

"MY FIRST JOB"

By Captain Jesse P. Hughes

"The steamboat landing was a half mile from my grandmother's home. My bare feet covered that distance whenever I heard a boat-landing whistle. Their stay at the landing was generally a short one, governed entirely by the amount of freight that was to be taken or discharged. The *Barnsdall* was the most frequent of all the boats that landed, and the large Cincinnati boats seldom ever stopped at all. I studied all the movements that took place, learned the identity of some of the boat crew members, and tried to familiarize myself with the whole proceeding. All through those long summer days, I watched and waited.

The boat's daily journey began each morning at the humble little settlement of Raven Rock, W.Va. The plain and unpainted buildings extended along beside the railroad at the lower end of a long, narrow stretch of river where a bluff hillside jutted out near the rocky shore. It was a small shipping point from which several dirt roads led out over the hills to the country beyond.

Country produce was hauled in for outgoing shipment, and groceries and other needs of life were brought each day by the packets in return. Four daily trains stopped at the little platform at the upper end of town that was called the station. The country store of Beaver and Barker sold everything from horse collars to safety pins and sow belly to dark brown sugar. It was the most important place in town. Aside from that, Raven Rock was just a handy place where the steamer tied up each night and departed again in the morning after the old cock had crowed.

The boat pulled out from Raven Rock each time virtually empty handed. The pilot, soon after leaving, sounded the boat's whistle on blast at intervals, in what was known as a begging whistle. This was just a friendly invitation for someone on either shore *to hail* the boat to land, and pick up a lone passenger, a calf, a case of eggs or other freight offering. This *hail signal* was usually a white handkerchief waved in daytime or a swinging lighted lantern, a burning newspaper or any other light that might be handy at night.

Each farmer had his landing or roadway to the River. The swinging stage on the steamer was adjusted and lowered into a convenient position as the boat's bow was shoved into a soft clay bank. The business was transacted quickly and the boat's bell tapped twice to tell the pilot that all details had been completed. The boat then backed away from the landing and proceeded on with little loss of time.

The important towns were regular landings each trip. The people ashore usually knew the crew by sight, especially the captain and clerk who were considered almost as home residents and trusted friends..."

"OLD OHIO STEAMBOAT DAYS, 1860-1890"
By William G. Sibley

"A great River is a powerful influence over the lives of all who dwell on its banks. When a river is intimately associated with the affairs of a small community, its whole population becomes conscious of it. So it was with boyhood in the late [eighteen] sixties and seventies, when spent in almost any village along the Ohio River between Pittsburgh and Cincinnati; a never-to be-forgotten experience, for in those decades the Ohio was *The Stream of the Empire* when the West was in the making.

Every village boy on the bank was acutely conscious of the Ohio River all the year around. It was so with me from young boyhood to manhood in the village of Racine, Ohio midway between Cincinnati and Pittsburgh—460 miles apart.

From spring to autumn in the late sixties, the great pine forests on the hillsides of the Allegheny and Monongahela Rivers floated down by the village in huge rafts of logs. In the seventies they were replaced by rafts of fragrant sawed lumber bound to ports on the lower Ohio and Mississippi. There was also the daily panorama of tow boats pushing ahead of them acres of heavily laden barges of coal from Pittsburgh, or great barges full of Pittsburgh and Wheeling industrial products for lower ports—a mighty volume of commerce that continued to ride the river until the country became a network of railroads...

The finest attraction of the river was the swift passenger packets; side-wheelers and stern-wheelers, half a dozen or more a day bound up or down-stream, full of people, with bands of music and all painted white from their hulls to their pilot-houses. The steamboat era was in its heyday then, with no competition for quick freight or passenger transportation. The stage-coach was passing out and the railroads were only in their beginning. Nowhere...did the steamboats travel in braver array, or mean more to the populations along the shores, than on the Upper Ohio. The villages and towns on the banks were the homes of the crews—masters, pilots, engineers and mates—whose standing was professional.

The river valley population depended almost wholly on the river for both freight and travel. When ice or low water suspended traffic, there were none but dirt roads along the banks, often impassable when winter thaws came. The river traffic built the towns from Pittsburgh down—Wheeling, Marietta, Parkersburg, Pomeroy, Middleport, Gallipolis, Ironton, Portsmouth and on to Cincinnati. Much capital was invested in them, and their business was cut up into 'trades'. There was the through trade from Pittsburgh to Cincinnati, the Wheeling and Parkersburg trade, the Wheeling and Cincinnati trade...Shorter trades existed between Ravenswood and Pomeroy, Gallipolis and Ironton, Ironton and Cincinnati; with another prosperous passenger express and freight trade between Pomeroy and Cincinnati; cared for by three fine, large side-wheelers that made tri-weekly round trips. Businessmen made frequent trips to Cincinnati to buy stock for their stores.

...For young people, it was an event to see 400 miles of the Ohio River...

The Steamboat *Andes* ...was famous for honeymooners, and Cincinnati, the one large city easily reached with the celebrated May musical festivals, drew thousands of music lovers from up and down the river.

The *White Collar* Line, plying between Pomeroy and Cincinnati, had three boats in operation all the time. The *Hummingbird* running between the Pomeroy Bend and Gallipolis, operated for many years.

Mark Twain gave the Mississippi River a place in literature with his book, *Life on the Mississippi*...It was a boy's classic in my youth that applied to the Ohio as well...The literature of the Ohio is scanty when one considers the prodigious volume of freight and passenger traffic it bore between 1860 and 1890, the heyday of steamboating on the Upper Ohio. In the nineties, the great decline set in.

Ohio River traffic, both freight and passenger, was important and exerted a powerful influence on social and economic progress along the shores. With its passing have gone many of the delights of travel."

"A RIVER BOY'S AMBITIONS IN THE 1870S"

By W. G. Sibley

"The boy who lived in a village or small town on the banks of the Ohio River in the 1870s had boundless ambitions, and they all had to do with the steamboats which were in the heyday of their popularity in that decade. The railroads were coming, but they had not arrived on the river banks. The steamboats did the freight business and carried the passengers.

The passenger packets did a particularly heavy business between Pittsburgh, Wheeling and Cincinnati. They all landed at the villages, towns and cities and most of them responded promptly to a 'hail' from the shore...

When a boat's musical whistle blew for a landing, all boy sports were suspended while they went to see the boat's hull plow into the mile-long sloping gravel beach, and to talk 'steamboats.'

Our particular ambition was to be a clerk. The individual who was the *mud* clerk, went ashore at every landing to check the freight delivered onto the beach or wharf boat, and the new consignments to be taken on board. He was always conspicuous and important, and not to be interfered with. He it was who nodded to the mate on the hurricane deck when the business was almost completed, and to ring the big melodious bell as a warning that departure was near. The deckhands hurried to the place where the big cable that held the boat to the shore was fastened. They untied it, and were the last to climb the big, broad stage plank. Then the pilot's bells rang and the boat backed out from shore and squared around to continue up or down the River.

After the boat left, the beach was a busy place with the teamsters loading their big wagons with freight destined for the local merchants: W. Cross and W.A. Ellis and Co., general dealers; J. Hayman, hardware; B.F. Sibley, drugs and J.R. Ellis, furniture; to get it all under cover before rain came.

Now the old beach is idle most of the time, except for the ferryboat...

The old river trade for passenger packets is done so far as majestic steamers are concerned. Now only fine excursion boats operate out of St. Louis, Louisville and Cincinnati, and serve to recall the former glories of Steamboating."

"THE HOUSE BEAUTIFUL"

By Mark Twain

"We took passage in a Cincinnati boat for New Orleans: or on a Cincinnati boat—either is correct; the former is the eastern form of putting it, the latter the western.

Mr. Dickens declined to agree that the Mississippi Steamboats were "magnificent," or that they were "floating palaces"—terms which had always been applied to them; terms which did not over-express the admiration with which the people viewed them.

...If Mr. Dickens was comparing these boats with the crown jewels; or with the Taj, or with the Matterhorn; or with some other priceless or wonderful thing which he had seen, they were not magnificent—he was right. The people compared them with what they had seen, and thus measured, thus judged, the boats were magnificent—the term was the correct one, it was not at all too strong. The steamboats were finer than anything on shore. Compared with superior dwelling houses and first-class hotels in the Valley they were indubitably magnificent, they were *palaces.* To the entire populations spread over both banks between Baton Rouge and St. Louis, they *were* palaces. They tallied with the citizen's dream of what magnificence was, and satisfied it.

…When he stepped aboard a big fine steamboat, he entered a new and marvelous world. Chimney tops cut to mimic a spraying crown of plumes—may be painted red. Pilothouse, hurricane deck, boiler-deck guards all garnished with white wooden filigree work of fanciful patterns. Gilt acorns topping the derricks; gilt deer horns over the big bell; gaudy symbolic picture on the paddle box…Big chandeliers every little way, each an April shower of glittering glass drops; lovely rainbow light falling everywhere from the colored blaring of the skylights; the whole…a bewildering and soul-satisfying spectacle."

"TORCH BASKETS"

"Old Times on the Upper Mississippi"

By George B. Merrick

"The advent of the electric searchlight has driven from the river one of the most picturesque of all the accessories to such scenes as we boys looked down upon, night after night during the busy times of 1854 and 1855 before I myself became part and parcel of it all. The torch by the light of which the work went on by night, was within an iron basket about a foot in diameter and eighteen inches deep, swung loosely between the prongs of a forked iron bar or standard; which could be set in holes in the forward deck, leaning far out over the water so as to allow live coals from the burning wood to fall into the river and not upon deck.

When a landing was to be made at a wood-yard or a town, the watchman filled one or perhaps two of these torch baskets with split lightwood or fatwood—southern pine full of resinous sap which would burn fiercely, making a bright light illuminating the deck of the boat and the levee for hundreds of feet around. As the boat neared the landing, the pine splinters were lighted at the furnace door, the torch being carried to place and firmly fixed in its socket.

Then came out the attendant who fed the burning smoking *jack* with more pine fatwood, and from time to time with a ladle of pulverized rosin. The rosin would flare up with a fierce flame followed by thick clouds of black smoke; the melted tar falling in drops upon the water to float away, burning and smoking until consumed. This addition to the other sights and sounds served more than any other thing to give this night work a wild and weird setting. We boys decided on many a night, that we would "go on the river," and feed powdered rosin and pine kindling to torches all night long, as the coal-black and greasy, but greatly envied white lamp-boy did, night after night, in front of our attic windows on the levee at Prescott."

"TIMBER RAFTS"
By Mark Twain

"On the great rise, down came a swarm of prodigious timber rafts from the headwaters of the Mississippi: coal barges from Pittsburgh, little trading scows from everywhere, and broadhorns from Posey County, Indiana freighted with "fruit and furniture"— the usual term for describing it, though in plain English the freight thus aggrandized was hoop-poles and pumpkins. Pilots bore a mortal hatred for these craft, and it was returned with usury. The law required all such helpless traders to keep a light burning, but it was a law that was often broken. All of a sudden on a murky night, a light would hop up right under our bows, almost, and an agonized voice with the back woods whang to it, would wail out, "Whar'n the— you goin' to! Cain't you see nothing, you etc. etc." Then for an instant as we whistled by, the red glare from our furnaces would reveal the scow and the form of the gesticulating orator, as if under a lightning flash, and in that instant our firemen and deckhands would send and receive a tempest of missiles and profanity. One of our wheels would walk off with the crashing fragments of a steering oar, and down the dead blackness would shut again. And that flatboat man would be sure to go to New Orleans and sue our boat, swearing stoutly that he had a light burning all the time, when in truth his gang had the lantern down below to sing and lie and drink and gamble by, and no watch on deck.

Once at night, in one of those forest-bordered crevices—we should have eaten up a Posey County family; fruit, furniture and all. They happened to be fiddling down below, and we just caught the sound of the music in time to sheer off, doing no serious damage.

One time, a coal boatman sent a bullet through our pilothouse when we borrowed a steering oar of him in a very narrow place."

CHAPTER 24

A Town and the Wilderness

"CINCINNATI IN 1815"
By Daniel Drake

"OAK, ASH, POPLAR, WALNUT and other native timber trees, squared or sawed into boards, plank and scantling are brought to market in wagons, boats or rafts.

ON THE PLAT OF CINCINNATI, there is at this time, July 1815, nearly 1100 houses exclusive of kitchens, smokehouses and stables...660 contain families; the remainder are public buildings, shops, ware-houses and offices.

THE FIRST COURT HOUSE stood on the eastern end of the public ground; erected in 1802, and burned down in 1814 while a company of soldiers were using it as a barrack. It was built of limestone with a wooden cupola with a balustrade.

PRESERVATION FROM FIRE: in 1808 the Select Council purchased a fire engine, and the Union Fire Company comprising nearly all the men in town was formed...An ordinance of the corporation requires each house to be furnished with a fire bucket...Each drayman shall furnish at every fire at least 2 barrels of water.

WATER: The borers of the town have a few indifferent springs, and on the hills are others, but none sufficient for distribution. The wells are of various depths. A large proportion of all that is used, is drawn up in barrels from the Ohio River. This is often impure and requires time to settle, but for most domestic purposes, it is preferred to well water.

FUEL: Wood is the chief article of fuel at this place. Beech, ash, hickory, sugar tree, oak, red maple, honey locust...Many teams are constantly employed in hauling wood into town from surrounding hills.

MARKETS: Cincinnati has four market days in each week: the supply of fish is not great, though in the Ohio River they are abundant. Perch, pike, eel, yellow-cat and sword fish are most esteemed. Venison is brought from the woods during proper season, and bear meat is now and then offered...

MANUFACTURES: As this town is older than the surrounding country, it has at no time had a surplus of laboring population or of capital. The former have been required to assist in clearing and improving the wilderness; the latter has been invested in lands.

Cincinnati has no iron foundry, but is well supplied with blacksmiths who fabricate in a neat and substantial manner, every article which those tradesmen usually take. Several shops are devoted to the manufacture of cut and wrought nails made in sufficient quantities for the town and adjacent settlements. Stills, tea kettles and other vessels of copper with a great variety of tin ware, are made in abundance. Rifles, pistols, dirks and gun locks of every kind are manufactured;

Plated saddler and carriage mounting of all kinds...Common pottery of a good quality...Manufactory of green window glass and hollow ware is about to go into operation...Clean sand of a beautiful white color has been found in abundance near the mouth of the Scioto...

The principal manufactures in wood are: sideboards, secretaries, bureaus, articles of cabinet furniture; all of which may be had of a superior quality, made either of our beautiful cherry and walnut or of mahogany brought by boat up the Mississippi.

Wagons, carts and drays; coaches, phaetons, gigs and other pleasure carriages, trimmed and ornamented...

There are four cotton spinning establishments, most small; contain 1200 spindles moved by horses.

Fur hats of a good quality are made in such quantities as to give a surplus for exportation to the Mississippi where they are exchanged for peltry. The tanning and currying of leather is carried on at six tan yards in this place...and the manufacture of shoes, boots and saddlery is extensive.

Flat-bottomed boats, keelboats and barges are the vessels in which the commerce of this place has been carried on...The latter will be in a great degree superseded by Steamboats of which two kinds are coming into use on the Western waters. From these inventions the people on the Ohio River anticipate many substantial advantages...all must admit that no Country on Earth equally fertile with this, can be more benefited by such boats.

Foreign and domestic goods: the different kinds of East Indian, European and New England goods with several manufactures of the middle states are received from Philadelphia and Baltimore... Whenever the General Government shall complete the road from the navigable waters of the Potomac to those of the Ohio, the expense of transportation by land will be so far reduced."

"NOTES ON A JOURNEY TO AMERICA"
Cincinnati, 1817
By Morris Birkbeck

"The hundreds of commodious well-finished brick houses, the spacious and busy markets, the substantial public buildings, the thousands of prosperous well-dressed industrious inhabitants, the numerous wagons and drays, the gay carriages...The shoals of craft on the Ohio River, the busy stir prevailing everywhere: house building, boat-building, paving and leveling streets; the numbers of country people, constantly coming and going, with the spacious taverns crowded with travelers from a distance—All this is so much more than I could comprehend from a description of a new town just risen from the woods, that I despair of conveying an adequate idea of it to my English friends.

It is enchantment, and liberty is the fair enchantress. I was assured by a respectable gentleman, one of the first settlers and now a man of wealth and influence, that he remembers when there was only one poor cabin where this noble town now stands."

"THE JOURNAL OF LIWWAT BOKE"
Journey Crossing the Atlantic Ocean

"We talked with various ship's reps, and took space on a sailing ship for Baltimore…We were here about 15 days, and obtained thru passage with other families; stalwart Catholic people from Vorden. In about 15 days we were on deck and got a cabin that was about like a sleeping alcove at our house with two drawers under the sleeping berths. It was to us, grand and also venturesome.

We were underway by sunrise. "The wind is right" they say. Sailing requires skill and wind. In the evening we anchored again. We are a little seasick; our heads go around. Today we are in the North Sea on the way to Heligoland. The wind is powerful and strong. The ship trembles and rocks and twists from side to side and then come great waves, end to end, and the stomach feels sick again.

DAY 2: We must endure the howling wind and all the shaking, and the noise mid decks, the children crying. People are very much afraid alone. We cooked once in our iron pot, such a little pot.

DAY 6: We are again under way sailing farther thru the straits between France and England.

DAY 7: The fog was thick and wet, almost like rain, the whole day was foggy and windy.

On the ship there are a variety of people, and a lot of families with little children. Two widows with children are going to Ohio.

DAY 12: We had a completely still wind the whole long day. The close association is getting us all now. We think about our new fatherland, and discover to our minds a counter stream of thoughts about our abandoned homeland. We are alone, yet mingled with unfamiliar people of every class. Frequently the children are friendly, completely agreeable. People are stingy with their laughter, never light-hearted.

...Always the mighty rolling and heaving of the ship...so that everything is thrown into a heap. One cannot remain sitting or standing. No cooking throughout the four days, only hardtack and black bread. We finally made soup...

DAY 56: The wind is weak and we are traveling in the channel toward Baltimore now, with a headwind and shallow water, with so much turning and steering. Yesterday evening our ship was visited by Americans.

DAY 57: This morning the anchor was weighed and we traveled in the entrance of the port where we again had to drop anchor, and the police and a doctor came to visit. Not a single person on the ship was sick...it was a profound, powerful experience for me. The first impression as I saw America: It is a joyful sight and a lovely land.

DAY 58: A long time since the departure from my home in Germany!"

Their Home in the Wilderness of St. John, Ohio
(The Boke Journal continues...)

"How different I and Natz seemed in those first times; how we struggled to overcome the dense, ominous, wet, silent forest, the streamlets, the creeks, the stones, the solitude....just we two against time, need and trees.

It is indeed an important notion to describe how hard and tedious it was; the time it took to clear the land of all these trees and underbrush. The forest is a vast attractive, wonderful sight to see and enjoy, but that one cannot eat or wear. Natz and I are thankful about our decision to immigrate to America. It is the best situation to live in the forest, also much better married to a nice fine man whom I love...One matures in this battle to take over the woods, but we did achieve it up to our expectation.

The usual food is wild game and little fish, not many from the streams here. Corn, beets, beans, soup beans, pumpkins, squash, cucumbers, melons, cabbage and turnips all the vegetables are from our own garden. We also use carrots and plant roots, fruits, nuts and berries from the woods.

We have no chickens yet. We need a chicken coop first; otherwise one cannot protect the chickens from the wolves, weasels and foxes.

It is so different here. Natz and I are white Europeans and also peasants. We are not Yankee Protestants, English, but no one is better than another, for the forest levels all the men in it to a raw lifestyle in work for food, clothes, buildings, plants, moving around. We had to adjust to different government regulations and to freedom. God's goodness provides here many prospects and much space.

Many strangers, men, families, who are on their way to establish a home come here. We help each one that passes here, especially our own people who are coming here all the time continually arriving from our old homes in Germany.

At Gast's house once or twice a month we usually have to walk; the forest is too thick for a horse to be able to get through...Usually someone gives a talk about God. Then we listen to one another with complaints, troubles, news and informative things like where, what and when about our work. We now have a horse, and Natz made a harrow out of wood with long iron nails or spikes. So many little and also large stones in the ground! It is exasperating to pick up 500 times.

Houses lie far apart from each other here in the forest. Right up to our doorsill and to those of our neighbors, reaches the huge, somber and vaulted forest. There are no openings to break up the overhang, nothing but endless miles upon miles of the shadowy wolf-haunted woodland. The great trees tower heavenwards until their individual crowns are lost among the many branches at the top...Here stand scattered proud beech trees, and pines, hemlocks, balsams and firs. Others: oak, chestnut, hickory, ash, walnut... The sunlight cannot get through the arches of the murmuring leaves...We people from Bieste in this thick forest feel as if our heads are hooded. All the countryside is monotonous in a tree-strewn land. Everything in it lies hidden. And farther on? No one can say, not even the brave hunters know how far to the west this forest extends; they have not yet gone through to the other end.

The husband is the provider and protector, his wife is the house-wife and mother. Man and woman, or woman and man...either way is correct...are equally important...All the people here have a little woods, 80-100 acres with a few essential animals. We are making fences between our farms.

The shoemaker comes around the community from house to house and remains until every foot's shoe is correct...The St. John community can barely survive even if everyone helps everyone else as in: log-rolling, house-raising, house-furnishing, corn shucking, quilting, roofing with the neighbors. Each family must do all that it can by itself.

Life is a long struggle. We must fell the trees, but also cope with droughts, deep snow, sudden flooding, cloudbursts, forest fire, swarms of deerflies and mosquitos and midges, snakes, wolves....

Squirrels in swarms eat up all the cornfields. In time, some people here go completely mad, changed, commit suicide. Countless people do not talk with their spouses; many women have miscarriages.

A stream with much water flow most of the time, crosses the way to St. John. Together we have installed a bridge on the path; more for the school children than for us parents. The bridge has stone abutments with oaken beams on both sides, and both ends and planks laid 4 inches thick...

From wood Natz and I have made many things for household use, such as: pancake rack, a soup cooking spoon of elm wood, meat forks...We also made a wooden rolling pin and handles at each end. Also various wooden pans in which to set anything for cooking, baking; wooden buckets with leather handles and hoops. We almost completed a wheelbarrow but the wheel didn't suit us, and there is presently no wagon maker here in St. John. So many things we need, so little time to make them. But we are both healthy, and by and with God's blessings, so fortunate here in this place to love each other.

In this new land, America, in this forest, often enough because of our ignorance, carelessness, neglect and half amateurism, if openly acknowledged, we both are driven into deep distress and worry. Yes, we take much time and energy for reading, having fun, drawing, writing, singing, praying, playing cards, and other pleasures that often are not related and tied in with farming and work.

It is sensible to first feed ourselves when we can, and that means to always nurture our minds, our intellect, our moods and our feelings as much as we nourish our stomachs.

Because of the violent deaths of men and sometimes women, either in the forest or from tools, or from guns and powder or from bulls or other wild animals, or from lightening, the expectation for violent death is a little more natural here than it is in cities.

The first year here in 1835: We had to walk everywhere and used the Indian path north and south. The path to St. John's Village we made with logs and branches. Wheat, corn and all things we carried or hauled by packsaddle on a horse to the mills ... to Sidney, Dayton, or Cincinnati there and back. One day each week Natz had to work for Marion Township, building bridges, culverts, roadways, dirt roads, dams.

Some kinds of wagon paths were necessary. The rivers and streams provided us the best means for hauling things.

Isolated here in St. John, we had to grind our own grain using the same primitive mortar and pestle which they used in ancient times, a thousand years ago. There are some farmers better located near grist mills, so they can easily haul their grain over rough pack-trails to the nearby mill.

HORSES: Without horses nothing would grow today. These work animals help us in everything, such as treadmills, plowing, harrowing, rolling, carrying, driving, riding, hay making, raking, wagon-pulling, hunting, visiting, traveling.

In the spring the children play in the warm forest, and carelessly they get turned around, don't recognize the surroundings; are lost! Often then a parent unthinking and so badly upset, also becomes lost in their urgent haste. Each neighborhood learns the vastness of the treacherous forest.

Self-concern is more common each succeeding summer and is now almost epidemic. The people, men and women are locked in the solitude of their own hearts and minds. The men want to chop down the forest in a short time for their small acreage of land, and it is not possible. The men fall short in their undertakings, and in their dissatisfaction, they are silent and sulky, sullen and pouty. Such behavior smothers the women's spirits, and they feel themselves alone, apart from the community, without friends and female companions. Some of the people here are alone in actual isolation, or are alone among other people or in crowds, because they think that no one is concerned, or that they cannot cope anymore. The women are not often praised so they feel themselves abandoned in the world facing their inner troubles.

In summertime many families are on the move. More and more new families from Europe and the eastern states are moving into the forest here. Other families move away from here to Indiana and Illinois...better land for farming, they say.

Now there are better wagon roads in the vicinity, and as far as Minster by the oncoming Canal. And the walking path is cleared; brush and thorns cut down, so that people travel more and carry back and forth the news.

In the last few years, we have gotten a new food bonus, sugar cane, which we plant in a cornfield. When it is cooked off and cooled down, it is skimmed off and is now molasses...This and English syrup we pour into shiny pails with lids which we buy from the peddler from Dayton who deals through here. This sweet cane has come here from southern America.

We women sew clothes, pants, shirts, underwear, jackets, towels, all winter long. A new American women's gathering is coming into use around here now. Six, seven, or eight visit, all at one house in the afternoon, and make quilts of matched patches sewed together. We sit on chairs and benches around a wooden form, talking, complaining, trading advice, troubles, and homesickness. The quilts are bright and useful. It is good medicine for all."

—Liwwat Boke

"CINCINNATI IN 1841"
By Charles Cist

"There are few places in the United States which more favorably impress a stranger who reaches it by water, the usual avenue, than Cincinnati. His eye glances upon that superb quay—our public landing, a space of ten acres nearly, and a front of almost one thousand feet; its whole front encumbered with packages of every description to an immense amount. The foreign imports, or the domestic produce of the valley of the Miami Rivers concentrate constantly at this point. The hurried arrival and departure, singly and in squads of whole battalion of drays; the unremitting and active labors of hands loading and unloading the vessels in port; the incessant ringing of bells as signals to passengers or the crews of the boats; the brief and abrupt interchange of business among the clerks on board, and those belonging to the mercantile houses of the city, with a great variety of sights and sounds; impress the mind of a stranger that he has landed at a place where business is carried on upon a large scale.

Let the stranger of whom I have spoken, next visit our workshops and notice the extent and variety of manufactures carried on, and he will no longer wonder at the manifestations of improvement which meet him on every side…and he will say,

'These people are building for ages to come not less than for themselves. I rejoice in their prosperity, for they are the trustees of the future destinies of our great republic.'

…The commerce of Cincinnati is so extensive with the navigation of the West, and its interior trade is spread over the whole extent of country between the River Ohio and the Lakes, north and south, and the Scioto and Wabash Rivers, east and west…Cincinnati affords the Ohio River country and the upper and lower Mississippi States and territories, with a vast amount of manufactured products not merely made here, but with which this market is extensively supplied from the interior. For there are received in return: sugar, cotton, rice, molasses, etc. from the South. Lead, shot, furs, honey from the Missouri and Upper Mississippi region; pork, flour, from Indiana…

…The eastern half of the State of Indiana is an important customer for foreign goods to this market, and the lower Mississippi country for our various manufactured articles. The products of other countries brought to this place, are purchased in New York and Philadelphia…In the great Ohio Valley there is no place so central in relation to its population and resources, as Cincinnati. This has had a great influence on its destiny and present prosperity. The Ohio River is 959 miles in length from Pittsburg to the Mississippi. From Pittsburgh to Cincinnati is 458 miles. From Cincinnati to the mouth of the Ohio is 501 miles so that Cincinnati is very nearly in the actual center of the valley."

Few, even of our own citizens, are aware of the extent and importance of the manufacturing interest in Cincinnati. Its operations have grown up so silently and gradually extending over the course of twenty years. The workshop of the mechanic with his two or three apprentices, to a factory with from thirty to fifty hands; and adding constantly, without parade, some new branch of industry."

MANUFACTURING IN 1859 CINCINNATI

"Articles for the Times"
By Charles Cist

"With the exception of Philadelphia, Cincinnati is probably the most extensive manufacturing city in the United States.

AGRICULTURAL MACHINERY AND IMPLEMENTS: Every variety of farmers' implements…such as ploughs, harvesters, mowers, rakers, reapers, grain threshers, harrows, corn planters, cultivators, hay presses.

STEAM ENGINES for driving saw and grist mills...

BUCKEYE FOUNDRY: *Bells:* During the past season, the Foundry have cast the chime of bells in St. Peter's Cathedral...three bells for St. Mary's Church, 3 bells for Trinity Church; 3 bells for St. Augustine's Church.

Bells

We have an extensive domestic market, stretching from the Muskingum to the Wabash, and from the Ohio River to the Lakes, whose population is continually increasing.

Let me begin then, with the bell and brass foundries of which *we have eight*. Cincinnati supplies the whole valley of the Ohio and of the Mississippi with bells of all sizes and for every use.

The bells cast here are finished; that is to say, they are mounted on a stand or frame, ready for setting up. Of course, all the iron work connected with the bells is completed before they are sent off. To every large bell made here, there are springs, by the action of which the tongue cannot touch the bell until it receives a full and distinct stroke on the upper side. The credit of this invention, alike ingenious and simple, belongs to one of our Cincinnati mechanics...

I have seen the bell, which may reach in weight three hundred pounds; it is the same which calls our citizens to meetings in the college edifice.

"There can be no doubt that we should not have been able to supersede the Eastern manufacture, if those made in Cincinnati had not equaled them in finish, in power and in sweetness of tone.

—Charles Cist

BELLOWS: three factories which supply this market for home and foreign demand, with blacksmiths' bellows.

BOOKBINDING: As the introduction of cotton rags into the manufacture of paper has been mainly of recent date; linen rags alone make a harsh, rough surface. The combination of the two is best...

CARRIAGES, BUGGIES, OMNIBUSES, SPRING WAGONS: Manufacture in every variety of wheeled vehicles...

CARVERS: WOOD, HENRY: Architectural carver and designer, executes Corinthian, Ionic and other capitals; brackets and every kind of ornament furnished in wood, iron...

STOVES, HOLLOW WARE AND OTHER CASTINGS for western and southern markets. Pig iron from Hanging Rock region [Ironton] is used exclusively. They smelt the best brands of iron.

Their first lot of hollow ware and stoves was made from the necessary supply of the Scotch iron, but having, by way of experiment resorted to the finer qualities of the pig-iron in Lawrence County, Ohio, they continue to make an article equal in smoothness to the Eastern castings of the same silver-gray color, but of greater strength and of a malleability which has no equal in any casting made elsewhere. ...An

Eastern man, walking by the door of this warehouse, where these stoves are kept, declared them 'as handsome as ours...'

STEAMBOATS: There are three steamboat yards. The building of steamboats has been declining here for years, but there is still and always will be a large amount of repairing and refitting of boats.

WARE, EARTHEN AND POTTER: Here a great variety of yellow and Rockingham ware is manufactured consisting of bowls, pitchers, jars of all kinds, milk dishes, baking dishes...

FURNITURE: Bedsteads, bureaus, tables, stands, wardrobes, desks, bookcases, cribs, sofas, settees, lounges, divans...the great bulk, beyond what is wanted for our own citizens, finds its market throughout the entire West, South and Southwest. Machinery is driven by steam...the escape steam is employed in warming the building in winter... Five million feet of lumber are annually worked up here into bedsteads. Poplar, sycamore, black walnut, and cherry are the lumber.

Oak, ash, poplar, walnut and other native timber trees, squared or sawed into boards, plank and scantling are brought to market in wagons, boats or rafts."

"A Raftman's Experience"

By Silas Robinson

"In the spring for six successive years, I took a raft from this mill, Braley, down to the mouth of Leading Creek, and then down the Ohio River to Cincinnati. I went out annually on the March rise, but sometimes had to wait for the necessary water until April or May. My raft consisted of stuff sawed out by the Braley brothers at the mill. I had four mill dams to run: Langsville, Smiths, Bingham and Skinners. At one time I took about 24,000 feet of fine lumber. I didn't usually have much trouble in getting out of Leading Creek. It took about three days and two nights to float down to Cincinnati. I got about nine dollars a thousand for bedstead stuff and thirteen for yellow pine. I had a pretty rough experience one night in floating down about Portsmouth. It was foggy—I couldn't see anything and I couldn't land. Occasionally the raft would rake against the bank brush, and then I would drift out into the river again. I endeavored to keep my bearings by throwing coal in the direction I supposed the bank to be. In this uncertain way, I drifted in the fog at night and couldn't see a thing till eight or nine a.m. My rafting was done in the 1840s and 50s."

"THE CINCINNATI LEVEE (100 YEARS AGO)"
By Harry B. Abdy, 1919

"We looked down on the beloved levee. How delicately beautiful it was in those few and fleeting moments of twilight! It was soft grey with the warm glow of cabin lights on anchored boats. An old red-walled warehouse stood at the levee top. The great suspension bridge was glowing with the many moving lights of an early autumn evening. The levee at Cincinnati is the busiest of all the river ports of the Ohio River. Long lines of freight toting darkies and knots of idlers...roustabouts working; roustabouts loafing. During the day and far into the night, passenger packets with crowded decks arrive and depart. We were glad to have an hour of twilight in which to see the river scenery just above Cincinnati. We saw further proof of the excellence of the location, the attractiveness and industrial importance of the Ohio River's metropolis. This region was prepared as a throne whereon to place its queen. In order for an important city to be founded on its banks, it must have a check to its rollicking twists and turns...and therefore the River straightened out a league or so above the prospective site, and became a long straight stretch of water, dignified and decorous, both in width of surface and speed of current."

CHAPTER 25

Small Towns Along the Upper Ohio

RIPLEY, OHIO

By Elise B. Stivers

"Ripley looked to the Ohio River for life. It was laid out in 1812, and in its early days Ripley was a center for steamboat building. Just below this land was the deepest water and the best landing along the river where flatboats could run along the shore and take on cargo. Steamboats could lie alongside the bank with ample water beneath their keels when fully loaded.

RIPLEY, OHIO LOCATED ABOUT FIFTY-TWO MILES ABOVE CINCINNATI...Although Marietta was the first permanent settlement made under the ordinance in 1788, it wasn't until after the defeat of the Indians by General Wayne in 1794, that settlers began to arrive...Ripley and the surrounding area are a part of this

Northwest Territory known as the Virginia Military District. The Commonwealth of Virginia reserved the tract of land between the Scioto and the Little Miami Rivers to fulfill all obligations to their Revolutionary War Veterans.

The name Ripley was in honor of General E. W. Ripley, an American commander in the War of 1812.

…The location provides deep water landing for boats on the Ohio River which is nearly one-half mile wide here.

…The Ohio River here runs about due north, causing the sun to set over the river above the beautiful Kentucky hills, the setting sun reflecting on the river.

Many Ripley residents remember the omnibus, a horse-drawn wagon-bus that took passengers to the ferry that crossed the Ohio River to meet the C & O trains.

The riverbank here was an ideal location for a shipyard. All around this spot were the best woods in the world for boat building; the banks gently sloping down into the deep water where vessels of any size could easily be launched.

Red Oak Creek was peculiarly adapted for mill sites, running out of the hills…There was unusual power back of the stream for manufacturing purposes. All these natural resources were important in pre-steam days. There was ample timber to make barrels for shipping grain, corn, etc. down the river." *(end Stivers writing.)*

In 1827, the local newspaper reported…"Ripley contains seven mercantile houses, all of which import goods regularly from the East: a number of groceries, three physicians, two attorneys, three hatting shops, three cabinet shops, three coopers, tanners, wool carding machines, a steam mill, and a large woolen factory."

One visitor related: "During a stay of about 40 hours at Ripley, eight steamboats passed that town, five or six of which stopped to put out and receive passengers. It was the first near view we ever had to their mighty prowess. Persons who have never seen them can form no correct opinion of their appearance, strength and speed. They appear to bid bold defiance to the established laws of nature; as if glorying in their own strength. The current of the majestic Ohio seems to offer no resistance to their speed."

Ripley historian Frank Gregg, stated, "If the Ohio River were straight and ran downhill for its thousand miles, the speed of its current would dash to the foothills of the Rocky Mountains.

...Stand with me at the Ohio's edge at Pittsburgh where the waters meet and the Ohio begins. Looking down the river you will see the bank has a long curve giving direction to the stream. When the water comes to the end of that curve, it shoots straight across striking the opposite bank, where it slows down and is diverted back across the river. Each bend thus acts as a brake. So the Ohio goes back and forth, slowing up at each bend, until it is held down to a navigable speed."

The Rankin House

"The residence, reached by a long flight of stone steps, was a [southern Ohio] station on *the Underground Railroad*. A lantern placed in an attic window could be seen for miles across the Ohio River, and served to guide fleeing slaves to safety. It was here, according to local legend that *Eliza*, in the novel, *Uncle Tom's Cabin*, fled across the floating ice from the Kentucky shore, and found temporary refuge in the Rankin home."

—*The Ohio Guide*

(Written by a son of the Rankins)
"All that my parents did in the aid of fugitives was to furnish food and shelter. Their sons, of whom there were nine, did the conveying away.

Some attempts were periodically made to search our house. One incident, on pretense of 'looking for a thief,' follows: Upon their starting to come for our door, my brother took down the rifle from over the door, cocked it, and called out, 'Halt!' 'If you come one step farther, I will kill you.' And they halted.

My brother David and myself had not yet returned home from conveying fugitives to the next station north, but we were soon on the scene. When word was sent to town of the perceived threat, in a short time our yard was full of friends.

The hunters were not allowed to pass out at the gate, but were taken by each arm, and led to the fence and ordered to climb, and they climbed!" (A *Henry Howe* quote)

SCIOTO COUNTY

Portsmouth, Ohio

"From these hills are magnificent views of the broad Scioto and Ohio Valleys and of the wooded Kentucky uplands...

After the coming of the steamboat, Portsmouth began to thrive as a port town. Between 1824 and 1834 six steamboats were built in or near Portsmouth...When the Ohio and Erie Canal was completed to Portsmouth in October 1833, and mule-drawn canal boats could make the trip from Columbus in 24 hours, the town became the busy southern outlet for the entire valley. Produce began to flow on regular schedule into Portsmouth where it was transferred to steamboats for Southern ports...

From 1832 to 1875 the river front from Scioto to Market Streets was jammed with boats unloading salt, flour and other merchandise and taking on pig iron, hollow ware and bar iron...

Since 1867 enormous quantities of stone for building and flagging have been quarried in more than 20 miles of ravines along the Ohio River, and shipped throughout Ohio, Indiana, Kentucky and West Virginia.

The city was placed so strategically that, as water traffic declined, it made an easy transition into an important railroad center...The Ohio and Erie Canal ran parallel with the west bank of the Scioto River."

—*The Ohio Guide*

"The Town Artisans of Early Portsmouth"
By Nelson A. Evans

"A lot between front and second streets: It had a blacksmith shop. Another was a residence and was convenient to the ferry which he maintained across the Scioto River where it meets the Ohio River.

There stood a big sycamore tree which was hollow and was used by the boys for shelter during storms. Mr. Glover was building a house for a hotel.

A one-story building was occupied by the cooper. A two-story brick house was occupied by a man who kept a tavern. One lot was occupied by a teamster who hauled goods up and down the river bank on a sled. On one lot was a residence and hatter shop; his brother an apprentice. Nearby was a small cabin kept by a tailor. One lot was used by Mr. Peebles for the manufacture of cut nails. On the east side of this lot was a small frame house where a brick maker had a brickyard.

On the sw. corner of 2nd and Jefferson streets was a store with a warehouse and stable. A cabinet maker's shop where "old smoking Johnnie Smith" worked. On the east part of the lot was a shoemaker's shop. A one-story building in which was kept a general retail store. On the remainder of the lot a dry goods and grocery store.

A small frame building in which Peter had a shoe shop. A small one-story frame house where David moved his school which had been conducted in a house. A two-story frame house was a dry goods and grocery store. In the second story was the commercial bank of Scioto with a president and a cashier. A one-story frame house was the Portsmouth Gazette…and a man established a book store and bindery.

A two-story log house: in that, one man conducted a carding machine and fulling mill. Opposite this lot in the center of Market St. stood the Court House, and about a hundred feet south of it was a public well, thirty feet deep.

A large elm tree in front of Prescott house: around it was the place for the militia to meet. The house was kept as a hotel. A log cabin was built on a lot. His wife was a great weaver…On the southeast corner of Washington and Front St. was a two-story log house on each lot. Darby used to make boat poles and oars for keel boats. On the west part of this lot two men had a wagon maker's shop.

A large cooper shop where three sons were coopers and employed three others. He also had two apprentices. He manufactured the entire cooperage of the lower end of the Scioto Valley.

One family was penniless except for a white horse; the father had died. A son built a sled and put a barrel on it, in which he and his brother conducted the water supply for a number of families who had no wells. He charged for each barrel a "flip," and with the receipts, the family was raised honorably."

The Reminiscences of James Emmitt

"It is next to impossible for the present generation to realize just how barren this country was of satisfactory methods of transportation for long distances prior to the opening of the Canal. In the early days; say up to 1822, we people in the interior had absolutely no means of transportation other than what was afforded by wagons drawn by horses or oxen, or by the primitive road that originated with Adam—afoot. The Ohio pioneers taught horses and oxen to draw themselves and burdens, and those living adjacent to navigable streams knew how to make rafts, and flat-boats, small craft and larger vessels useful. The people living along the sea coast, the lakes and rivers, enjoyed great advantages over their fellowmen in the interior country. They could ship their surplus products to markets at their command and could secure to themselves from other points, such produce or manufactured stuffs as were beyond their own immediate resources.

When that happy day arrived when we had a surplus, we had no home market of any consequence, and what corn we couldn't get off to New Orleans by flatboat, we could feed to hogs and cattle which could be driven, instead of transported to the eastern markets. But the condition of affairs was terribly unsatisfactory and commercial progress was well-nigh impossible.

You see, the pioneers of Scioto Valley developed in this way: they came out here from Virginia, Pennsylvania and the East, and settled in the wilderness, generally in the neighborhood of some river. A cabin was built, a clearing was made, and as soon as possible a crop put in. The rifle supplied the table with an abundance of choicest meats, and pretty largely, the male population with clothing. A few hogs and a cow or two were finally secured; the crops came on, and what corn was not needed for seed and meal was fed to the animals, and the animals were fostered and bred to the best advantage. Each succeeding year the clearing was extended, and the amount of grain put in increased accordingly, and after a while, the fields produced more than a family and stock could consume. Here was a surplus, to be turned into money or merchandise. But there was no place to sell it. Every man's neighbor was in a similar condition to himself. There was no market for the surplus. Everyone wanted money and manufactured goods; everyone had something that could be converted into these necessities could they get their surplus to a point where there was an excess of manufactured goods or money and a scarcity of produce and meats. But it was impossible to make the exchange owing to the lack of transportation facilities.

The great need of that early day—and it is the need of every new section of country at the present day—certain and cheap communication with the business world.

Dewitt Clinton offered a partial solution of this all-important problem when he built his great New York and Erie Canal which pointed the way by which interior places could find an outlet other than by wagon, to the points where their surplus was in demand. Out of it grew the really stupendous project of building the Ohio and Erie Canal to bring the Great lake regions and consequently the East into business relations with a vast and fertile interior region, and on through to the Ohio, the Mississippi and great marts of the South.

It was a great and daring conception for those days, and the prospect of its ever becoming a reality sent a thrill of joy through the people of this valley. Everyone knew that, with its coming would dawn such an era of prosperity as this valley had never known and hardly dared to hope for. Everyone had some well-thought plan devised to put into execution 'when the canal's built.' That expression qualified almost every utterance of a business scene. The people here, in the slowly yielding wilderness, looked upon the Canal project as the Jews did upon Moses. It was to get them out of the woods and bring them to the promised land of business, life and prosperity. And really, all these extravagant hopes were justified, for the isolated and transportation-bound condi-tion of our people, at that time, was most harrowing. The railroad was not dreamed of at that time, and the canal seemed to afford a marvelously convenient, rapid and economical method of getting over long distances...products to a profitable market.

The law authorizing the construction of the Ohio-Erie Canal was passed in the winter of 1824-25. It was to cost fully six mil-lion dollars."

—James Emmitt

Citizens' Reflections on the Early Days

"The ground now occupied by the city of Portsmouth was, when I first saw it, and for some time thereafter, almost an unbroken forest. The timber consisted of white oak, burr oak, black oak, beech, sugar, walnut, hickory, hackberry, maple, gum, elm, honey locust and buckeye. Along the margin of the streams; sycamore, elm, cottonwood, birch, maple and willow; the undergrowth of pawpaw, swamp alder, spice, dogwood and sassafras."

—A contributor who signed his name 'Scioto'

"There was only one road from the town to the Ohio River until about the year 1809-1810. ...At that time there was no such vehicle as dray, cart, or wagon in or about Portsmouth. Everything brought from the river was either hauled on sleds, packed on horses or car-ried by hand.

For the want of roads, the only transportation of the coun-try was by the navigable rivers in flat boats and keel boats, and the Scioto River forming its junction with the Ohio at that place, and the business men having established themselves there, it had become the principal landing for boats.

The first settlers ground their corn on hand mills, usually working at their respective occupations all day, and shelling and grinding corn in the evening or on rainy days.

At first, and for some years, the citizens sent to Chillicothe for their coffee, tea, salt, powder, lead, flour and store clothes. Their sugar and molasses were made from the sap that flows from the forest trees...Camps were built and those who engaged in the business left their houses, and during the sugar making season lived entirely in these camps. Men, women and children, taking their guns, dogs, cows and horses with them.

W.H., F.M., and U.B. were all owners and commanders of keel boats, with which goods and merchandise were transported from port to port. Those boats were pulled and warped up the Scioto River to Chillicothe and Circleville, when that furious stream was at a high stage. Darby made poles and oars such as were used in the management of these boats, in his log house."

—'Shelawoy' (a contributor)

"In 1791 St. Clair was defeated, and from that time until Wayne defeated the Indians in the fall of 1794, it was absolutely impossible for anyone to live on this north bank of the Ohio River between Marietta and Cincinnati, unless in a fortification.
In 1791, Nathaniel Massie and others built block houses, and fortified them with pickets at Manchester, on the north bank of the Ohio River."

—'Scioto'

"In addition to flints, large bullets, pieces of gun barrels and locks; stone axes, arrow heads of various sizes, glass beads and broken vessels made of clay or stone, were found at many places, and especially at and about the junction of Front and Scioto Streets.

The marks of the claws distinctly seen at so early a day on the back of the beech trees occupying the site of Portsmouth, were proof positive that the woods in that region were once inhabited by those animals. In fact, bear skins were as common among the first settlers in the making of beds and robes, as are buffalo skins at the present time…Almost every teamster and boatman carried with him his bear skin… some persons salted and smoked bear meat, converting it into bacon…

While the men were in the army during the War of 1812, squirrels in countless numbers swam the Ohio River from Kentucky to the Ohio shore, traveling north, and many families subsisted almost entirely on them and corn pone, and before that harvest was over, some families had a barrel each of squirrels salted down for future use. It requires no great stretch of the imagination to compare those squirrels to the manna sent from on High to relieve the wants of the children of Israel in their time of need. Few persons of the present day have any idea of the hardships their forefathers underwent, especially those who first settled the west.

When you are informed of the fact that the first settlers of that section of Ohio packed salt from Chillicothe and other points on horses, you will become aware that it was an important item with them. It was said that efforts were made to sink a well and manufacture salt, just below the Scioto on the bank of the Ohio River before Portsmouth was thought of.

The mechanical branches pursued by M. and H. argues strongly in favor of the latter having built the first boat…if indeed either one of those gentlemen did ever build one at Portsmouth. The most reasonable conclusion is the extreme scarcity of saw mills, lumber and ship carpenters considering that the *keel boats* were all built higher up on the Ohio River and brought here containing the families and moveable goods and property of their owners.

John McDowell…was not what is termed a "Sunday Christian," but he carried his religion into his business and daily transactions. It was found in his commission house in his prices, in his books, and in his weights and measures, as well as at his family altar, and in the house of worship."

—'Shelawoy'

PIONEER SKETCHES

C. CADOT: "Started as an emigrant to Gallipolis, arriving in fall of 1790. He engaged in keel boating with Mike fink for 63 cents a day. He followed this for four years and saved enough money to buy a quarter section of land. He found a ready market for all his produce having located near the busy furnaces in the *Hanging Rock* region of Ironton. He would go with a keel boat from Pittsburgh to Nashville and sometimes walk back."

E. GLOVER SR.: "His first visit to Ohio was in 1799 when he crossed the river to buy furs for his father's hat store in Kentucky. With another man, Crane, he went in a pirogue up the Scioto River to Chillicothe. On their way back, at the head of a mill race, the boat struck a snag, turned over and Crane lost all his furs. Afterwards this spot was called *Crane's Defeat.*"

W. EACH: "Born 1794 in N. Carolina. In about 1800, his family immigrated to Fleming County, Kentucky using three horses. The mother rode one, carrying a child. Two children rode another, and the third was used as a packhorse. The dad walked. He did land surveying in their neighborhood."

H. KINNEY: "He was born in 1815. His father gave him a farm when 21 which he sold, and with a brother started west to invest in real estate. It was their intention to invest in Chicago which at this time, was a mere cluster of huts and seeming a swamp. They decided not to invest there. He became a trader on the Mississippi River, buying produce and livestock, and transporting it to New Orleans to market. During one of these trips, the party became wind bound and narrowly escaped an encounter with the land and sea pirate, Lafitte, whom they learned a few days previously captured a flat boat loaded with cattle and murdered the crew. When he gave up flatboating, he returned to his farm and raised small fruit. In 1826 he went to Cincinnati and got a dozen grapevine cuttings. He was said to be the second man in Ohio to cultivate the grape."

J. WAIT: "He was born in 1811 on the shore of Lake Champlain. The family came to Ohio in 1814 from Vermont: They traveled by wagon to Pittsburg, and on to Portsmouth by the Ohio River. Young John decided to learn the trade of cabinet making and went to Pittsburg for that purpose. He remained two years, then went to Cincinnati and completed his course. He was very skillful and clever in designing and constructing furniture. He opened a combined shop and dwelling in Portsmouth where he made furniture, chairs, and for many years doing all the work by hand. Some of the finest mahogany goods in the way of sideboards, tables and parlor chairs were made here and they were so well made by his superior skill that some of them are in use to this day."

J. BACCUS: "About the year 1805, a widow living in Pennsylvania, sold her little home in the Monongahela hills, and with proceeds in pocket, set out for the wilderness of Scioto County. She came down the Ohio River with a few others, bringing her horse and a light outfit, and after her arrival, made a journey on horseback to the Government Land Office in Chillicothe, and entered Section 23 in Porter Township."

A. BOYNTON SR.: "Made the trip overland from N.H. to their new home in 1810; traveling in the family carriage and wagons, and were on the journey for six weeks... They did much to develop the country. He built a mill for grinding wheat and corn. The mill was run by horse power, and the bolt turned by hand. Often those who came to get the grinding done would furnish their own horse power thereby saving toll. It was difficult to get money for farm crops, so he built a flat boat in order to take cargo of produce to New Orleans, returning by steamboat."

SON, W. BOYNTON: "Bought the Ironton ferry and conducted it across the Ohio River."

MR. FUNK: "He lived on the old Chillicothe road and entertained waggoners to and from Chillicothe, and made much gain in that way. His home was a general stopping place. Mrs. Elizabeth Funk was an excellent cook, and a most efficient nurse in sickness. Many of those attacked with malaria resorted to her home and remained there till cured. She fell victim to malaria prevailing in 1822, and died that year at the age of fifty."

JAMES EMMITT: "If they had seen this country around here, as it was when I first saw it, they would understand why the first settlers took to the high ground. The growth of weeds and underbrush was wonderfully dense, and when floods would come and cover the bottoms, several inches of water would remain in these brakes of weeds for months…When land was cleared of timber, the sun speedily converted it into workable condition. Fever and ague became less prevalent."

D. HAHN: "At the age of 14 he left home, and being large for his age, he became a stage driver driving four horses over the Alleghany Mountains. He was a born driver and drove over the principal lines of the United States. He had a knack of managing horses. He came to Portsmouth when a young man, and became a driver on the stage line between Portsmouth and Columbus. His stage horn has waked the morning echoes many a time in front of the sign of the *Golden Lamb* on Front Street in Chillicothe. When he passed on, the notice was in all dramatic papers, and was stated that in driving over the Alleghenies, he had carried Gen. Jackson, Henry Clay, Pres. Harrison and Tyler."

LACROIX: "A French emigrant. He built a cabin and cleared ground for peach orchards. When a crop of peaches ripened, he distilled them and sent containers of peach brandy in flatboats to New Orleans. He gave attention to fruits; had orchards of apple trees. He had an encounter with a bear on the hills back of Franklin Furnace. The two rolled down the hill together."

J. SHAFER: "The family left Germany in 1819. They took a sailing ship at Amsterdam, Holland. After being out at sea for about a week, the vessel sprung a leak and had to put into the port of Lisbon temporarily, then out to sea bound for Baltimore. They arrived in 1820. He had spent all his means on the voyage and three of his oldest daughters *were bound out* at Baltimore from three to five years to pay for their passage of eighty dollars each. The others of the family proceeded by wagon to Brownsville on the Monongahela River, and thence to Portsmouth by flatboat. Mrs. Schafer died soon after their arrival. In August 1823, Geo. Schafer, one of the sons, walked to Baltimore to bring out his sisters. He made the trip one way in fourteen days. He brought his two elder sisters out in a wagon. The younger sister remained in Baltimore eight years longer; then came along."

"On Being Bound Out"
by James Emmitt

"There was a system in vogue then under which ship owners or speculators, would carry emigrants from their native country to America, providing the emigrants would enter into an arrangement permitting the person who had furnished them transportation, to sell them into bondage; giving of their labor for a certain length of time…to pay for their passage—which as may be imagined was always placed at an exorbitant figure. On reaching New York, they were sold to contractors…The grossest wrongs to emigrants were perpetrated under this system."

IRONTON, OHIO

"The city spreads over a crescent-shaped flood plain, hemmed in by the river and the hills. It became a strategic center for the iron industry because of extensive ore pockets in the vicinity: quantities of timber, coal, clay and limestone in the hills, and transportation by the Ohio River.

The ore deposits in the Ironton district were discovered about 1826. A Virginian who had come to Ohio and freed his slaves, set up the *Union,* the first charcoal furnace north of the Ohio River and began to make pig iron. Forty of these furnaces were erected throughout southern Ohio before the Civil War.

…During the Civil War, iron from this Hecla region was used for casting heavy ordinance and field guns because of its exceptional strength…The celebrated gun known as the *Swamp Angel at Charleston Harbor* was cast from Hecla iron.

As the Pittsburgh-Youngstown iron region rose, Ironton slowly declined."

—*The Ohio Guide*

"Iron Ores"

By Walter Havighurst

"An Empire within an Empire. The iron ores of Ohio are of small economic value at present, but in the pioneer days they were important factors in the development of the settlements and adjacent country.

'Insistent as was the demand for salt, the need for iron was even more imperative. Axes, hoes, scythes, sickles, log-chains, plow shares and augers were required even on the more primitive farms; while hollow ware, ranging in size from the smallest skillet to the ninety-gallon salt kettles, was almost as necessary. Nails and other building hardware were in demand as the log cabins were supplanted by frame houses. Bar iron from western Pennsylvania found a ready market in Ohio with the appearance of the first blacksmiths.'   —*William Utter*

Ohio is rich in common rocks and minerals needed for economic progress. The high development of the State is due in large measure to the abundance of mineral resources, and to their intelligent employment for many purposes...

By a generous gift of *geography*, the Great Lakes offered a transportation route in the midst of huge natural resources...Vessels carried copper from the rich mines of Lake Superior, limestone from the quarries on Lake Huron and Lake Erie, and oil from the wells of Pennsylvania.

But the greatest cargoes were iron. At the beginning of the age of steel, when some men were still fevered by the search for gold and silver, Andrew Carnegie made a quiet comment, "Gold is precious, but iron is priceless."

...A surveying crew on the rough south shore of Lake Superior found their compass needle swinging wildly. They found the first iron outcrop that led to the rich deposits of the Marquette range.

So, in 1853 they shipped the first iron ore, in barrels across Lake Superior. They portaged it in creaking wagons around St. Mary's rapids. They reloaded it in wind-born schooners for the port of Cleveland. Ultimately the Sault St. Marie Canal (The Soo) was opened, and in 1855 the Brig *Columbia* passed through the locks. On the deck was carried in little mounds like refuse, 132 tons of red iron ore. It was the first bulk shipment of iron ore down the Lakes. In 1943, less than a century later 80,000,000 tons of iron ore passed through great new locks of the Soo Canal."

—Havighurst

"At Cleveland, Lorain, Toledo, Ashtabula, and Conneaut, the Lake freighters unloaded their cargoes of Iron ore. To these same docks, long trains brought their heavy loads of coal from the mines of Ohio, Pennsylvania and West Virginia.

On their return voyage [to Lake Superior region], the empty hatches of the ore freighters were filled with coal for the homes and towns of the Northwest, just as the railroad cars were refilled with Lake Superior iron ore for the iron furnaces of Youngstown, Pittsburgh, and Steubenville.

The ports of Lake Erie were thus the meeting places of iron ore and coal, two of the most essential raw materials in manufacturing."

—William H. Van Fossen

"That lake-shipped ore went into railroad tracks and the loco-motives that ran on them. It went into harvesting machines and barbed-wire fences. It went into bridges and built the hulls of steamships. It was strung across the continent on telegraph poles. It went into motorcars and airplanes; into axes, saws, and hammers, bolts, nails and hinges, razor blades, the girders of skyscrapers and armor plate of dreadnoughts.

As the demand for iron ore grew, new sources of supply were uncovered to meet the urgency. Lake Superior was found ringed in iron hills: the Marquette range, the Menominee, the Gogebic, the Vermilion, and finally, the giant range, Mesabi...with its vast ore bodies lying just beneath the ground—All poured out their age-old ores to build the United States of America."

—Havighurst

GALLIPOLIS, OHIO

Breckenridge, in his recollections, gives some reminiscences of Gallipolis related in a style of charming simplicity. He was at Gallipolis in 1795, at which time he was a boy of nine years.

"Behold me once more in port, and domiciled at the house, or the inn of Monsieur, or rather Dr. Saugrain, a cheerful, sprightly little Frenchman, four feet six, English measure, and a chemist, natural philosopher, and physician, both in the English and French signification of the word...

This singular village was settled by people from Paris and Lyons; chiefly artisans and artists, peculiarly unfitted to sit down in the wilderness and clear away forests. I have seen half a dozen at work in taking down a tree; some pulling ropes fastened to the branches, while others were cutting around it like beavers. Sometimes serious accidents occurred in consequences of their awkwardness. Their former employment had been only calculated to administer to the luxury of highly polished and wealthy societies. There were carvers and gilders to the king, coach makers, freizure and peruke makers, and a variety of others who might have found some employment in our larger towns, but who were entirely out of their place in the wilds of Ohio.

Their means by this time had been exhausted, and they were beginning to suffer from the want of the comforts, and even the necessaries of life. The country back from the river was still a wilderness, and the Gallipolitans did not pretend to cultivate anything more than small garden spots; depending for their supply of provisions on the boats which now began to descend the river, but they had to pay in cash and that was becoming scarce.

They still assembled at the ballroom twice a week. It was evident, however, that they felt disappointment, and were no longer happy. The predilections of the best among them, being on the side of the Bourbons, the honors of the French Revolution; even in their remote situation, mingled with their private misfortunes which had at this time nearly reached their acme, in consequence of the discovery that they had no title to their lands, having been cruelly deceived by those from whom they had purchased. It is well known that Congress generously made them a grant of twenty thousand acres, from which, however, but few of them ever derived an advantage."

—From: Gallia County History

[The following is from *The History of Gallipolis* by Waldeurard Meulette, one of the colonists:]

"When at last the distribution of the lots of the French grant was achieved, some sold their share; others settled on it or put on tenants, and either remained at Gallipolis, or went elsewhere.

But how few entered again heartily into a new kind of life, after having lost many of their lives and much of their health amid hardships, excess of labor, or the indolence which follows discouragement and hopeless efforts! Few of the original settlers remain at Gallipolis; not many at the French grant."

MEIGS COUNTY
Pomeroy, Ohio

Log Cabin Reminiscences

The following are reminiscences of citizens of Pomeroy and Meigs County which were printed as a series in the Pomeroy newspaper, The Leader, beginning in 1898...The brief autobiographies of families, tell of events reaching well back into the early 1800s.

Their responses to the Leader's request were compiled into booklet form and titled, 'Log Cabin Reminiscences,' which was published by "The Meigs County Pioneer and Historical Society," in 1992. Their value lies in the uniqueness presented; not likely to be found in a general history of the United States. One can envision how they seemed to take deprivation in stride, and encountered hardships with the best means available to them; at the same time catching a glimpse of hope when a new invention or one of the great new innovations appeared on the horizon.

"The territory was covered by a vast wilderness, with but one road leading to the Ohio River...The little children had to be kept in the house as a protection from the fierce wolves, while the older ones had to herd the sheep from the beasts. There were but two houses in Pomeroy. I have seen corn growing where the city now stands. Corn was topped and bladed, leaving the ear on the stalk until a jolly corn husking party helped to gather it in...

The mode of traveling was on horseback by those who had horses. If they had no horses, then afoot. Oxen were used for farm work. Mr. Roush hauled goods to Athens with a double team which was the only way of getting goods into Athens." —R.J. Hiland

"I was born in 1816. We moved to Meigs County in the year '17 and occupied a cabin. I knocked about as all boys did in the woods at that time till I was 14 years of age when I went to Pomeroy to work for Mr. Horton who had a little saw mill at the mouth of Naylor's Run. We cut saw logs all along the present site of the city of Pomeroy. On the river banks where Pomeroy now stands, were the biggest paw-paw trees I ever saw. The trees of large size growing within what is now the city limits were sycamore, elm, beech, poplar and oak. Out of these trees, I helped cut the timber that entered into the construction of the old Moredock Mill. At this time deer were skipping all along the Pomeroy Bend, and it was no uncommon sight to see these animals at the river's edge or on the hills nearby, eight to ten in a herd. I have seen flocks of wild turkeys about where Pomeroy now stands fully as large as the flocks of tame turkeys now frequently observed on Meigs County farms. There were no buildings in Pomeroy then except a few shanties…The 'bend' did not then look as if it would ever be possible for a town to be built on it. There were no stores worth speaking of. There was a little grocery at the mouth of Kerr's Run carrying only the necessaries of life. Horton's little mill had a sash saw and was run by steam. He cut timber for barges and for the buildings the people had then begun erecting.

There was no road then along the banks of the Ohio River where Pomeroy stands—only a bridle path. And if there had been a road, there would have been no wagons or buggies to travel it… I have a cane made in 1792 which belonged to Gen. Matson, a great uncle of mine who served in the Revolutionary War, and was wounded in the Battle of Bunker Hill."

—D. M. Bailey

"Meigs in 1838: When we landed where Pomeroy now stands, I remember seeing a goat on the rocks, high up and expected it to tumble, but it was at home on the high hill. I can see the dear old cabin with its big fireplace with its blazing fires around which the neighbors would sit when they came to spend winter evenings…The pan of turnips and apples were brought in from the garden where they were holed up for winter use, but were brought in for the visitors to eat while they enjoyed the evening. No matter how many children came to stay all night, the two trundle beds would hold them all.

When I was very little girl, my father made me a present of a little spinning wheel to spin flax on.

We had to have our shoes made by shoemakers. Father would buy leather, make the pegs, and mother would spin the thread to make the shoes with. When there were a great many ahead of us, we would have to wait for our shoes till our turn came and sometimes it would be near the middle of winter. All shoes looked alike.

When I was nine, my brother plowed with oxen and then I drove the oxen while he planted a field of buckwheat.
Teacher played a fiddle and smoked a pipe during recess and noon. There was no main road, and we had to go to school through the pine woods and how lovely it looked covered with snow."

—M. Anderson

"The small stream which passes into the river was quite a stream which often during a storm became a rushing torrent. This stream was crossed by a rough bridge of logs. The children who often came miles to this school, placed their dinner pails among the rocks at the edge of the water where shaded by the willows, their milk kept fresh and cool. During one storm the stream arose, and carried off their lunches which created quite a panic."

—A Pioneer Granddaughter

A Brief History

"In 1833, Mr. Pomeroy having purchased most of the coal land on the Ohio River for four miles, formed a company and began mining on a large scale. They built a steam saw-mill and commenced building houses for themselves and their workmen. In 1834, there were twelve families in the town. In 1835, the steam tow-boat Condor was built. The coal was carried out of the hillside in cars on railways, and emptied from the cars on one grade to that below; until the last cars in turn emptied into the boats on the Ohio River.

A tragedy in 1834 turned the Pomeroy mines into an immediate success...A cholera epidemic struck the Ohio Valley, including Meigs County...Someone in Cincinnati decided Pomeroy coal could slow the spread of the disease because of its high sulfur content. For that reason, Cincinnati started burning the coal on every street corner. It was not effective, nonetheless it gave the Pomeroy mines a needed boost in business. The increased business meant more available jobs, and Irish, Welsh and German immigrants filled the need.

By 1870 Pomeroy with a population of five thousand, was a rather prosperous town. River traffic was heavy. There were machine shops, an organ factory, buggy and wagon factory, cooper shops, tanneries, cobbler shops, blacksmith shops, boat builders, and millinery shops.

Products from these industries were shipped up and down the Ohio River from Pittsburgh to Cincinnati, and those, as well as many passengers, crossed the bustling wharf boat; probably the most interesting and exciting place in town.

'The extreme rise and fall of the rivers made fixed piers impractical. Many towns and cities paved their landings with stone, and embedded mooring rings into the pavement. They were expensive to build and maintain.

Wharfboats were the most practical alternative. They were old steamboat hulls with the machinery removed. All or part of the structure was remodeled to accommodate storage for perishable goods, freight consignment offices, and rooms for waiting passengers. Since they were tied to the shore, they rose and fell with the River and made excellent docks.'

Here at the wharf, the river boats nudged their way to the landing; aiming for the wharf boat. The 124x40 foot wharf boat had an apartment upstairs for the care-taker of night traffic. The night steamboat pilot was guided on his course by oil lamps hung on high poles at the bends of the River.

People learned to distinguish boat whistles such as the Bonanza, Tacoma, or Klondike, coming around the bend. At the wharf, incoming freight was quickly unloaded and outgoing was re-loaded.

Meigs County had always been closely tied to the steamboat era. Early farmers made money hauling wood on small wood-boats. The boats would go out to passing steamboats, nudging alongside of them, and whoever was willing, would assist in the transfer of wood. The Condor was built at a Cincinnati boatyard, and was the first boat in the world to successfully use coal for fuel rather than wood.

The Steamboat advanced civilization along The Ohio River.

It was a pretty sight to travel by boat along the Pomeroy bend at night, and see the twinkling of village lights reflecting on the Ohio River."

—Meigs County Pioneer and Historical Society

Pomeroy (from an old postcard)

MEIGS COUNTY MEMORIES

From: Log Cabin Reminiscences

"We lived on a farm about a mile from Reedsville. At that time all roads were dirt, and as there was no school bus, we walked to school, and when the roads were muddy, we walked through the fields. There was always a cross cow in at least one field. We had a creek to cross, and when it rained that was always fun. The school and church were the only places we had to go. In the winter my father would hitch his horses to a big sled and pick everyone up and take them to church. Later the showboats came on the river and sometimes we were allowed to attend a show. In summer we

345

swam and fished in the Ohio River. On my 10th birthday, Dad took me by train to see my first circus."

—Major Reed

"While attending Portland Elementary school, I first rode in a school wagon pulled by horses. My grandfather was a produce man shipping produce: vegetables, eggs and chickens from Portland to Pittsburgh on the steamboat *Senator Cordell*. He owned and operated a ferry from Kenauga to Point Pleasant W.Va. for many years."

—M. McDade

"Away back in the '50s, I remember mounting our gentle old horse and riding around the lane to the tannery while my father walked across. He was a tanner by trade. The building was a large one having several compartments. One large room was devoted to dressing hides and finishing leather ready for market. A large and well-ventilated room upstairs was kept filled with dry tan-bark ready for use. In a large room in one end of the building stood the bark mill; a huge iron hopper with a long sweep attached. Father would break up a quantity of bark, hitch the horse to the sweep, tell me to keep the hopper full, then leave me to grind while he went to his task of dressing leather. My task would become a little irksome, and I would amuse myself by riding around the well-beaten track on the sweep by the side of the horse. I helped my dad lay away many a vat full. It took six months in those days to tan a pack of hides.

He was one of the kindest of fathers. I never remember from him giving me a cross word…One time the girls hid his apron, and He watched his chance to blacken their faces with lamp black. Those were days of anti-slavery and the fugitive slave law. My dad longed for the chance to help a poor fugitive from bondage to freedom on the so-called, "Underground Railway."

—Aunt Nine

"One of the most important duties of a teacher at that time was to make a quill pen. Parents were then almost compelled to keep a few geese to get quills for their children to take to school…I needed a first Reader. Mother placed two dozen eggs in a little basket and let me go to Bungtown to get the book. Eggs were worth three cents per dozen, and the price of the book was six cents. I had about one mile to go and went in a hurry. I slipped and fell and broke nearly all my eggs. I went into the store amid my sobs and tears and told the store keeper all about it. "Well Bub, you shall have the book." I went home happy a boy as you ever saw. In later years when I think of the occurrence, how I love that man for his kindness to me when I was a little boy." —J.P. Stancart, Bedford

"I have known my father to ride to Gallipolis on horseback to get a metal plow-point. He could not get one nearer. I have seen him plow with a wooden mold-board plow. I never rode in a buggy until 1846."

—W. Humphrey

"Groceries were scarce. We would take a sack of wheat to Gallipolis, a distance of 18 miles, and trade it for groceries. After putting in our crop, we would go to the [Ironton] furnace, and cut cord-wood, stay in a shanty, and do our own cooking. Our meals were composed of corn bread, meat and coffee."

—G. M. Spires

"My father was a blacksmith, and made a great many bells for the neighbors to put on their cows so they could find them, the woods were so extensive. The men used to take their wives on a horse behind them, and go three or four miles to spend the evening with other pioneer settlers. They had no buggies, no railroads, no farming machinery, no steam mills.

Look at the great oil fields and the grand old hills for grazing cattle and sheep where they can lie down under the beautiful shade trees. Those hills were filled with coal for future generations where the majestic poplar and oak grew abundantly."

—C. Stevens

"My grandfather left eastern Pennsylvania in the spring of 1796 in company with other emigrants for the then "far West"—the Ohio Valley. They drove ox teams. Their mode of travel was to drive till evening when they would halt, and turn out their oxen; the boys watching them that they didn't stray off from camp. The old folks and the girls would sleep in the wagons, and the boys slept under the wagons. As soon as it was light, they drove up the cattle and when breakfast was over, and everything packed up, they would hitch up and drive on, day after day till they got to Duquesne, now Pittsburg. They sold their teams and got a boat and floated down the Ohio River."

—unknown

"My grandfather emigrated from near Utica, N. Y., and settled about one mile west of Chester in Meigs County in 1816 with a family of ten children; my father was four...Father engaged in tanning together with farming on a small scale, boat building and merchandizing in the village dealing in goods which were in demand in those days: groceries, dry goods, Queensware, hardware and ammunition...Twice a year he would go to Kerr's Run, *hail* the first up-bound Steamboat, and go to Pittsburgh to lay up his stock of goods.

In early times the merchandise laid upon the bank until the teams came to haul it away. The whole county seemed to have cognizance of the date of their arrival, and his store for two weeks was the center of attraction. For weeks, sometimes months, calicoes, factory goods, ammunition and iron could not be had until the new goods came in.

In 1840 at Chester there were various 'mechanics'. One carded wool and made it into rolls available for farmer's wives. Two were blacksmiths; there were stone and brick masons...millers, tanners, chair and furniture makers, attorney, farmers, a wagon maker, a cabinet maker, and one was learning the tailor's trade. There was a physician, a shoe maker, hatter, harness maker and a sheriff. They told of the songs that were sung in their Vermont homes, and of 'oats, peas, beans and barley growing on the banks of the beautiful Ohio'...of the grandeur, the beauties and fertility of the land...

Not only from my relatives, but from numerous old settlers, I learned that my life had missed the severe deprivations of the early settlers of Ohio.

In my young days, among those early settlers, I saw old Revolutionary War Soldiers. They came to the 4th of July celebrations always held in Chester. They came to the old time 'militia drills,' and turned out to hear the great orators of the political campaigns. Everybody came to hear the latest views. Those old heroes have long since disappeared, and few of us old fellows have it to tell to our grandchildren that we, with our own eyes, saw Revolutionary Soldiers, talked with them, and shook hands with them."

—J. Hull

LOG CABIN REMINISCENCES

"Dr. Brown served the surrounding area of Dexter, Salem, Langsville and Rutland as country doctor. He grew many of the plants used in making his medications. When dried, they were reduced to powders by mortar and pestle. Among plants grown were poppies, foxglove, lobelia, delphinium, catnip, peppermint, boneset, and ginseng. He delivered boy babies for three dollars and girl babies for two dollars.

When I was seven, I plowed as much as any man. At that time my father had a practice of 30 miles, and had to ride on horseback following cow paths through the timber. I well remember making a solemn vow that I never would be a doctor as I had to get out at all times and kinds of night to get and take care of father's horse."

—Stevenson

"Dr. Hensley made house calls in a buggy, and after a hard day, he would tell the horse to go home and then he fell asleep till they arrived.

I worked at my trade making wagons between three and four a year. I moved to Meigs County in 1848. I also built a log cabin for my shop. I worked at my trade in one end of the cabin, part of the time being after night; our light being a piece of muslin twisted, put in a saucer, with grease poured over it."

—C. B. Harkins

"Those were days that I look back to with fond remembrance, and when someone tells how they used to go to mill, it makes me think how I used to be put on the old horse's back, and my sack of corn on in front, and how it would fall off, and I would have to go to the nearest house, and get someone to go with me, and put it back on again. And how we used to go to the neighbors to pumpkin parings, corn husking and apple peelings. What fun we used to have! And how I used to go after the cows and how I got lost for a day and had to be hunted up by my folks."

—M. K. Roush

"The logs for the building had been previously hauled with oxen or horses and put in place upon the ground. At an early hour the neighbors of the community began to arrive on foot and on horseback, and in a very little while, there were dozens of men ready for work.

The conduct of men in those days was apparently quite different from today. They were all on a level. They were all back-woodsmen. They were industrious of course, and were content if they had plenty to eat, drink and wear. They were dressed alike. They all had cow hide boots or shoes, jeans pants and flannel shirts. They were neighbors in the truest and highest sense of that magnificent term. They laughed, joked, played pranks on each other, and had the liveliest and jolliest of times from the minute the first two men got together upon the ground until the last two left for their homes. The passage of almost every log from the ground to its place upon the building was attended by many explosions of wit and humor. And how everybody at spells, did laugh. The laughs were of the vigorous sort and made the forest ring."

—"X"

CHAPTER 26

The Erie Canal

PROPOSAL, CONSTRUCTION AND
CONTRIBUTION TO NEW YORK

"At the close of the 18th century, the population in the United States was confined largely to the Atlantic coastal region. Movement of settlers westward and of produce eastward was sharply limited because of poor roads; scarcely more than forest and mountain trails which made transportation costs almost prohibitive. By 1800 in Massachusetts, New York, Pennsylvania, Maryland and Virginia, serious consideration was given to proposals for the development of land or of water transportation from the Atlantic Seaboard to the West including construction of canals...that the great central valley west of the Appalachian Mountains could be settled rapidly.

In 1810 DeWitt Clinton, later governor of New York, supported a water route across the State to open transportation from Albany to Lake Erie at Buffalo. He traveled to Washington, D.C to seek aid for his project, but was unsuccessful. However, the citizens of New York refused to abandon plans for a canal, and in 1817 the legislature authorized the expenditure of $7,000,000 on the credit of the State for the construction of the canal.

Construction: The Canal was 363 miles long, 40 feet wide and 4 feet deep. The route west from Troy and Albany followed the Mohawk valley through a wild and sparsely settled region…It carried boats over a more than 500 ft. rise in elevation from Troy to the Lake Erie water level by the use of 82 locks. The canal was built solely by horsepower and man power. No roads existed over which supplies could be hauled. The canal was built through Montezuma swamp, and was carried across several streams in watertight aqueducts. In several places it was necessary to cut though rock; aided only by the use of black blasting powder.

On October 25, 1825, the Erie Canal was opened. The canal boat, "Seneca Chief" left Buffalo for Albany with Governor Clinton and other officials. On board, were two kegs of Lake Erie water; later poured into the harbor at New York to signify the merging of inland Lakes with the Atlantic Ocean.

The Erie Canal contributed directly, not only to the development of the entire region through which it passed, but also to the growth of New York City, Albany and Buffalo. It served as the main artery for both freight and passenger traffic between New England and New York, and the rapidly growing States of Ohio, Indiana, Illinois and Michigan…To the western terminus of the canal at Buffalo, were hauled supplies for westward moving settlers; machinery and other manufactured goods. Increasing amounts of grain grown by those new residents, was freighted to Buffalo for shipment through the Canal, to Albany, to the port of New

York and thence to European markets. The number of lake boats entering and leaving Buffalo harbor increased 150% during the first two years of the operation of the Erie Canal…Transportation time from Albany to Buffalo was cut from 15 days by wagon to 6 days by Canal."

—The Encyclopedia Britannica

LOCKPORT

"One of the most difficult feats of the entire project was the climbing of the Niagara Escarpment, a solid rock ridge at the west end of the route. Here, Roberts pierced a solid mixture of limestone and flint using black blasting powder to cut a flight of five double locks, each with a lift of twelve feet; thus producing the famed Lockport Locks. It took two years to do it, but when completed, every man on the job was proud of every lock that they had blasted out of nearly solid rock. This was the major obstacle to join the canal with the waters of Lake Erie at Buffalo. When the Canal was opened on October 26, 1825, the populace of the entire State declared a holiday."

—"Best of American Canals"

In 1843, stated in honor of the rise of the village of Lockport:

"Oh! Rock enthroned! Fair daughter of the West. …Thou art here, so full of commerce, busy, bustling, gay! The splashing of a hundred water wheels, the hum of industry of a thousand hammers, the sharp clink, and all the varied forms of wealth-producing industry—that one may almost turn the ear incredulous at the great changes. See! Through thy streets, how Erie's waters come, wafting the golden wealth of the Great West, and dashing down thy mountain, bearing away a tide of plenty on toward Hudson's tide."

—*The Niagara Democrat*

"DIVINITY ATTRIBUTED"

"Historian Burns stated that the New Yorkers of 1817-1825 who completed the Erie Canal, altered the whole pattern of economic and social development of the United States: The function of the Canal; that of uniting our inland rivers with our ocean ports."

E. WATSON: "The argument was hard to counter that this was indeed a Divinely created pathway…The passageway through the mountains and the phenomenon of the Hudson River Valley gave the New York State Canal planners their essential link with the Atlantic Ocean. Before geology attempted to figure out the reason for things, *Divine Intent* was credited as sufficient explanation for both of these God-given routes."

—Russell Bourne

PROFESSOR MCNALL of Genesee Valley, "The Lakes with their natural outlet through the St. Lawrence, together with the Mississippi and its branches, presented to him such a scene of inland navigation as cannot be of parallel in any other part of the World.

'No situation on the globe offers such extensive and numerous advantages to inland navigation by a Canal as this.' So favored a condition Hawley attributed to the *Hand of God*:

'Nor do I conceive the idea to be vain, or even incorrect in saying that it appears as if the Author of Nature…had in prospect a large and valuable Canal to be completed at some period in the history of man, by his ingenuity and industry.'"
—*Hosack,* Memoir of DeWitt Clinton

"Most of the materials needed for construction were found near the canal. The engineers discovered a clay or *muck* called, 'the blue mud of the meadows' which served as a canal lining in order to prevent water seepage."

—Ronald Shaw

"A young engineer, Canvass White, was sent to Europe in fall of 1817 to inspect the canals of the Old World. He returned with copious notes and drawings and new instruments. Proper cement for the stone locks could be procured only from Europe and at great expense. The decision was made to put the blocks together with quicklime mortar, and use the expensive European cement only for 'pointing.' Within a few months after his return from abroad, White discovered a deposit of stone near Chittanango on the line of the canal from which an excellent grade of hydraulic cement could be made. Factories to manufacture the cement were built."

—*"Best of the Canals Number V"*

"BRITISH TRAVELERS TO THE GENESEE COUNTRY"

"In the young village [of Rochester] there was not to be found in 1827, a single grown-up person born there; the oldest native not being then 17 years of age. The population is composed principally of emigrants from New England...Countries represented also: Germany, England, Ireland and Scotland.

We strolled through the village of Rochester under the guidance of a native of this part of the country. Everything in this bustling place appeared to be in motion. The very streets seemed to be starting up of their own accord, readymade, and looking as fresh and new, as if they had been turned out of the workmen's hands but an hour before...The canal banks were at some places still un-turfed; the lime seemed hardly dry in the masonry of the aqueduct in the bridges...In many of these buildings the people were at work below stairs, while at the top the carpenters were busy nailing on the planks of the roof.

... Here and there we saw great warehouses without window sashes, but half-filled with goods and furnished with hoisting cranes, ready to fish up the huge pyramids of flour barrels, bales and boxes lying in the streets. In the center of the town the spire of a Presbyterian church rose to a great height, and on each side of the dial-plate of a clock, the machinery in the rush had been left at New York. I need not say that these half-finished, whole-finished streets were crowded with people, carts, stages, and cattle.

Rochester is the best place we have yet seen for giving strangers an idea of the newness of this Country. In 1815 there was a population of 300 persons. Now it amounts to upwards of 8000, and this morning we have been to see various manufacturing carried on: pails, window sashes, etc., besides sawmills and flour mills and everything bespeaking activity and industry."

—Basil Hall

"I was informed that more than 12,000 bushels of wheat were daily ground in these mills; the produce is chiefly sent to New York. The most singular feature of this bustling infant town is the condition of the environs, which are still very much in a state of nature.

The transition from a crowded street ... to the forest is so sudden that a stranger, by turning a wrong corner in the dusk, might either be in danger of breaking his neck over the enormous stumps of trees, which as yet, there has been no time to clear away; or, escaping that calamity, might soon be entangled in the labyrinth of the woods which environs this place.

Amidst all this grinding of corn, shipping of flour, unpacking and retailing of manufactures, felling of trees and building of houses, we found the refinements of life were not neglected. Music was taught to all the young girls, and in a ballroom over the apartment in which we dined at the hotel, Monsieur was giving dancing lessons."

—James Boardman

"The Canal route has its peculiar beauties and attractions; every few miles brings you to a village or a hamlet—and the elegant church spire or commodious belfry tells you...that you are in a Christian Country among an opulent and religious people."

—William Mackinzie

"Of the *aqueduct,* a Spaniard, de la Segra wrote, 'The canal passes over an artificial bed of prodigious height in such a fashion that from the road, we watched the boats laden with passengers and merchandise moving along at a height of 70 feet above our heads.'"

—*The Rochester Historical Society*

TRANSPORTING PRODUCTS ON THE ERIE CANAL

"When the canals were first completed, many farmers who lived nearby built their own boats to carry their produce to market. Farmers loaded their own boat, and started for a town such as Utica or Harrisburg to sell grain or produce…One boat loaded with wheat; another loaded with corn; others carrying barrels of cider, molasses, salt pork, bags of corn meal, crates of eggs, and hams or bacons smoked in little smoke houses out on their farms.

Another boat is nearly full of bags of wool, clipped from sheep which graze on the prairies of Indiana and Illinois. We see large rolls of leather, too, tanned by men who own little tanneries…One of these rolls of leather is very important to such a man, and he is very anxious about it until he hears that it has been delivered, and he receives his pay for it.

One day in 1825, an Erie Canal boat passed Albany with a thousand turkeys, ducks and geese on board. These fowls would be shipped to the West Indies.

From Syracuse where there were great salt factories, you saw whole boatloads of salt going this way and that. Rochester had several large flour mills, and many boat-loads of wheat came into that town, and with many loads of flour going out.

Brick, lime, cement, lumber, and other things used in building houses were also carried in large quantities.

From cities like Boston, New York and Philadelphia came boats loaded with manufactured goods and things from foreign countries—machinery, tools, farm implements, hardware, sewing machines, sugar, coffee, and many other kinds of freight.

A great deal of freight carried on the Erie Canal was going to or from New York City. From Albany where the Canal ended, the route was down the Hudson River to New York. Boats which came through the canal fully loaded with freight for New York City, did not unload it at Albany, but were towed down the Hudson River to New York, by steamboat.

A group of four or more canal boats were tied together by ropes making a sort of fleet, and the steamboat towed them down the Hudson. When the boats were unloaded at New York, the captain or owner of each boat tried to get a load of merchandise to take back."

—Alvin Harlow

"Hundreds of bills of lading are preserved. In 1836, the boat Venice of Rochester…carried 38,000 pounds of merchandise to canal ports between Troy and Buffalo. In 1842, the boat *Massachusetts* of Elmira carried seven passengers, 100,000 pounds of flour and smaller amounts of tallow, cheese, apples, lard, ashes, peaches and high wines from Buffalo to Albany. *Equity* of Rochester carried 13,332 pounds of furniture from Albany to Buffalo. At Holley the boat picked up two dozen eggs and half a barrel of molasses, and at Rochester, five and a half barrels of fish, a cask of oil and a cask of butter. Passengers were picked up for trips of varying lengths. The interesting addition to the clearance, "30 Dutchmen migrating."

—Clearance of boat *Equity*, Collector's
Office, *Albany Comptroller Papers*

"Canal boats filled with emigrants, and covered with goods and furniture, are almost hourly arriving. The boats are discharged of their motley freight…to purchase necessaries, or to inquire the most favorable points for their future location. Several steamboats and vessels daily depart from Buffalo for the far West literally crammed with masses of living beings to people those regions...As I have stood upon the wharves and seen the departure of these floating taverns, with their decks piled up in huge heaps with furniture and chattels of all description...and to witness this spectacle year after year, for many months of the season, I have almost wondered at the amazing increase of our population, and the inexhaustible enterprise and energy of the people! What a Country must the vast border of these Lakes become! And Buffalo must be the great emporium and place of transit for their products and supplies."

—*Rochester Daily Advertiser*, June 1832

"Our steamboat is crowded with goods, and 200 passengers left Buffalo. We have been favored all the way with agreeable captains and good company. The Lake looks green but is perfectly calm; evening had a fine shower. Called at Erie and Cleveland, small villages. The fifth day in the morning we heard plenty of music. Sandusky lights were in sight, and we landed about 11 in the evening; just two weeks since we left Jersey...I remembered my friends in Jersey, and felt happy to think although widely separated, the same bright luminary of the setting sun was shining on them."

—Sibyl Tatum

"Farmers and mechanics are best adapted for the country, and if they are industrious, they are sure to succeed. The term *mechanics* includes a great variety of occupations, but the most important embraced by our subject are *masons, brick layers, carpenters, cabinet makers, blacksmiths* and generally all classes calculated for building houses, making implements of husbandry, erecting mills and machinery. Emigrant mechanics are constantly going from the eastern to western states."

—John Melish

"BUFFALO"

By Frank Oppel

"Approach Buffalo from the harbor side. In the foreground stands the most imposing row of bread distributors on the Lakes. The mammoth grain elevators of Buffalo Creek, nearly 40 of them, a mile long; the combined storage capacity of 9,250,000 bushels. The power of receiving from Lake vessels, and transferring to canal boats and cars daily: 3,000,000 bushels of wheat...It is not uncommon to see a large Lake vessel unloading and two canal boats and two trains of freight cars loading at the same time.

In 1842, J. Dart from Buffalo built the first steam storage transfer elevator with power to raise 1,000 bushels an hour; today 19,000 bushels an hour: Watch the legs of the two towers of this huge elevator drop upon a mass of wheat in the hold of a lake vessel moored at its wharf, and the buckets dip down into the grain, and rush with lightning speed up into the roof of the building where they deposit their load into the bins."

The harbor of this queen city of the Lakes will vie with that of Liverpool in its endless docks and warehouses."

—F. Oppel, 1885

"THE TIDE OF HUMAN FREIGHT WESTWARD"

"If he desires a most charming water trip, he embarks also via Buffalo on one of the handsome steamboats which ply the Lakes between this city and Chicago, and steaming down the length of Lake Erie, up through the narrower St. Clair and the broad Huron, he passes the wooded shores of Mackinac's beautiful Island, surmounted by its old fort, and enters Lake Michigan. In due time he is landed on the breezy Milwaukee banks, or is set down within that maelstrom of business, named Chicago. Indeed, after Chicago, Buffalo is the ranking city of the Lakes."

—Willard Glazier

"THE FANCY PATENT AND OTHER FLOUR INTERESTS"
(A poignant, humorous tale)

"Upon the warehouse floors is written a history of our commerce. They are dented by contact with freight from all continents, and strewn with samples of the products of every climate: Tea and coffee and cinnamon, fragrant oils and cloves and spices.

Half of the building is devoted to the flour interest, and each one of the hundreds of samples is carefully labeled. Some of the names of the brands are serious, but many are fanciful and funny. Flour is *Patent Process, Fancy Patent, Standard, Choice and Extra Choice, Old Glory, Minnesota Pride, Sublime,* and so on. Everybody here is nearly as white as a miller before the morning is over. You observe a grave-faced man with his whiskers all meal, take some flour in the hollow of his hand, pour upon it a few drops of water from a silver tankard, and solemnly work it into dough, which he kneads and pats and rolls, folds, and worries, judging by the result how good a loaf of bread it will make. He takes another brand of flour and repeats the operation…We saw sold 20 carloads of wheat bought by a gentleman who intends shipping it to the English market in a Liverpool steamer."

—Harpers Magazine; 1877 New York

"A CANALLER'S DIARY"
By William E. Charles, age 18

"It was a grand sight to see the harbor full of ships and the great buildings and the traffic and movement everywhere about us. One thing we did see that was hard to believe, were street cars in New York still drawn by horses. We came back to the boats after an interesting time. Our boat is unloaded. Late in the afternoon a tug comes and picks us up and takes us up the East River, gathering boats here and there. It is glorious to see the city in the twilight and to watch the lights come on as the night sets in. During the night we are taken down to Elizabeth, New Jersey."

"THE CANAL BRIDE"
By Dorcas Robie

"Several years after my Grandfather Adams' death, a leather-bound ledger was found in a trunk of his. It contained a few scattered pages of a diary in a delicate, feminine hand. Who the diarist was I do not know; perhaps a relative." (From: "Grandfather Stories" by Samuel Adams.)

"You, Dorcas!" My weeping mother said, "Daughter of an honorable judge. Graduated at great cost from a Female Academy of Elegant Learning. You, to throw yourself away upon a rough and rude canaller! Reflect, my child, reflect, ere it be too late."

"My father bewailed that I should be sundered apart from all ties with decent home-keeping, dry-land folk. Could they but see me now, as I sit easeful and ladyish upon my spotless foredeck!

One hundred feet ahead, our senior hoggee guides the tandem sorrels that draw on. The younger boy is currying down the relief team between decks. The deckhand is fishing over side with a slab of salt pork. My husband, captain and owner, stands watchful at the tiller. Though I make my boast, and who should not, there is no master upon Erie Water more macrooni and personable than Captain Angus Robie of the *Starry Flag*...

We are now in the Long Level, having passed through the massive five-fold locks at Lockport. For sixty-three miles to the Genesee River there is neither lock, block, nor stay to traffic. We could make our fifty miles a day were it not that we must stop to take on freights.

Before me the stupendous prospect charms the eye. Forty feet from bank to bank the canal spreads. Its depth of four feet can support the mightiest bottom afloat. The hand-built towpath is three hundred and sixty-five miles long. As for the traffic, not all the argosies of Greece could equal this spectacle. There are line boats, packets boats, gala boats, counter-sterns, dugouts, arks, flats and always the slow rafts; all transporting such cargoes as were never before conceived of.

Albany to Buffalo by wagon, the *Starry Flag*, freights for six dollars in a fourth of the time. Where are now the malcontent politicasters who dubbed this greatest of man-made achievements, "Clinton's Folly," and declared that the "Governor's Gutter" would go dry for lack of patronage?

Utica is our port. Below decks we carry cargo for the asheries, both pot and pearl; and fifty bales of cedar shingles for the fast-building town of Rome. Amidships we have fresh fish in barrels for delivery in Rochester, and such general merchandise as turnips, cloth in bales, gin in pipes, mirrors, furniture, axes, saws and mauls, and ten fine head of merino sheep. Every few miles we are hailed by farmers, standing on their private docks and offering us goods for transportation or wishing to bargain for what we have aboard.

We pass through a wild and ragged land. Few are the clearings. The farmsteads are mostly rough cabins. Everywhere the roadless forest stretches. Only the Grand Erie Canal brings to this desolate region the blessings of commerce and civilization.

Night falls while we are still in the wilds. Half asleep, I hear the steersman's call, "Look for a post," and the weary hoggee's grateful answer: *Post-O! Snub in*, the steersman orders. We ease over against the berm for our night-berth. The gangplank is run out. The tandem tramps aboard, for we are no rich packet boat with fresh relays every twelve or fifteen miles. We carry our own draught-stock.

Nearby from a thicket comes a piggish grunting. A bear is busy with his nightly concerns. From afar the wind brings the desolate howling of wolves.

FRIDAY: A rude awakening this morning. My husband's musket, with which he conquered the redcoats in 1813, has shot a skulking wolf, and now jumps ashore to skin the animal which will put a ten dollar bounty in our money-box. As everyone aboard is roused by the clamor, we make a timely start...

SATURDAY: How happy I am to be in Rochester! Only a few years ago the town was derided as 'an emporium of mud and outcasts.' Now it is the swiftest-growing city in our great Nation. Here we shall take on fifty barrels of white flour from the water-powered mills along the Genesee River. We shall lay up in the basin. Other boats will be moored there. I shall visit and be visited by the wives of other captains. From them I shall hear what goes on in this fine, new water-world of ours...

SUNDAY: This is the Sabbath. No keel stirs along the length of Erie Water, save only their cockahoop high-mightinesses, the *packet* boats, by special privilege of the Canal Commission. Honest trading craft must remain wharfed or basined at whatever risk and damage to their freights, while the through *packets* break God's Holy law at four miles per hour.

Though bells are ringing in the nearby village of Perrington, we worship on the Gospel Raft of the Wembley brothers, equally powerful in prayer, exhortation and song. This day no less than two hundred canallers of all sects have attended. Captain Robie and I worshipped at morning service...and evening service. Now at 11:00 p.m., the good brothers are holding their Refreshment of Song. Across the waters are the harmonies of their lap organ. I shall sink happily to sleep soothed and exalted by those distant voices singing...

MONDAY: East of Rochester we pass through a new world improved and nurtured by the canal traffic. Where before there was desolation and wilderness, we now come to a region of thriving villages, wharves, basins, frequent occupation bridges, and waterside taverns.

Here the towpath has become a free-to-all highway for a vagrant world…all the riff and the raff of the itinerant trades.

Item: A knife-grinder with cart and bell. "Sharpen 'em up, lady? Whet all your cutlery for sixpence."

Item: A goose-girl with a dozen of her charges, arguing in Dutch, against the Pathmaster's angry English, that her birds should have privilege of the path.

Item: A puppet show of Punch and Judy; mortal visible for a penny …

Item: Three felonious woodsmen on their way to jail in the charge of a constable, for felling the state's trees…

Truly, a great and wonderful world. Where, otherwise than on the Grand Erie Canal could one witness such a human panorama!

A hoggee of the packet, *Storm Queen* was bitten on Saturday by a rattlesnake taking its comfort in the warm dust of the towpath. A doctor on a passing boat bled…purged him and applied a cataplasm of bread and milk upon a wilted cabbage leaf, thus saving his life and haply, his leg.

THURSDAY. The dawn is cool and crisp, and I pray that it may so hold. For now we approach the five-mile crossing of the Great Montezuma Marsh, a wasteland of tall water reeds, quick-sands, and the ravening marsh mosquitoes. Here the building of the Canal came near to being terminated by these pests. Under their savage attacks the Irish mechanics went mad and sickened and died and finally deserted their camps and abandoned their contracts, so that for four weeks not a spade rose or a pick fell. Nor would the survivors return until the frosts killed the bloodsuckers. The crossing was finished with the sturdy Irish toiling knee-deep in icy sludge...I have a sovereign defense against the venomous buzzers in my basket of fresh pennyroyal leaves, which I rub into hands and face and neck. No mosquito can abide its spicy odor.

FRIDAY. "Daily I return thanks to *Divine Providence* that I am a canal wife. Truly, life on the Erie is enviable. Consider, dear Diary, my day. Unless there is special cause for an early start, I keep to my easeful bed often as late as six o'clock. While the horses are turned out and the '*Starry Flag*' cast off, I light the fire in Mr. Burden's patent stove from Troy, dispose my pots, and pans and skillets, and get breakfast for all hands...The meal may consist of a pike or bass, fresh caught upon my overnight trawl line, a steak, bacon, sausage or ham; a platter of scrambled eggs, baked potatoes, boiled cabbage and squash...

With my dishes washed and restored, I draw my water buckets and sluice out our cabin with the soft soap...I am proud of my Canal home. Our cabin on the foredeck is of oak, painted in blue and gilt. Every window has its curtain of striped dimity, work of my own hands. Outside stands my Dutch Wasserbank of maple, gay with potted ferns, marigolds, geraniums and the handsome though poisonous tomato. This my floral display is the advertisement to all and sundry that Captain Angus Robie of the *Starry Flag* has taken a wife.

Land wives must go to market. My market comes to me. Before I am done with my morning survey, the farm children are paddling alongside in their homemade bateaus. They offer eggs, fowls, vegetables and fruits in season, milk, butter and maple syrup. These farm folk, whose local medium of barter is flaxseed, goose down, or gun-powder, are mortal impressed with the sight and feel of a shilling…

Dinner is at eleven o'clock. The towpath hoggee has his carried out, hot supper at five is soon out of the way. Again, I have my leisure spell. Other boats may be moored near us for the night. Then there will be polite visits back and forth and the exchange of the news of the day, very excitable, lasting as late as nine o'clock. I go to bed, grateful for all my mercies and asking myself what other life could be so affording and pompous as that on The Grand Erie Canal!"

—Dorcas Robie

A WEST-BOUND FAMILY SETTLES IN WISCONSIN

"My Boyhood and Youth"
By John Muir (1836-1914)

"1849, in crossing the Atlantic before the days of steamships, or even American clippers, the voyages made in old fashioned sailing vessels were very long. Ours was six weeks and three days… No matter how much the old ship tossed about and battered the waves, we were on deck every day, not in the least seasick, watching the sailors at their rope hauling and climbing work; joining in songs, learning names of ropes and sails; helping them far as they would let us.

On our wavering westward way, a grain dealer in Buffalo told father that most of the wheat he handled came from Wisconsin, and this influential information finally determined my father's choice. On that hundred-mile journey, just after the spring thaw, the roads over the prairies were heavy and miry, causing no end of lamentation, for we often got stuck in the mud. Father found the land for a farm in a sunny, open woods on the side of a lake.

Coming direct from school in Scotland while we were still hopefully ignorant and far from tame, getting acquainted with the animals about us was a never failing source of wonder and delight. At first my father, like nearly all the backwoods settlers, bought a yoke of oxen to do the farm work, and as field after field was cleared, the number was gradually increased until we had five yoke. These wise, patient, plodding animals did all the plowing, logging, hauling, and hard work of every sort. We worked with them, sympathized with them in their rest and toil and play, and thus learned to know them. We soon learned that each ox and cow and calf had individual character.

The humanity we found in them came partly through the expression of their eyes when tired, their tones of voice when hungry and calling for food, their patient plodding and pulling in hot weather...By learning a smattering of languages, Scotch, English, Irish, French, Dutch as required in the faithful service they so willingly, wisely rendered; by their alert curiosity, manifested in listening to strange sounds, their love of play, the attachments they made, and their mourning when a companion died: we got to know them.

Men and boys, and in those days, even women and girls, were cut down while cutting the wheat. The fat folk grew lean, and the lean leaner... We were called in the morning at four o'clock and seldom got to bed before nine, making a seething day seventeen hours long, loaded with heavy work while I was only a small boy, and a few years later my brothers and my older sisters had to endure about as much as I did.

None of our American neighbors were so excessively industrious as father; though nearly all of the Scotch, English and Irish worked too hard, trying to make good homes and to lay up money enough for comfortable independence. Excepting small garden patches, few of them had owned land in the old country. Here their craving land-hunger was satisfied, and they were naturally proud of their farms and tried to keep them as neat and clean and well-tilled as gardens. The American settlers were wisely content with smaller fields and less of everything; kept indoors during excessively hot or cold weather, rested when tired, went off fishing and hunting...gathered nuts and berries, and in general tranquility, accepted all the good things the fertile wilderness offered."

—John Muir, (Naturalist)

The Ohio-Erie Canal at Roscoe Village

CHAPTER 27

The Ohio-Erie Canal

OHIO-ERIE CANAL DOCUMENTS (EXCERPTS)

John Kilbourne 1832

"For many years after the termination of the Revolutionary War, nay, even after the adoption of the Federal Constitution, this now populous and promising State, was one extensive wilderness.

The cataract of Niagara barred all movement from Lake Erie to the Ocean and the only remaining outlet for heavy articles which necessarily include the grand staples of our Country was through the Ohio and Mississippi Rivers to New Orleans.

Our contemplated Canal completes the line of communication between the Mississippi and its tributaries; the upper and lower Lakes, the St. Lawrence and the Hudson River of North America forming more than 16,000 miles of connected inland navigation and opening to the whole extended west, an easy access to the city of New York, already the grand emporium of North American commerce.

'CITIZENS OF OHIO—The grand work which in this day is begun in our infant State, yet in the cradle of prosperity:...Great as is the undertaking, your powers are equal to its completion; be but united, firm and persevering, and if Heaven smile on your labors, success is sure. We join in thankfulness and gratitude to the Ruler of Nations, for the past blessings which He has showered upon our favored and happy Country'...

—Mr. Ewing

'The Union of the States will be as firm as the everlasting hills; and from this great epoch in our history, we may dismiss all fears of a dismemberment of the American Republic.'

—Dewitt Clinton

The Scioto and Sandusky Route

We are fully of opinion that the upper levels of the proposed Sandusky and Scioto route cannot be supplied with water in dry seasons, by any other means than that of constructing an extensive artificial reservoir on the summit. Nature has presented us with no safe and convenient place for the formation of such a reservoir in the vicinity of the summit...

The Muskingum and Scioto Route

The line upon which the engineer has been engaged during the latter part of the season, may be termed the Muskingum and Scioto route, which will cross the State from Lake Erie to the Ohio River, passing through the upper part of the Muskingum, the Licking and the lower part of the Scioto valleys. The advantages proposed by this route, are, that it will offer a navigable communication from the Ohio River to the Lake, affording also a cheap and safe outlet for the surplus productions and mineral treasures of the richest and most populous parts of the valleys through which it will pass.

On this line there will necessarily be two summits: that between the head waters of the Muskingum River and the Lake, and the summit between the south branch of Licking and Little Walnut Creek...This part of the Country seems as if it was calculated by nature for our use in the prosecution of the project. About two miles westerly from this is the ...swamp, which can be constructed into a reservoir, in which may be deposited 400 million cubic feet of water should it be necessary. [Buckeye Lake]

When we consider the geographical position of Ohio; being as it is, the connecting link between the eastern and western States; between the great inland seas on the north and the navigable waters of the Mississippi on the south; the fertility of its soil, the mildness of its climate, its extensive and rapidly increasing population; we can entertain little doubt that a canal through the State, connecting the waters of Lake Erie, with those of the Ohio River, must become the channel of an extensive commerce...

Should the contemplated works be completed, we shall see canal boats towed by steamboats on the Ohio River to the southern termination of the Ohio Canal at Portsmouth; thence through that canal by boat and horse power to Cleveland. Across Lake Erie by steamboats, through the Grand Erie Canal in New York in the ordinary canal-boat manner to the Hudson River at Albany; then towed by steamboat down the Hudson River to New York.

In returning, they will pass in the manner before described to the place of destination on the Ohio River. Thus, conveying their freight through the whole length of the route without re-lading...

Sandstone everywhere abounds in the hills which skirt the Tuscarawas Valley; and limestone is also found in the same hills. Stone may be obtained for the security of such banks as are exposed to the current of the River, and also for the construction of aqueducts, culverts and locks, with the greatest ease, and in the greatest abundance, all along the Tuscarawas and Cuyahoga valleys.

Suitable stone for the construction of these locks abounds in convenient situations particularly near the head of this line, and at one point six or seven miles above Dayton.

...Adjoining hills and bank are composed of loose masses of stone, gravel and other materials necessary for the construction of the embankment or wall....

"AN ACT TO PROVIDE FOR INTERNAL IMPROVEMENT BY NAVIGABLE CANALS"

...'The expense of constructing the Ohio Canal will not be, on an average of its whole length, more than half as much per mile, as that of the Erie Canal of New York. This difference arises chiefly from the great difficulties which were encountered on some parts of that canal, and from which ours is happily exempt. We have no mountain ridges of solid rock to cut through, nor precipitous ledges like those of the Mohawk to encounter. The abundance of materials which are almost everywhere found in the vicinity of our line, and the wonderful ease with which they are procured and fitted for use, also contribute greatly to this difference in cost. Such are these facilities, that forty locks are now under contract on the Ohio Canal, almost all of them to experienced and able contractors—'.

Our canals pass through countries at least as fertile, and capable of yielding as great a quantity of productions, for market, as those of New York; and, although our situation is more distant from the place of market, the same necessity exists of reaching that market, with all such articles as will bear transportation. It is true, the Erie Canal terminates in tide water, and leads to the city of New York; ours, also is directed towards the same point. That canal connects the Ocean with the Great Lakes; ours will connect the same Great Lakes with the extensive navigable waters of the Ohio and Mississippi, and through them with the Gulf of Mexico and the West Indies. The New York Canal connects distant countries, situated nearly in *the same* latitudes, and yielding the same productions. The Ohio canal will connect distant countries, lying in *different latitudes*, each abounding in productions not common to the other, making an interchange through this channel mutually beneficial to both." —John Kilbourne, 1832

"*The Albany Daily Advertiser* says that one of the canal boats which arrived in that place on the 22nd ultimo from the city of New York, contained goods for the States of Pennsylvania, Ohio, Kentucky, Tennessee, Indiana, Illinois and the territory of Michigan."

"THE PASSING OF THE FRONTIER 1825-1850"
Francis P. Weisenburger

"At Licking Summit, Clinton turned the first shovelful of dirt for the Ohio Canal, followed by a second shovelful turned by Governor Morrow of Ohio. It was hoped that the Ohio Canal would permit the marketing of Ohio's surplus farm products in New York City; hence work was first started in earnest on the part of the route nearest Lake Erie. On July 4, 1825, work on the canals was started. By late November, fifteen hundred to two thousand men were working on the Ohio Canal northward from Portage Summit.

The primitive character of the country and the necessity of working at times in knee-deep water caused malaria. Many Irish immigrants found their way to Ohio [having first worked on the Erie Canal]. The city of Akron arose from shanties which had housed the Irish and other builders of the canal.

Exactly two years after the ground-breaking ceremony of 1825, on July 4, 1827, the northern part of the Ohio-Erie Canal from Akron to Cleveland was opened to traffic with jubilation. Forty-one locks and three aqueducts had been built in this section of the Canal. A wide variety of agricultural products were transported by this route to the eastern markets, and woolen cloth, formerly conveyed by wagon to Baltimore or Philadelphia, now found its way overland from the mills of Steubenville to Massillon on the Canal, and thence via the Canal to Lake Erie.

Portsmouth, Ohio 1827: "Business of every kind is very dull here; but we all hope to live on milk and honey and without labor when we get the canal." By summer of 1830, navigation was open as far south as Newark, and during 1833, the entire length of 333 miles from Cleveland to Portsmouth had been completed.

Cities along the canals grew with phenomenal rapidity. Property increased in value especially in the canal counties...The value of agriculture increased. Consequently, new lands were opened up, and the products of forest and mine, as well as of field and meadow, found their way to profitable markets.

With the building of the canals, side roads leading to the canal and main roads were demanded for areas untouched by the canal."

"CANALS"

By Harlan Hatcher

"Canals were the thing for Ohio...A State once rolled and scoured to a level by the glaciers as though God were fashioning it to order for the canal builders. Canals would enhance the service upon Lake Erie by opening it to Ohio farmers.

Locating the canal across Ohio was rigorous and dangerous work. Much of the route was uninhabited wilderness. The men had to fight their way through miles of forest, through low swampy ground and along damp riverbanks. Their sufferings duplicated those of Moses Cleveland's first surveying party. Few of them were able to keep healthy for more than a week at a time....

By Thanksgiving, 1825 about two thousand men were swarming in the Cuyahoga Valley...Men and animals worked from sunup to sundown. All along the valley they cleared out the trees, brush, roots, grass and herbage so that the canal banks, as the contracts specified, might 'unite securely with the solid earth beneath.' They dug the ditch at least six feet deep. The specifications called for a minimum of four feet of water at all points on the canal, and the banks had to be not less than two feet and not more five feet above the water level...They dug it twenty-six feet wide at the bottom and they sloped the banks so that it would be at least forty feet wide at the water level. On one bank they fashioned a towpath that was ten feet wide at the surface...

On the level stretches, it was largely a matter of digging a ditch and piling up dirt for the banks. But in some places a way had to be blasted through rock...

At forty-one spots along the route other men were digging special pits, hauling in stone, chiseling it into blocks, and laying it to form the walls of the locks. Through these locks the canal boats would drop down over the 400 foot difference in elevation between Akron and Cleveland...

Still other workmen were hewing out timber and constructing the aqueducts which carried the canal over the three tributary streams which flow into the Cuyahoga from the east...

In addition to...farm produce, the canals made possible the flow of coal to the lake just at the moment when manufacturing was beginning and when William Otis was founding the first ironworks (1840) in Cleveland—portent of the meeting of coal and iron which was to lift this port to its position of eminence. For another fifteen years the canals hauled the freight in and out of the Reserve in ever-increasing quantities. By that time the developing railroad system was in a position to divert traffic to the cars, and by its growing network, to serve a wider area."

—H. Hatcher

AKRON (A BRIEF TALE)

"Akron is at the highest point on the old Ohio and Erie Canal. Akron proper owes its existence to the canal. After the canal was opened to traffic in 1827, the town grew quickly. For some time prior to the opening, carpenters in the boat yard on Lock No. 1, just south of Akon had been hurrying to get the *State of Ohio* ready for service. On July 3, 1827, this first packet on the Ohio and Erie Canal moved away on its journey to Cleveland...

...The Old Empire Hotel catered to travelers coming in by packet boat on the canal. On the old Empire was a cupola, manned by a watchman who notified the management when boats approached. Immediately hotel employees jumped into action making arrangements for the new guests."

—*The Ohio Guide*

The Ohio-Erie Canal in Millersport

"UP AND DOWN THE OHIO CANAL"
Memories of Canallers
By Lewis Cook

"J. Soliday of Pickerington remembers much about the dry dock as it was her girlhood playground. Her father would send her to Lancaster with horse and buggy to buy a bale of oakum for caulking. The oakum was rolled out, and driven into cracks in the boats. Boats were caulked, rebuilt, and some new ones made at this dock in the Baltimore, Ohio basin.

Baltimore was a great shipping point for various goods. Grain was hauled to the warehouses for shipment to Cleveland. Wool, farm products and tobacco packed in barrels also went up the canal.

The oldest man in the township remembers when his father rode horseback to Cleveland to order white pine lumber for a new house. He rode along the towpath. The lumber arrived by canal boat, and was found to be in the rough. They built a kiln and dried the lumber, then worked it into shape and a carpenter built the house.

G. Littlejohn for a time worked on state repair boats. On various trips he went as far south as Chillicothe; up north to Cleveland and down the Hocking Canal to Athens and up the Columbus branch. For nearly 26 years he kept a grocery in Columbus. He remembers many of the canal boats owned by local men... The *Star* made regular runs to Columbus, hauling mostly eggs and butter.

He also recalls that stone for a Columbus church was hauled by canal boat from Lancaster. On a back haul from Columbus, he brought down the girder, a long timber beam for the same church.

The timber was longer than the boat and stuck out over the bow of the boat.

Other memories of Littlejohn. The twenty-one locks at Akron. Hauling wheat to Cleveland at 25 cents a bushel, and then hauling a full back haul of cheese and white pine lumber.

The basin at Havensport served as swimming pool for boys during summer, and winter quarters for some of the canal boats in which to 'freeze in'.

West of the basin, the road crossed the canal by a bridge with stone abutments. A trap door was cut in the floor of this bridge so that wagons loaded with grain could unload into boats and so save on handling the grain. Canallers delivered grain to Newark and brought coal up from the Hocking Hills.

The canal was the life of the community. The stores, taverns and warehouses all tried to attract the canal trade. The favored business spot was a lot on the towpath side of the canal, so the building might face the canal.

J. Norris came from Baltimore, Maryland as a teamster over Zane's Trace, and for some time freighted goods from the East. When the Canal was constructed, Norris and Black built a mill, and did considerable business both in grinding flour and feed and in the carding of wool. The canal was the playground of his children. They had skiffs with which to travel along the canal, and the lock was the swimming pool for the boys. As the locks were floored with the best of oak timber...the boys were well provided with swimming facilities. People came from miles to have their wheat ground. Sad were the times when the Canal was so low that no water came over the state gauge to run the mill. The only mill that enough water to run occasionally was the old Bright Mill on

Poplar Creek, fully five miles from the Norris Mill. Many of the mills along the Canal had but a six-foot drop—the level of one lock, but the Norris mill had an 18 foot drop.

South and east of the Norris Mill stood the lock tender's house. This lock tender had charge of the first 8 locks and the guard lock. It was his business to keep the locks in repair as much as one man might, and to call for the help of the state repairmen when he was unable to care for the lock leaks or breaks in the bank. He was a sort of track-walker for the Canal.

The towns and villages along the Canal were all boom towns. Canal Winchester enjoyed the following businesses between 1830 and 1840: Grocery store, tavern, tailor, physicians, grain dealer, cabinet shop, brick yard and masons, tailor, and shoe shop.

One entry line in an account book of January 4, 1842: 'The tavern cared for man and animals.'

Groveport offered dry dock facilities and Carroll was a junction point, so the boats tried to reach one or the other point before being 'frozen in.' ... During the winter the boatmen would build an ice-breaker and when a thaw came, would load it with stone so its bow would stick above the surface of the ice. They would hitch all their teams to it, and put three or four hardy men aboard to rock it from side to side, and go crashing, yelling along the canal breaking up ice so boats could move sooner.

Gen. Speaks recalls the time when boats ran day and night on the canal.

One night he was given a bedroom with windows facing the Canal on the towpath side. The sounds of teams and passing boats were not strange to him so he soon went to sleep. But he awoke very much frightened when a strong-voiced driver put his head in the bedroom window and yelled. 'Hey! Do you know where I can I get some hay?'

One man had a short experience as a boatman. He signed on as a driver. The cargo was a load of ear corn from Winchester that he hauled to the starch factory at Columbus. Allen who is now eighty-one years old still shakes his head over his experience as a night driver. He by no means enjoyed blundering alone with a team in the dark.

The canal boats furnished passengers a means of travel for some years. Then came the Stage Coaches running from Columbus to Lancaster and on down the valley. These were displaced by the Hocking Valley Railroad. Cleveland was booming with the Canal trade."

"A Branch of the Canal Entered Columbus"
By Lewis Cook

"When the Ohio Canal was projected, a branch was planned to run into Columbus from the main Canal. In April 1827 work was begun on the branch and four years were necessary to complete it...Here was a center of business and canal activity.

A hundred yards from a mill stood a warehouse, not the ordinary type of canal warehouse used for grain, but a warehouse for transferring freight. A boat going from Portsmouth to Cleveland might pick up some freight for Columbus along the lengthy canal pathway. The freight would be unloaded into this warehouse, and the original carrier would then travel onward to Cleveland, assured that the freight would be picked up by a boat going into the Columbus branch.

On September 23, 1831, the *Gov. Brown*, first canal boat to reach Columbus, was greeted by a salute of cannon. The next day the *Red Rover* and *Cincinnati* both from Cleveland, entered the locks and were towed by their mule-team up the Scioto River to the Broad Street Bridge; amidst much jubilation.

'The first canal boats seemed like little fairy palaces,' one person said. 'They were painted white and the windows had green shutters and scarlet curtains, while the inside panels of the cabins contained mirrors and pictures. The cabin was a dining and sitting room in daytime, but converted into a sleeping apartment at night.'

Soon the canal was the busiest part of the village of Columbus. At the foot of Main Street and just west of Canal Street were the locks. Below Main Street and on the west bank of the canal stood an elevator. A loaded boat towed by 3 mules in tandem one day came down the canal...A towpath ran along the east bank of the Scioto River from Main street to Dennison and all the businesses alongside were served by the canal. From Town Street to the north side of Broad Street bridge stretched a wharf where boats were loaded and unloaded of general freight.

Since Columbus was the capital of the State, the Canal was more than a means of freight transportation. The Legislature, governors, and everyone used the packet boats as a means of reaching the city.

...The best marker of the Columbus feeder is the four-mile lock. From Buckeye Lake to Columbus, this is the only lock which still has its gates standing. (July 1940)

Nowhere on the Canal is a greater contrast between the canal days and the present apparent, than at west Main Street where, standing near the site of the lock, one looks up across the levee walls to see the tower of the A.I.U. Building [Lincoln-Leveque Tower] standing like a figure of white smoke rising over the City; while to the south, the low ground of the former canal channel can be roughly followed. It is only to imagine with what amazement an old boatman of the past century came suddenly to life, and would view the wonders of the present age and the changes to Columbus.

In conclusion, permit me to voice my respect for and thanks to the men of the past who, by means of the Canal, opened the State of Ohio to the development which has culminated in the present State, and whose debtors we are." — *Lewis Cook*

(FROM) "A HISTORY OF THE STATE OF OHIO"
By Caleb Atwater

"From Columbus downward, the traveler almost everywhere sees the canal with its boats. They hear the sound of their horns and see the Scioto wending its way along toward the Ohio River. This is the Scioto Country famed in all of time since man dwelt on its surface for its beauty and fertility. Here the wild animals lived in the greatest numbers, and we have placed our Capitol on the most beautiful spot of the whole Scioto Country."

CHAPTER 28

The National Road

"Packhorses laden with merchandise...through the day plodded on through the forest, scaling steep acclivities, fording rivers, enduring all the toils of an arduous march and encamping at night in the wilderness. These were merchants carrying their wares to the forts and settlements of the west...They deserve a high place among the founders of western settlements, as they furnished the supplies of arms, ammunition, clothing, and other necessaries, which enabled the inhabitants of the frontier to sustain themselves and their families." —James Hall[1]

---

1   Hall, James "Letters from the West" H. Colburn, London 1828.

"THE NATIONAL ROAD"
by Philip Jordan

"Once the idea of utilizing income from the sale of public lands for road building took root, actual plans went forward rapidly; although not without difficulty and dispute. The Enabling act of 1792, by which Ohio became a State, stipulated that five percent of the proceeds from the sale of Ohio land be set aside for construction of roads.

News of increasing land sales and of the proposed road thrilled western Maryland, Virginia, Pennsylvania and Ohio. Men wondered just where the road would run...The route was to be governed by the shortness of distance between navigable points on the Eastern and Western waters. That was the first consideration. It must touch an advantageous point on the Monongahela River and a site on the Ohio River which would combine certainty of water traffic with road accommodation...

Surely their crisp logic served notice that the road was not generally to jog and jag in deference to political whim and sectional interest. Western Marylanders rejoiced when they learned that the highway would start at Cumberland. Located at the junction of Will's Creek and the historic Potomac; Cumberland was a gateway...

Long, hard years were to pass before even the first few miles west of Cumberland were completed, and before ever-increasing numbers of wagons rolled along its narrow roadway...

From Cumberland to Brownsville and on to Wheeling and then across the interior valley, surveyors trudged...

"When's that road comin' through?" Worthington's only answer was that progress was being made. He had seen axmen hacking a trail west of Cumberland in 1807. He was elated when he could announce that the first construction contracts had been let on May 8, 1811.

The mountain heights over which the road must run were high and difficult. Will's Mountain, not far west of Cumberland, jutted up more than 5,800 feet...Terrain then gradually sloped to the Big Youghiogheny River only to climb again to over 1,500 feet at the peak of Laurel Hill. Grubbing, the roadbed was leveled 30 feet in width.

First, a strip 66 feet wide was cleared of all trees and underbrush; that meant weeks of work in heavily timbered sections... Oxen and horses strained at chains fastened to huge stumps... Twenty feet of the road's surface was covered with stones ranging from 12 inches in depth to 18 inches. Over all was strewed stone broken small enough to pass through a three- inch ring...Base stone was broken to go through a seven-inch ring. Gangs of men sat patiently, their legs straight out, and their hands bandaged, hammering rock to proper size. They damned the specifications while banging their hands.

As gangs of road workers cut and grubbed and ditched and surfaced; others hauled rock for bridges. Carpenters worked on superstructures, and masons fitted rock into foundations...

Slowly the hope of the West inched forward, mile by mile and section by section until by the end of December 1813, two years after the initial contracts were let, Shriver was able to report the completion of the first ten miles. 'The banks and sideways are dressed,' he wrote happily, 'and the whole of the accounts settled and paid.'

An enthusiastic farmer watched the building of the road between Braddock's Grove and Uniontown. 'I was there to see it located before a shovelful of earth was displaced, and also to see that great contractor...with his immortal Irish brigade, a thousand strong, with their carts, wheel-barrows, picks, shovels and blasting tools, grading those commons, and climbing the mountain-side... and leaving behind them a roadway good enough for an emperor to travel over.'

Wheeling residents watched engineers in 1818 bring the road over the hill east of town and carry it down to the banks of the great River. The Ohio had been reached, and the vision of Mr. Worthington and countless frontier families was realized...Wheeling, a village of only 120 houses and 11 stores was to develop into one of the most important western entrepots."

—Jordan[2]

EARLY TRAVELERS WHO DESCRIBED THEIR EXPERIENCES

"So here we are, nine in number; one hundred thirty miles of mountain country between us and Pittsburgh. We learn that the stages which pass daily from Philadelphia and Baltimore are generally full, and that there are now many persons at Baltimore waiting for places. No vehicles of any kind are to be hired, and here we must either stay or walk off. The latter we prefer, and separating each our bundle from the little that we have of traveling stores, we

---

2   Jordan, Philip D. "The National Road." The Bobbs-Merrill Company, Indianapolis.

are about to undertake our mountain pilgrimage—accepting the alternative most cheerfully after the dreadful shaking of the last hundred miles by stage.

To give an idea of the internal movements of this vast hive, about twelve thousand wagons passed between Baltimore and Philadelphia in the last year...add to these the numerous stages, loaded to the utmost, and the innumerable travelers on horseback, on foot, and in light wagons, and you have before you a scene of bustle and business, extending over a space of three hundred miles, which is truly wonderful."

—Morris Birkbeck[3]

"I counted 30 regular stage wagons engaged in the transportation of goods to and from Pittsburgh. They are drawn by four strong well-fed horses; are made upon the model of English wagons, but about one third less in size. They are from 20-35 days in effecting their journey. The articles sent from Philadelphia are hardware and dry goods, and include all articles of woolen, linen, cotton and silk. Farm products especially flour, return.

Emigrants prefer traveling in companies securing assistance when needed. In getting over mountains, ropes were useful in stabilizing wagons. One wagon had broken down; the husband was at a distant blacksmiths. She had been seated in the open all night; her comment: 'Oh sir, I wish we had never left home.'"

—Fearon[4]

3   Birkbeck, Morris. "Letters from Illinois in 1818". Notes on a Journey to America, from the Coast of Virginia to the Territory of Illinois. London, 1818.

4   Fearon, Henry B. "A Narrative of a Journey through America in 1817." London, 1818.

"The road begins to ascend immediately and passes through a rough and mountainous country thickly covered with forest which is chiefly oak; also pine and cedar; the spare ground between the trees being covered with large mountain laurel. This is so abundant and luxuriant in some places, that the woods seem almost impenetrable. Deer, bears, wolves and wild turkeys and indeed all kinds of wild animals are plentiful. While the stage was stopping a short time to water the horses, and to allow the passengers to take some refreshment at a small inn on this mountain, I observed two hunters just come in with some turkeys. A great quantity of merchandise is brought to and from the Ohio River along the National Road."

—Blane[5]

"There is one feature in this National work which is truly fine,— I allude to the massive stone bridges which form a part of it. They consist either of one, two or three arches; the center arch being a foot or two higher than those on either side. Their thick walls projecting above the road, their round stone buttresses and carved keystones combine to give them an air of Roman solidity and strength. They are monuments of good taste and power that will speak well for the Country."

—Hoffman[6]

---

5   Blane, William N. "An Excursion through the United States and Canada During the years 1822-1823." London, 1818.

6   Hoffman, Charles F. 1806-1888: "A Winter in the West 1833-34 by a New Yorker." New York, 1835.

"The road is of immense advantage, especially to stages and wagons; the latter of which are capable of drawing on it with their six-horse teams and six tons. It is indeed the grand thoroughfare between the west and Baltimore, and I suppose on the course of the route I must have seen a hundred, perhaps a hundred and fifty heavy wagons loaded with produce and merchandise. This is the country for cream and butter and fine cows. How I longed to have two or three of the latter which I saw on the road, safe in my yard at home. Mary might milk them. After dinner leaving Washington, (Penna.), we reached Wheeling at 10 o'clock; distance from Washington, 32 miles. The distance from Baltimore to Wheeling is 287 miles. For the drivers on this route, I can say that I found not one that was contrary or mulish, but polite and good and careful men."

—Wills[7]

"Wheeling was a river port where overland travelers often sold their wagons and oxen for boats. Tavern talk: 'Are there snags? How wide is the channel? Is it very deep? How fast is the current?'

The town lies in so narrow a strip along the Ohio River that the ridge on which you stand, you will hardly notice it is crowded with buildings. That first view of the lovely River of the West is worth a journey of a thousand miles.

I went out to enquire about a steamboat. The only one at the wharf ready to go down was the 'Pensacola'. I accordingly had my baggage on board, my berth taken and passage to Cincinnati

7   Wills, Willliam H. "A Southern Travelers Diary in 1840." Southern History Association Publications. Vol. 7, no.6, November 1903.

paid ready to be again moving, but I found here and subsequently; that none of the boats on the Ohio are prompt. Freight being their principle object, they wait as long as they can and stop frequently at the intermediate ports."

—Hoffman[8]

"The National Turnpike passes through Wheeling, and with little variance from a straight line, through Columbus and Indianapolis, crossing a very level and fertile Country, compared with the country from forty to a hundred miles south of it, where the gorges cut by the streams descending into the Ohio River, become deep and precipitous." The Wheeling Times June 9, 1845

"Wheeling certainly is the nail city. I have never seen so many in my life." One day he counted, on the National Road, a fleet of twenty wagons each crowded with casks filled with nails and all moving westward. In his journal he wrote that 100 Ohio Towns ought to come into being because of that one procession. Local coopers, he found, were working day and night to make kegs strong enough to hold the heavy loads of nails."

— Jordan[9]

"Congress had appropriated $150,000 for the extension of the Road through Ohio. The new section as far as Zanesville would be built using a new technology devised a few years earlier by Scotsman, John *McAdam*. . . .

8   Hoffman, Charles F. 1806-1888: "A Winter in the West 1833-34 by a New Yorker." New York, 1835.

9   Jordan, Philip D. "The National Road." The Bobbs-Merrill Company, Indianapolis.

Indiana 1816 and *Illinois* 1818 had become States, and had compacts with the government for extending the road through their capitals, Indianapolis and Vandalia...the then capital of Illinois."

—Wills[10]

WAGONNERS

"Men who hauled merchandise over the road were called wagonners. As a rule, the horses were rarely stabled, but rested overnight in the wagon yards of the old taverns...Feed troughs were suspended at the rear of the wagon bed and carried along year-round. Wagonners carried their beds rolled up in the forepart of the wagon, and spread them out in a semicircle on the bar room floor in front of the big fire place. Some of the old barroom grates would hold as much as six bushels of coal, and iron pikers 4-6 feet to stir fires. The 'pike boys' had some hard times, and they had some good times. They were generally very fond of sport and mostly tried to put up where the landlord was a fiddler, so that they could take a hoe-down. Everyone carried his own bed, and after they had all the sport they wanted, they put their beds down on the floor in a circle with their feet to the fire, and slept like a mouse in a mill. They were generally very sociable and friendly with each other."

—Thomas B. Searight

"To get up and down the hills: they had no trouble to get up, but the trouble was in getting down, for they had no rubbers then, and to

10   Wills, Willliam H. "A Southern Travelers Diary in 1840." Southern History Association Publications. Vol. 7, no.6, November 1903.

tight-lock would soon wear out their tires. They would cut a small sapling-pole about ten feet long and tie it to the bed with the lock chain, and then bend it against the hind wheel and tie it to the feed trough or the hind part of the wagon bed just tight enough to let the wheels turn slowly. Sometimes one driver would wear out 15 to 20 poles between Baltimore and Wheeling.

When there was ice, they had to use rough locks and cutters and the wagon would sometimes be straight across the road, if not the hind end foremost. The snow was sometimes so deep that they had to go through fields and shovel the drifts from the fences and often had to get sleds to take their loads across a mountain… Those of us who had to go through the fields were three days going nine miles. This was near Frostburg, Maryland.

There were no bridges then, across the Monongahela or the Ohio River. Wagonners had to ferry across in small flat boats, and sometimes to lay at the river's edge for some days until the ice would run out or the river freeze over…

The pike boys were bitterly opposed to railroads and so were the tavern keepers. Before this writer became a pike boy, he plowed many a day with a wooden mold board plow."

—John Deets

"It was for the great wagons and their waggoners to haul over the mountains and distribute throughout the west the products of mill and factory and, [on return] the rich harvests of the fields, and this great freight traffic created a race of men of its own, strong and daring, as they well had need to be…

The fact that these rulers of mountain ships had wagon houses of their own where they stopped, tended to separate them into a class by themselves....

Waggoners frequented only those inns where decent provisions regularly were offered to horses... Hundreds of wagons went to Walker's establishment at Etna, Ohio; one whose praises were sung by drivers. Catering to drovers and waggoners, Walker promised on a hand-bill:

> "Oats, Corn and Hay, I always have on hand
> For plenty, I always raise on my own land;
> And if I should keep two droves of animals at once,
> It wouldn't lower my oat-bin much."

What They Hauled

"From the 'West': Every type of agricultural product.

Bills of lading listed bacon, bagging, bale rope, beans, butter, beef and buffalo robes, cotton, corn, cheese, candles, cider and coal, feathers, and flaxseed."

"From the East came rough and cut nails, stills, kettles, copper vessels, tin-ware, firearms, saddler and carriage mountings, clocks, pottery, glassware, furniture, cooperage materials, hats, snuff, soap, candles, millstones and iron: rolled, cast and in bars."

—Philip Jordan

"A SPEECH DELIVERED IN CONGRESS JUNE 6, 1832"

"This Road, Mr. Speaker, is a magnificent one—magnificent in extent; it traverses seven different States of this Union, and its whole distance will cover an extent of near eight hundred miles. Magnificent in the difficulties overcome by the wealth of a Nation, and in the benefits and advantages and blessings which it diffuses, east and west, far and wide through the whole Country. It is a splendid monument of *national wealth* and *national greatness*...a source of never failing prosperity to millions yet unborn.

Let me call attention to the amount of merchandise transported to the Ohio River in a single year after its completion:

In the year 1822, shortly after the completion of the road, a single house in the town of Wheeling unloaded 1,081 wagons, about 3500 pounds each, and paid for the carriage of the goods $90,000. At that time there were five other commission houses in the same place...there must have been nearly 5,000 wagons unloaded and nearly $400,000 paid as the cost of transportation. But further, it is estimated that at least every tenth wagon passed through that place into the interior of Ohio, Indiana, Illinois... which would considerably swell the amount. These wagons take their return loads and carry to the eastern markets all the various articles of production and manufacture of the West—their flour, whisky, hemp, tobacco, bacon and wool. Since this estimate was made, the town of Wheeling is greatly enlarged; its population nearly doubled; the number of its commercial establishments has greatly increased, and the demand for merchandise in the West has increased with the wealth and improvement and prosperity of the Country.

Before the completion of this Road, from four to six weeks were usually occupied in the transportation of goods from Baltimore to the Ohio River. Now carried in less than half the time and at one half the cost. Before its completion eight or more days were occupied in transporting the mail from Baltimore to Wheeling. It was then carried on horseback and did not reach the western country by this route more than once a week. Now it is carried in comfortable stages, protected from the inclemency of the weather, in 48 hours and no less than twenty-eight mails weekly and regularly pass and repass each other on this Road."

—Thomas B. Searight

THE PONY EXPRESS

"In 1835 or 36, A. Kendall, being Postmaster General, placed on the road a line of couriers, called the *Pony Express*. It was intended to carry light mails with more speed than the general mail carried by the coaches. The Pony Express was a single horse and a boy rider, with a leather mail pouch thrown over the horse's back; something after the style of the old- fashioned saddle bags. The route for each horse covered a distance of about six miles on average. The horse was put to his utmost speed, and the rider carried a tin horn vigorously blown when approaching a station. ...Three riders afterwards became stage drivers; one an employee of the Baltimore and Ohio Railroad. The Pony Express did not remain long on the road, but when it was on, old pike boys say, 'It kicked up a dust.'"

—Thomas B. Searight

THE STAGECOACH AND DRIVERS

"Excitement followed in the wake of the coaches all along the road. Their arrival in the towns was the leading event of each day, and they were so regular in transit that farmers along the road knew the exact hour by their coming without the aid of watch or clock. They ran night and day alike. Relays of fresh horses were placed at intervals of twelve miles as nearly as practicable. Ordinarily a driver had charge of one team only which he drove and cared for.

Mail drivers often drove three or four teams which were cared for by grooms at the stations. Teams were driven rapidly to the station where a fresh team stood ready harnessed and waiting on the roadside. The moment the team came to a halt, the driver threw down the reins, and almost instantly the incoming team was detached; the fresh one attached, and the reins thrown back to the driver, who did not leave his seat and away again went the coach...

The *Postilion*: A groom with two horses was stationed at the foot of many of the long hills, and added to the ordinary team of four horses to aid in making the ascent. The summit gained, the extra horses were quickly detached and returned to await and aid the next coming coach. He was a tall spare man four miles east of Brownsville.

Mr. Stockton established a coach factory in Uniontown where many of the coaches of his line were made...and repaired. Blacksmith shops were also set up in connection with this factory where the stage horses of the Stockton line were shod. Many mechanics in different lines of work were employed in the stage yard. One a coach trimmer, another was a painter and ornamented coaches...others were workers in wood.

An incident in the early career of Mr. Stockton was that he formed a race between a horse and buggy against a steam locomotive, [named *Tom Thumb*] from the relay house to Baltimore, in which he came out ahead."

—Thomas B. Searight

Passenger at an Inn

"We reached our resting place for the night, if no accident intervened at 10 o'clock and after a frugal supper, went to bed with a notice we would be called at three a.m. Whether it rained or snowed, the traveler must rise and make ready by the help of a horn lantern and a farthing candle, and proceed on his way over bad roads, sometimes getting out to help the coachman lift the coach out of a quagmire or rut."

—Clarence Hornung

"Hughes, an old stage driver, is still living in Washington, Penna., vivacious and sprightly despite the weight of years piled upon his back. He was an expert and trusty driver, well-known along the road, and cherishes the memory of the stirring times when the road was the great highway of the Nation, and he and his fellow drivers rode on the top wave of the excitement incident thereto."

—Thomas Searight

TAVERNS AND INNS

"The house looks old and dingy, and no wonder for it has withstood the wild dashes of numberless mountain storms. It is situated at the foot of the eastern slope of Laurel Hill...it will soon be gone. The old host too, is showing the marks of time and age...He is universally esteemed for his honesty. As a tavern keeper, he enjoyed an excellent reputation and many a weary traveler has found consolation and comfort under his hospitable roof.

Night after night in the prosperous era of the road, the ground all around it was crowded with big wagons and teams, and the old barroom rang out with the songs and jokes of the jolly wagoner.

Opposite the house a large water trough is kept full and overflowing from a spring nearby called the *Monroe Spring* in honor of President Monroe. One time the president passed along the road, and a public dinner was given him here.

About a mile down the western slope of Laurel Hill, we come to the famous watering trough. Here Wm. Downard lived for many years in a stone house built against the hillside. He did not keep a tavern for he had no ground for teams to stand upon and no stabling that was accessible, but he always maintained the big water trough that was in good condition pro bono public, and it would be almost impossible for big teams to make the ascent of Laurel Hill in hot weather without water.

The mountain division of the road was a long division covering 200 miles including glades and valleys. Surprise is often expressed that there were so many good taverns in the mountains remote from fertile fields and needed markets...The old taverns of the National Road have never been surpassed for bounteous entertainment and good cheer. It may seem a trifling thing to be written down in serious history that the old taverns of the mountains excelled all others in the matter of serving buckwheat cakes; but it is germane and true. There are men and women still living on the line of the National Road who often heard the great statesman, orator and patriot, Henry Clay, praising the good qualities of the buckwheat cakes furnished by the old mountain taverns.... Another memorable feature of the mountain taverns was the immense fires kept constantly burning in the bar room during the old time winters. In many instances the grates were seven feet in length with corresponding width and depth and would contain an ordinary wagon load of coal. When the fires were stirred up in these immense grates, and set to roaring, the jolly old wagonners occupying the bar rooms paid little heed to the eagerness of the howling mountain weather. The old landlord of the mountains took special pride in keeping up his barroom fire. He kept a poker from six to eight feet long and did not allow it to be used by anyone but himself."

—Thomas B. Searight

"THE WAYSIDE INN"
(of Sudbury, Mass.)
By Henry W. Longfellow

One autumn night, in Sudbury town,
Across the meadow bare and brown,
The windows of the Wayside Inn
Gleamed red with fire-light through the leaves
Of woodbine, hanging from the eaves.

It was a region of repose it seems,
A place of slumber and of dreams,
Remote among the wooded hills…
Across the road the barns display
Their lines of stalls, their mows of hay.

…From the parlor of the Inn
A pleasant murmur smote the ear,
Like water rushing through a weir:
Oft interrupted by the din
Of laughter and of loud applause,

And, in each intervening pause,
The music of a violin.
The fire-light, shedding over all
The splendor of its ruddy glow,
Filled the whole parlor large and low;

Before the blazing fire of wood,
Erect, the rapt musician stood;
And ever and anon he bent
His head upon his instrument,
And seemed to listen, till he caught
Confessions of its secret thought,

The joy, the triumph, the lament,
The exultation and the pain;
Then, by the magic of his art,
He soothed the throbbing of its heart,
And lulled it into peace again.

Around the fireside at their ease
There sat a group of friends, entranced
With the delicious melodies;
Who, from the far-off noisy town,
Had to the Wayside Inn come down,
To rest beneath its old oak trees.
The fire-light on their faces glanced,
Their shadows on the wainscot danced..."

TOWNS ALONG THE WAY

"Just as the Ohio River brought its settlers to build the scores of cities and towns in the valley, so did the National Road open the land route into the heart of the State, and shift the center and the flow of population northward from the Ohio River Valley...There is no way to exaggerate the importance of the National Road as a life-line of the Republic in the crucial middle decades of the 19th Century."

—Harlan Hatcher

Until the completion of the National Road, the journey through the mountains was spoken of as "going into or coming out of the west; as though it were a giant cave."

"In the same year that work was begun on the National Road at Cumberland, Maryland, the *New Orleans* was launched at Pittsburgh (1811). It was the first Steamboat on the Ohio River... Before the National Road had reached Wheeling in 1818, the Steamboat was there to join hands with it in providing transportation into the West."

—William Van Fossen

"When ground was broken at ST. CLAIRSVILLE, Ohio, on July 4, 1825, the program included reading of *The Declaration of Independence*. A volley fired by the Belmont Light Cavalry, and an eloquent address by W...who prophesied that the road was destined to reach the Rocky Mountains."

—Norris Schneider

"West of St. Clairsville, *US 40* wends along the ridge, now dipping into shallow valleys, now rising to orchard-crowned hilltops…"

—The Ohio Guide

Cambridge

"CAMBRIDGE had been only a town of cabins in the midst of a forest in 1806, but it was given new life by traffic on the highway. It was named for Cambridge, Maryland, from which had come many of the first settlers.

Merchants along the way could order from waggoners the needed supplies from the East to stock their stores. Teas, calico, pots and pans, stoves and all manner of merchandise that home owners desired.

Every town had at least one blacksmith to service horses and oxen along the route. Wagon makers and wheelwrights repaired road-worn wagons and damaged coaches."

—The Ohio Guide

Zanesville

Mr. Zane and Mr. Mcintire laid out the town in 1799-1800. There was a pleasant little grove of sugar trees near the Muskingum River with a road in front leading to the ferry. Their cabin was the first hotel in Zanesville…

Travelers going west took the ferry boat… The two ferrymen would often keep travelers overnight in their cabins. The reputation of the Muskingum was considered one of the best streams in the land. Game such as bear, deer, wild turkeys were also plentiful in this valley when the first settlers arrived. There went east across the mountains, reports from adventurers, scouts, and hunters that away beyond the Alleghenies was a fertile country with forests, streams, hills and valleys; with a rich soil and healthy climate. Those men who had fought the battle bravely and won the prize, turned toward the west."

—*E. H. Church*

"The great National Road, is of importance itself as the trunk of the tree is to its branches, but there never was a trunk from which more *numerous branches* projected than this. Scarce a mile of the road is found in the State from which does not diverge a road leading to important towns, villages and farms."

—*The Wheeling Times*, June 9, 1845

Hebron

Hebron, also on the National Road, is where, at *Licking Summit*, the ground-breaking took place for construction of the OHIO-ERIE CANAL. Thousands of people assembled there on July 4, 1825, to witness the ceremony. So overwhelmed were some, the historians recount that "tears fell from manly eyes."

—*The Ohio Guide*

Perhaps those so moved to tears had learned that on the same day, July 4, 1825, a ceremony was being held at St. Clairsville, commemorating the entrance of the National Road into the State of Ohio. In October, of the same year, 1825, THE GRAND ERIE CANAL was completed. The National Road would reach Columbus in 1833; the same year the Ohio-Erie Canal would be completed to its destination of Portsmouth.

The National Road would intersect with the Ohio-Erie Canal at Hebron. At this point, was a stagecoach stop, where one could either remain and travel to Columbus, or transfer from the National Road, to a canal boat northward to Cleveland or downstream to Circleville, Chillicothe or Portsmouth and the Ohio River…where they might like to transfer to a steamboat for Cincinnati—assuming the Miami-Erie Canal had not yet been built; in which case if completed, (in 1841) they could continue on the National Road through Columbus to Springfield/Dayton area, and reach Cincinnati via Ohio's Miami-Erie Canal.

(Edna Millay wrote in her time: "There isn't a train I wouldn't take no matter where it's going.")

"KIRKERSVILLE AND ETNA"
By Morris Schaaf

"The building of the National Road gave employment for many men and teams, as all the stone for the bridges and for *macadamizing* had to be hauled from quarries eight and ten miles distant. It was a busy scene as the road made way between the two towns of KIrkersville and Etna.

In winter of 1830… My father bought a farm in Etna at a little clearing of a few acres in the midst of primeval woods. He contracted with someone for the construction of a cabin, and toward the end of a November day, just as a light snow began to fall, his two-horse wagon, containing all their worldly goods, drew up to the cabin door. The house was not finished, and I have often heard my mother say, recalling that long first night, that she saw the stars gazing down on them through the loosely laid clapboard shingles. In that home, were six boys born. They brought with them two cows driven behind the wagon, one named Cherry and the other Blossom; their descendants still jangling the same old bell that was in the family when I was a small lad.

Our mother would tell us how the camp-fires of the workmen lighted up the night all along the line; about the bustle, the teams coming and going. As the road was completed, the stream of emigrants—we called them 'movers' began, which for over 30 years poured along it...

White canvas-covered wagons of the movers, I remember them almost with tenderness. How often did I sit by the roadside or on the doorstep and watch them file by. The man of the house, or one of the grown-up boys, drove the team, the women and children walking sometimes ahead and sometimes behind the wagons; sometimes driving a few cows and small herds of sheep...Parties on horseback...Along would come heavily loaded freighting wagons with four or six horses...

No boy reared alongside will ever forget the great droves of cattle, hogs, sheep, horses and mules that were driven over it on their way to Pittsburg, Baltimore and Philadelphia...

As soon as the National Road was finished, the town rose into local importance, for it was made the point where the horses were changed on all the stagecoach lines. When I was a boy, there were two taverns ...till the stages were taken off, there was not a lighter-hearted town then 'Kirk' from one end of the National Road to the other."

Alexis de Tocqueville, from his book titled, *Democracy in America*: "This gradual and continuous progress of the European race toward the Rocky Mountains has the solemnity of a *Providential Event*. It is like a deluge of people rising unabatedly, and daily driven onward by the Hand of God."

"THE VERY EARLY VILLAGE OF COLUMBUS, OHIO"
By Alfred E. Lee

"Judge Swan has left us a picture of the country of the early 1800s. 'When I opened my office in Franklinton in 1811,' he says, 'There was neither church nor school house, nor pleasure carriage in the county; nor was there a bridge over any stream within the compass of a hundred miles. The roads at all seasons were nearly impassable; there was not in the county a chair for every two inhabitants, or a knife and fork for every four.'

Merchandise was brought up the Scioto River from the Ohio River in flatboats or canoes. In his first report to the Scioto Company in 1802, Mr. J. Kilbourne spoke of the Scioto as a navigable stream. If the intent was to travel further west, a person built a boat, descended the Scioto River to the Ohio River, and floated onward and upward the Wabash River perhaps, and might settle in Vincennes, Indiana.

Columbus has the unique distinction of having been born a capital. Its origin dates from the hour when the General Assembly of the State passed an act making it the seat of government.

The town of Columbus is situated on an elevated and a beautiful site on the east side of the Scioto River, immediately below the junction of the Olentangy River. It is opposite to Franklinton, the seat of justice for Franklin County, in the center of an extensive tract of rich fertile country, from whence there is an easy navigation to the Ohio River.

'Proprietors of the town of Columbus will, by every means in their power, encourage industrious mechanics [blacksmiths, carpenter, cooper, wheelwright, shoemakers] who wish to make a residence in the town. All such are invited to become purchasers.'

The influx of settlers when that season opened and during the remainder of the year 1813, was considered large; an increase to about 300…A good many were from Chillicothe and other settlements down the valley. A dry goods, hardware and grocery were combined in a small brick building erected on the site of the block known as *the Broadway Exchange,* a few rods north of the present Neil House. A general store about the same time traded in a small log cabin. *The Pioneer Inn* of Columbus was opened for guests in 1813.

The future seat of the State government was by law established in Columbus in 1812…The city was named when the site on which it was to be built was simply a densely wooded tract without even a good wagon road through it.

During the winter of 1813, a school was kept in a cabin on the public square. Travel between Franklinton and Columbus across the Scioto River was by ferry. A roofless wooden bridge was erected in 1816. In following the crooked paths which led through the village clearings, the nightly pedestrian found the use of a tallow-dip or lantern necessary. Trees, logs, stumps and ponds of water alike disrupted the walk.

S. Barr and Co. announced a stock for his store, of all kinds of clothes and dry goods, notions, paper hangings, boots and shoes, books and shawls, saddles, bridles and Bibles, looms, and groceries, glassware, tin ware, spices, drugs and dyestuffs.

In 1818 when *The National Road* reached Wheeling, W.Va., merchandise from Eastern cities could be freighted by Conestoga wagon to the commission houses at the Wheeling port, transferred to steamboats and shipped to Portsmouth; where they would be trans-shipped on the Scioto River by keelboat or in skiffs north to Chillicothe and upstream to Columbus or Worthington.

In front of every store, says Mr. G., was a post and rail for the convenience of the country people to hitch their horses when they came to town. So numerous were the animals, saddled and side-saddled; hitched in rows up and down High Street particularly on Saturdays, that they were commonly spoken of as *the cavalry*."

The Postal Service began in summer of 1805: A 13 year-old carrier's experience

"I was the first appointed carrier, and did carry the first mail to Franklinton, employed about one year during the winter and spring; having twice to swim Darby and Deer Creek carrying the small mail bag on my shoulders. I commenced carrying the mail at 13 years old. There was no house but Wm. Brown's on Big Run, between Franklinton and Darby, and but one cabin at Westfall and Deer Creek to Chillicothe. It was rather a lonesome route for a boy."

—Lee's *History of Columbus*

"A PIONEER ENTREPRENEUR"
By Christian Heyl

"I succeeded in getting a very rough cabin on the southeast corner of Rich and High Streets where the Eagle Drug Store now is. The accommodations were very poor indeed, but still I had to pay $125. rent and the cabins were not worth $20. ...In the fall of the same year, I moved to Columbus. We were three days on the way from Lancaster to Columbus; [30 miles] the roads were very bad indeed. We had two heavily loaded wagons with a five-horse team to each, and they had very hard work to get along.

The second day, we intended to get as far as Williams' Tavern, about five miles from Columbus on the old Lancaster road, but we did not reach it, and so had to camp on the banks of the Big Belly as it was then called. On the last day, we arrived at Columbus about three o'clock in the afternoon. The road from the old W. Merion farm was laid out, but the logs were not rolled out of the way. We therefore had to wend our way as best we could. When we came to South Columbus, as it was called, at McGowan's Run, the road was fenced. Old Mr. McGowan refused to let me go through his gates. I tried to prevail on him to let me pass through. I also found that the old man was fond of a little good old whisky. I promised to make him a present of some, and the gates were at once opened.

We then passed on without any further trouble, and arrived at my great hotel, which I opened, and built a fire and got my widowed sister to cook some supper while we unloaded the wagon. After all was unloaded, I set the table which was the lid of my dough tray laid across two barrels of flour set endwise. I rolled barrels of flour on each side for our seats, and we made out to take our supper, and as we were very hungry, I think it was the best meal I ever ate in Columbus. Old Mr. McGowan did not forget to call the next day for the prize I had promised him...

I then went on and built myself an oven to carry on the baking business. I had to get all my supplies from Lancaster, Fairfield County for a number of years; this being a new county and Franklinton the headquarters of the army, where a great many troops were located, and consequently, provisions scarce...

We had to go to Franklinton for all our dry goods, as there was at that time no store in Columbus. In the spring of the year 1814, Green & McLene started a small dry goods store in a cabin on the same lot where I lived. A second store was opened in a little brick house by the Worthington Manufacturing Company, and was managed by Joel Buttles...

The first winter that I was in Columbus, I had my firewood very convenient as I cut it off of the lot where I lived. My cabin was divided into three rooms, or, more properly, into three stalls. A widowed sister kept house for me, and having fixed up the old cabin pretty comfortably, I carried on the baking business quite briskly. In May 1814, I married E. Alspach in Fairfield County, Ohio. When she first saw my great hotel, she seemed a little surprised, but she soon became contented. I did business in the old cabin for two years. I then purchased a lot on the same square, and built upon it the house that is now *The Franklin House*. I kept a hotel there for twenty-eight years, and then traded it off for a farm five miles northeast of Columbus on Alum Creek."

"THE NATIONAL ROAD ARRIVES IN COLUMBUS IN 1833"

By Alfred E. Lee

"The National Road enters Columbus from the east on Main Street, now Route 40. Turning right onto High Street, it passes the State Capital on the right and the Neil House on the left. Continuing north a short distance the road turns left and heads west on Broad Street. [toward Springfield] The road will open up trade with the East, the people had said, 'It will help Ohio grow.'

Columbus was second only to Cincinnati in size and had the advantage of being the State Capital since 1816. Since it was on the National Road, as well as being the capital, it was said to have 'bustled with a constant stream of traffic.'

Manufactured products were brought in from Eastern cities in Conestoga wagons. The variety becoming over time, more and more sophisticated: Hardware, glass and mirrors, stoves, agriculture supplies and implements. Those wagons carried back flour from Columbus mills. One of the large wagons could carry about thirty-four barrels. They also carried farm produce to eastern markets.

A major part of Columbus' business centered about the emigrant trade and new settlers. In any inn or hotel, fellow travelers were oftentimes 'craftsmen', and small shopkeepers with their families. Carpenters, blacksmiths, wheelwrights, saddle makers, gunsmiths, harness makers, coopers and shoemakers did an ever-increasing business establishing shops for the traveling public, and began building little homesteads. Grocers, starting out in a small log cabin, gradually expanded to a frame building and supplied both settlers and travelers with seeds, beans, flour, and produce from farmers who had bartered for coffee, tobacco, sugar, or yard goods. Reports went back to the East Coast that carpenters were needed in *the West.*

> 'The sidewalks are broad, paved with brick and present quite a busy scene, and the middle of the street is kept in a state of constant and lively animation by the endless train of wagons, horses and horsemen—long-springed, four-horse stagecoaches; horns announcing arrivals.'

But the countryside of central Ohio bore many of the earmarks of a pioneer region…Although the soil was excellent, poor cabins and log huts with roofs and clapboards were the usual abodes. Excellent timber land abounded and easterners were especially impressed by the giant sycamores.

A wooden covered bridge crossed the Scioto River and connected Columbus with Franklinton: This Broad Street Bridge was built in 1832, and stood until replaced by an open iron bridge in 1882.

When the bridge was finished, the question arose as to its strength…One of the largest of cattle droves came along a few days after the completion of the bridge. R. Cowling of London, Ohio stopped overnight in a tavern in Franklinton, and the next morning arrived to examine the bridge before driving his herd across. He concluded it could not bear the burden, and was making arrangements to swim them over. The engineer of the bridge assured him that it was plenty strong enough, and told him the government would pay for all the loss of the cattle if the bridge broke down. He decided to venture it with the whole seven hundred head. There was some trouble in getting the cattle started through, but when they began there was a virtual stampede. The bridge creaked and settled but held firm. The bridge remained in use for 50 years.

Many who arrived on the National Road intended to stay in the growing village of Columbus; others had bought land further west in Indiana, Illinois or Iowa, and continued the journey. The road reached the western border of Ohio in 1840. As the road approached small villages along its pathway; inns, blacksmith shops, grocery stores, hardware stores and wagon shops began appearing along with the new and changing scenery."

—Lee's *History of Columbus*

"WESTWARD TO SPRINGFIELD"
By Reverend Read

"An English minister in 1834 wrote: 'Springfield is a flourishing town, built among the handsome hills that abound in this vicinity. It is one of the cleanest, brightest and most inviting that I have seen. But all the habitations were as nothing compared with the forest. I had been travelling through it for two days and nights, and still it was the same. Now you came to a woodsman's hut in the solitudes; now to a farm; and now to a village, by courtesy called a town or a city, but it was still the forest. You drove on for miles through it unbroken, then you came to a small clearance and a young settlement, and then again you plunged into the wide everlasting forest.'"

"BY STAGECOACH: ZANESVILLE TO FREDERICK, MARYLAND ON THE NATIONAL ROAD"
Mary Reed Eastman, 1833

"The bridges over the numerous creeks are all of stone, & very handsome as well as durable. There is no road in the United States equal to this, extending more than 100 miles in such perfect order. We reached Wheeling on Thursday at 12 not much fatigued; heard the cholera was in Pittsburg, and the people generally alarmed there. We concluded to go directly to Baltimore...

At 3 o'clock we left Wheeling. Although we were still on the National Road, it was not so good as in Ohio. It has been made many years and was originally formed of large stones; spaces between which were filled with sandstone, but this now worn off and the earth around them washed away, and we were constantly riding over large rough rocks...At daylight we crossed the Monongahela at Brownsville in a flat boat, which was 'poled across'.

About 6 miles before we reached the breakfast house, a gentleman and lady joined us, who were in a 'stage' that broke down the evening before, and soon we began to ascend the mountains. At the foot of Laurel Hill, 2 more horses were attached to our team; on one of which sat a little boy to guide us, and then we went up and up and up 3 miles... the vast mass of forest trees around, above and below us, and afar off in every direction as far as the eye could reach, surpassed in beauty anything I had ever seen.

The collection of dwelling houses, the fields cultivated with grain of different kinds, and all distinctly visible by their several colors, formed a most beautiful picture...The road was generally good. Many were employed breaking stones to cover it or repair it

where it was worn...We reached Cumberland with no other accident than breaking the iron of the wheel.

What could be more romantic than to be on the Alleghenies in
a fine moonlight night? The view was indeed sublime. We stopped
at Hagerstown, a pretty place and reached Frederick at 12 noon.
We are well accommodated at the hotel and after so much jolting
and tossing, it is a comfort to be alone with my own thoughts, on
the eastern side of the Alleghenies."

"ON THE ERA OF CALVACADES AND INNS"
By William Rideling

"Octogenarians who participated in the traffic, will tell an inquirer
that never before were there such inn keepers, such taverns, such
dinners, such bustle or endless cavalcades of coaches and wagons
as could be seen or had, between Wheeling and Frederick in the
palmy days of the old National Pike. No other post road in the
country did the same business as this fine old Highway which
opened the west and southwest to the east.

Besides the coaches and wagons, there were men traveling
singly in the saddle, with all the accoutrements of the journey
stuffed into their saddle bags, and there were enormous droves of
sheep and herds of cattle which raised the dust like a cloud along
their pathway."

"A STAGECOACH JOURNEY TO LAKE ERIE IN 1848"
By John L. Peyton

"The Xenia station, where I secured a ticket for the first train to Columbus, was a rude shed constructed of timber, and everything connected with the spot indicated the haste in which it was built. A well-dressed gentleman of about fifty...inquired where I was bound. Replying Chicago, he seemed unexpectedly surprised and pleased saying, 'I shall be your travelling companion, as it's my own destination.'

From Xenia we travelled to Columbus, the capital of the State, and then to Tiffin, a small town which had recently sprung up like a mushroom among the logs and stumps of a forest. From this point to Sandusky on Lake Erie, there was no railway, only a stage coach...

The other passengers having made themselves *snug,* according to the advice of the driver, we dashed forward to the music of his voice, the screeching of wheels, and the flapping of the aged curtains.

Pursuing what was called our road, though the traces of a road were slight, we soon found that we were in the midst of a dense forest, with no guide but the blazes or cut spots upon the sides of the trees. After going about fifteen miles, all such slight traces as existed of the road were lost, and to add to our embarrassment the blazes forked or diverged in opposite directions. The driver now acknowledged that he had taken the wrong road...

We set off again over roots and stumps, across creeks and swamps, uphill and downhill, and by following the blazes of the trees, finally returned to the main road. No sooner out of one difficulty, however, than we plunged into another. At this point one of our wheels gave way, and we were turned into the road to think of an expedient for getting along with three. The driver was not at all disconcerted...and proceeded to supply the defect. Felling a small tree, he took from it a log ten feet long, one end of this was, with the assistance of the passengers, secured upon the front axle, and passed back so as to hold up the body of the coach sufficiently high to admit of the wheel on the opposite side turning upon its spindle. This done, the passengers were coolly informed that it would be necessary for them to make the residue of the journey, a distance of twenty-five miles, on foot...At the end of three miles we came upon a farmhouse, and here the driver borrowed a wheel from the farmer's ox-cart which was placed upon our coach...We soon entered upon a *corduroy road,* on which the jolting is truly formidable. A corduroy road as all western travelers know, consists of small trees stripped of their boughs, and laid across the road, touching one another, and without any covering of earth. As the marsh underneath is of various degrees of solidity, the whole road assumed a kind of undulating appearance. Somewhat in this fashion, we made the entire journey of forty miles to Sandusky, having had three upsets and one turn-over. No lives were lost, no limbs broken, and consequently no one thought seriously of such an every-day accident... Arrived at Sandusky, we were informed that the boat from Buffalo for Detroit, in which we purposed sailing, would not be in port till the following morning...

Sandusky's chief importance arose from the harbor where vessels navigating the lakes occasionally called. Good firm roads however were projected, and had been commenced in town...While Sandusky was a comfortless place, it was obvious that it only awaited a share of the immense bodies emigrating west to become a place of no small consequence...The existence during a certain portion of the year of intermittent fevers and ague and the necessity for drainage, deterred many from stopping here.

While there, for the steamer not arriving at the appointed time, we were detained two days. I walked much in the neighborhood. I saw a tall handsome German of about twenty-five years of age, trembling and shuddering with the chill which precedes the fever in the ague. He was a miserable, woe-begone looking object, or rather a fine object under distressing circumstances...'The want of health was,' he said, 'the only difficulty in the way of the early improvement and rapid progress of this portion of Ohio.'

'You will not find,' he continued, 'precious stones or metals here, but innumerable dangers, discomforts and toil; but these are inseparable from a new country, and if surmounted by industry, any man can accumulate a fortune. The soil is of extraordinary fertility, and the facilities for market by the Lake are all that could be desired.'...I saw at once that he possessed the judgment and perseverance which assure success. He informed me that he was a native of Dresden in Saxony...The history of this young man is that of thousands of others who have sought homes on the western prairies of America."

"THE CHILD-WORLD: MEMORIES OF THE NATIONAL ROAD"

By James Whitcomb Riley

"A Child-World, yet a wondrous world, no less,
To those who knew its boundless happiness.

A simple old frame house; eight rooms in all—
    Set just one side the center of a small,
But very hopeful Indiana town.
    The upper-story looking squarely down
Upon the main street, and the main highway
    From East to West. —historic in its day,
Known as *The National Road*; old timers, all
    Who linger yet, will happily recall
It as the scheme and handiwork, as well
    As property of Uncle Sam, and tell
Of its importance, long and long afore
    Railroads wuz ever *dremp* of—Furthermore
The reminiscent first inhabitants
    Will make that old road blossom with romance
Of snowy caravans in long parade,
    Of covered vehicles, of every grade
From ox-cart of most primitive design,
    To Conestoga wagons, with their fine
Deep-chested six-horse teams, in heavy gear,
    High hames and chiming bells—to childish ear,
And eye entrancing as the glittering train
    Of some sun-smitten pageant of Old Spain.
And in like spirit, haply they will tell
    You of the roadside forests, and the yell
Of *wolfs* and *painters,* in the long night ride...."

"ASSESSING THE PREVIOUS 10 YEARS"
By Charles Cist

....But descend with me again—TEN YEARS AGO [1849]—and where? Why, we had risen to the rank of a mighty people, doubling in number the entire population when the Nation sprang into being. Our voice was heard with attention in the halls of national legislation. The tide of emigration at first feeble and slow, had now rolled toward us in a mighty volume...like bees, they had swarmed, and were migrating. Our giant strides had astonished our Eastern brethren, and they were reaching out their hands in friendly salutations. Turnpikes and Canals were stretched out toward us from all directions with tenders of intercommunication and traffic. At a bound, we covered the land with population, from river to lake and from lake to river. Instead of struggling feebly toward the West, as we had struggled to this point; by adding settlement to settlement, and county to county, we marshaled into line by platoons of States.

But we must pass the last decade, and then pause and meditate, *where are we now?* [1859] The chief feature which distinguishes this period from others which preceded it, is the clear development of that law of gravitation, and of the operation of the new forces under it, which the last decade has principally introduced. It will probably be known in coming time, as *The Railroad and Telegraph period.*"
                                                               —Charles Cist

CHAPTER 29

The Railroad

"THE STEAM LOCOMOTIVE"

By Bourne and Benton

"No invention has had greater influence on American history than that of the Locomotive. For this the world is chiefly indebted to George Stephenson, the son of an English laborer. The story is told that in 1807 he wished to go to America, but found that he was too poor to pay his passage. As an engineer at a coal mine he learned all about the Watt steam engine. Stephenson thought something like it could be used on the railroads which were being built for horse-cars. About 1814 he invented his first locomotive; a rough, noisy, weak machine, but he proved that it could draw cars for everyday business. By 1825 he was able to secure its introduction in place of horse-power on the new railroads, which were short lines about a dozen miles in length.

In the United States: The Erie Canal proved of so great benefit to business in New York City that other cities were anxious about their share of the western trade. Charleston, South Carolina was the first to use one of the new locomotives on a railroad some six miles long. This was in 1830. Four years later the line was extended westward 37 miles to the Savannah River near Augusta. Meanwhile the owners of the short horse-car lines built from Baltimore and Philadelphia toward the west, adopted the new power.

The locomotives were improved and gradually took the place of horses on all railroads. At first the locomotives could not climb steep grades or run very swiftly. Fourteen or fifteen miles an hour was the best they could do. Railroad builders were slow in learning how to build the tracks in order to endure hard usage. At the hills the locomotives, and stationary engines with ropes dragged the cars up an inclined plane to the top, where another locomotive took the cars on the journey. Philadelphia used this system on part of the state highway to Pittsburgh which was built to offset the advantage given to New York by the Erie Canal.

Other regions became eager to have railroads. New York businessmen began short lines parallel to the Erie Canal. In 1841 Boston men began a railroad which was soon to reach Albany. The Baltimore and Ohio Railroad was steadily extended westward. By 1840 nearly 3,000 miles of railway had been built in the United States."

"THE *BEST* FRIEND"
By William H. Brown

"Mr. Matthew, who was foreman of the hands fitting up machinery in the West Point Foundry, had charge of fitting up the *Best Friend*." [Matthew in a letter to Brown]: "It was the first locomotive built in America, and was exhibited at our shop under steam for some time, and visited by many. The Locomotive was shipped to Charleston on board of the ship *Niagara*, in October, 1830."

"The Best Friend's Maiden Voyage: Charleston Welcomes the Best Friend"
by Horatio Allen, Chief Engineer

"Since the locomotive was to be used in the night, and during the whole night on the South Carolina Railroad, it was thought well to make trial of such running by night...For such trial, two platform cars were placed in front of the locomotive. On the forward platform was placed an enclosure of sand, and on the sand a structure; somewhat of urn shape. In this structure was to be kept up a fire of pine-wood knots. ...The day preceding the evening of the trial closed in with a heavy fog as I have ever seen. But the fog did not prevent the trial when the appointed time came.

The country to be run through was very level, and on the surface rested this heavy fog, but just before we were ready to start, the fog began to lift and continued to rise slowly, and as uniformly as ever curtain left the surface of a stage, until about eighteen feet high. There it remained stationary, with an under surface as uniform as the surface it had risen from. This under surface was lit up with

429

radiating lines in all directions with prismatic colors, presenting a scene of remarkable brilliancy and beauty.

Under this canopy, lit on its under surface, the locomotive moved onward with a clearly illuminated road before it. The run was continued for some five miles with no untoward occurrence, and I had reason to exclaim, "The very atmosphere of Carolina says, 'Welcome to the Locomotive!'" —H. Allen

"The *Best Friend* continued to do the necessary work of the railroad, hauling materials, workmen, ballast, and lumber used in the construction, and during all of that time under the charge of those who had put it together."

—William H. Brown

"THE RAILROAD: EARLY DAYS"
By Edward Channing

"On July 4, 1828, three years after the completion of the Erie Canal, Charles Carroll of Maryland, the last survivor of the signers of the Declaration of Independence, drove the first spike on the *Baltimore and Ohio Railroad*, the earliest line designed for the conveyance of both passengers and freight…At the outset, these roads were designed to connect towns already in existence,…Afterwards the railroads were generally built first, giving the means of settlement to a new section of the country…In this manner, the interior began to be settled away from the rivers. In the decade 1840-1850, five thousand miles of railroad were built; but it was not until after 1850, that the push of the railroad into new sections was done with great vigor…

By 1845, the American life, in the North at least, may be said to have thrown off the Colonial guise, and to have taken on its modern form."

"THE NEW INVENTION CONCERNS"
By David S. Muzzey

"The appearance in 1830 of *a* steam locomotive on the new 23 mile track of the Baltimore and Ohio Railway gave promise of the network of nearly 250,000 miles of railroad track which covers our Country today, bringing the Pacific coast within five days of New York City.

It is an interesting coincidence that while the steam locomotive was being tested, and its advocates were laboring to overcome the foolish prejudices against its adoption, statesmen in Congress were ridiculing the idea of our taking any interest in the Oregon country beyond the Rockies, on the ground that it would take a House-Representative a year to make the journey to Washington and back...

'The locomotive,' it was said, 'would spoil the farms by its soot, and ignite barns and dwellings by its sparks. Its noise would frighten the animals so that hens would not lay, and cows would refuse to give their milk.'

This improvement in transportation over wagon and canal, stimulated business in every direction. The demand for the products of American farms and factories increased with the extension of the railroad.

As the volume of freight traffic grew, cities began to develop rapidly."

"**The New York Central Railroad** never succeeded in driving the Erie Canal out of business, for so large is the traffic from the West through New York State, that at times, even railroads and canals together accommodate the traffic with difficulty.

Says Professor Coman, comparing canals and railroads: 'Canal traffic was safe and cheap, but slow and liable to be interrupted by slack water, floods, or frost. The Erie Canal, for example, freezes over in winter, and navigation is stopped from four to five months of the year. A railroad can be built through mountainous country at one-third the cost of a canal."

—Emerson Fite

"THE FIRST LOCOMOTIVE IN NEW YORK: THE DEWITT CLINTON"
By Brown & Matthews

"August, 1831, when what was represented and known to be the first American locomotive ever run upon a railroad in the State of New York…It was the third locomotive built in America for actual service. This engine was named the *De Witt Clinton*, and is thus described by Mr. David Matthew, in his letter to the author in 1859."

—William H Brown, (author and passenger)

"American engine No. 3 was called the 'De Witt Clinton.' It was contracted for by John B. Jervis, Esq., at the West Point Foundry, and was commenced by me to fit up in April, 1831, soon after the engines 'Best Friend' and 'West Point' were completed and forwarded to Charleston.

I left New York with the 'De Witt' on the 25th of June, 1831, and had steam on to commence running in one week from that time. The 'De Witt' had two cylinders, five and a half inches in diameter and sixteen inches stroke; four wheels, all drivers, four and a half feet diameter…This engine weighed about three and a half tons without water, and would run thirty miles an hour with three to five cars on a level, with anthracite coal, and was the first engine run in the State of New York on a railroad."

—David Matthew

W.H. Brown described the first trip

"On this first excursion on the 6th day of August, 1831, as no such officer as a conductor had been required upon the road, where hitherto no connected train of cars had been run, but where each *driver* officiated as collector of fares, Mr. John T. Clark, the first passenger railroad conductor in the north, stepping from platform to platform outside the stagecoach cars, collected the tickets which had been sold at hotels and other places through the city.

When he finished his tour, he mounted upon the tender attached to the engine, and sitting upon the little buggy-seat, he gave the signal with a tin horn, and the train started on its way…It was not that quiet, imperceptible motion which characterizes the first impulsive movements of the passenger-engines of the present day. Not so. There came a sudden jerk that bounded the sitters from their places, to the great detriment of their high-top fashionable beavers, due to the close proximity to the roofs of the cars.

This first jerk being over, the engine proceeded on its route with considerable velocity for those times when compared with stage-coaches, until it arrived at a water station, when it suddenly brought up with jerk No. 2, to the further amusement of some of the excursionists.

Mr. Clark retained his elevated seat, thanking his stars for its close proximity to the tall smoke-pipe of the machine; thereby allowing the smoke and sparks to pass over his head. At the water-station a short stop was made, and a successful experiment tried to remedy the unpleasant jerks. A plan was soon hit upon and put into execution. The three links in the couplings of the cars were stretched to their utmost tension; a rail from a fence in the neighborhood, was placed between each pair of cars and made fast by means of the packing yarn for the cylinders. This arrangement improved the order of things, and it was found to answer the purpose, when the signal was again given, and the engine started.

In a short time, the engine, after frightening horses attached to all sorts of vehicles causing capsizes, arrived at the head of the inclined plane at Schenectady amid the cheers and welcomes of thousands assembled to witness the arrival of the iron horse and its living freight."

"THE HISTORY OF THE FIRST LOCOMOTIVES IN AMERICA"
By William H. Brown

"During the past forty years, while railroads were stretching forth their iron arms over vast sections of our Country, and indeed of the civilized world, and even through the wild and thinly populated domains where exist vast forests and hitherto pathless deserts of sand; locomotives, those absolute essentials to the economy and success of these enterprises, were in like manner, making giant strides in the way of improvement: from the "Rocket" of Stephenson in England, and the "Best Friend" of Charleston in this country, to the perfection which characterizes the first-class locomotive of the present day. When we compare the performances of these and their readiness at all hours, and under all circumstances, to brave the torrents, the winds, and the snows of the most terrific tempest, we cannot but call to mind an advertisement in a Philadelphia paper in 1832...

'NOTICE TO THE PUBLIC: The engine with a train of cars will be run daily, commencing this day when the weather is fair. When the weather is not fair, the horses will draw the cars. Passengers are requested to be punctual at the hour of starting.'

When we contemplate the rapid march made upon the continent alone, in railroad and locomotive improvement, it seems like the work of enchantment. The mind is bewildered and almost carried away in its efforts to keep pace with or follow its giant strides.

Let us, by way of illustration conduct our reader for a few moments to some imaginary eminence, from which his eye could command in one sweep the entire surface of our country; let him turn his gaze toward the north, the south, the east, or the west, even across the Rocky Mountains to the shores of the broad Pacific, and he will behold a scene of life and industry which few could be prepared to believe had been developed in less than half a century. And then let him predict the future—if he can. Lead his mind back to the period just forty years ago, when on the 15th day of December, 1830, the first locomotive built in America for actual service upon a railroad, and known as the "Best Friend of Charleston," started out upon its solitary journey, a few miles only in extent, upon the unfinished track of the South Carolina Railroad—the second railroad commenced in this country for commercial purposes, and the first railroad in the world built expressly for locomotive power. Let him contemplate this scene for a moment, then turn his mind to the one presented to him at the present day: All over the wide expanse of our Union, behold the countless railroads extending for thousands of miles in every direction, bearing upon their rails their droves of iron horses of every imaginary form and pattern, dashing with lightening-speed from city to city, with their long and heavy trains of living, breathing human creatures, or with their lengthened trains of freight cars, loaded with thousands of tons of the products of the industry of the people, adding millions to the trade and commerce of the Nation, rushing on, overcoming all obstacles, crossing wide, deep and rapid rivers; ascending the steepest grades, or driving headlong through lengthened tunnels—then ask the beholder if we have reached summit, the consummation, the ultimatum of this great instrumentality in the advancement of the trade and commerce of our prosperous Republic...

We cannot quit the subject without again drawing before our readers a comparison between the locomotive passenger trains of the present day and those of forty years ago, when the old fashioned stagecoach body pattern was the model for the first-class passenger cars...When we compare these vehicles with the splendid drawing-room, sleeping and dining room cars now coming into use upon some of the principal railroad thoroughfares and soon to become universal; and when the old familiar voice of the conductor, announcing 'Twenty minutes for dinner', will no longer be heard, but instead thereof, the traveler will be ushered into a splendid dining-saloon attached to the train and vying in elegance with the most sumptuous apartment, furnished and provided with all the concomitants of a well-appointed hotel, a table of well-prepared provisions, followed by all the luxuries of the various seasons through which they travel, served by polite and attentive waiters; and at length, at the end of a well-enjoyed meal, the traveler will find himself some twenty-five or thirty miles farther advanced upon his journey,.. all, all seems like the work of enchantment!"

JOHN H.B. LATROBE, was introduced by the author who described him as, '*The eminent counsellor of the Baltimore and Ohio Railroad,*' at a banquet given in Wheeling in 1853 on the successful completion of that great enterprise.

LATROBE: "We talk of the *Course of Empire*. Its type is the locomotive and its train, whose tread is the tread of a giant, from hill-top to hill-top. We speak of the array of a conqueror: where is there a conqueror like steam? Its panoply, too, is of iron; man has made it not less than mortal as it performs the work of one hundred thousand of men's hands, and as it is impatient of delay, it rushes through the bosom of the hills; its white and feathery plume is the ensign of a daring, a courage that treads its way through the forest, or climbs the side of the mountain…That the fruition of these hopes will disappoint no reasonable expectations, but surpass them all, who of us can doubt? The west built up Baltimore; first with the pack-saddle, then with the county road, then with the turnpike; as it is now about to employ the greatest agent of modern times to realize for us the destiny appointed by *Providence*, when the waters of the fountains of the Potomac are made to flow from the same hills that sent their tribute to the Ohio."

Again, on this memorable occasion: the completion of the Baltimore and Ohio Railroad, and the arrival of the first locomotive and train from Baltimore at Wheeling, a guest from Cleveland, *James A. Briggs*, Esq., made these remarks in allusion to the march of internal improvements in railways and locomotives:

"The men of Maryland and Virginia and Ohio, and Pennsylvania, have met here to commemorate the completion of one of the great lines of trade and travel between the Atlantic Ocean and the Ohio River. This line of railroad is a great work. It was originated by men who had the capacity to conceive great designs and the courage to execute them. The work is finished. The iron horse has traveled on his iron pathway from the Monumental City over the Alleghany Mountains to this, not long since frontier settlement, but now the flourishing city of Wheeling. Here, in this room are men who have heard the war-whoop of the Indian on this very spot, and today they have heard the shrill whistle of the locomotive. How wonderful that such changes have come within the memory of those who still live! And this is a change—not of cities desolated, and villages ruined, and fields laid waste—but of the progress of the arts of peace, of the advancement of a high order of civilization and of the onward course of Christianity, freighted and innumerable blessings for the whole world-wide family of humanity...It is one link in the chain which binds us together as a Nation. While I am speaking, the locomotive is thundering along on his iron tracks from the Queen City of Ohio, and from the far-off prairies of Illinois; long trains freighted with people and products of the rich fields of the West, are heading to Eastern markets..."

POETRY AND PROSE COMMEMORATING THE RAILROAD AND THE MEN.

Short stories and poems commemorating the Railroad, and the men who dedicated their lives to the great cause of keeping locomotives running.

They made possible for the citizens of the United States, for the first time, to experience our vast and open country-side, and to watch small towns in the great West grow from cabin in the woods to villages, and for those so destined: into vibrant cities.[11]

Canal Winchester, Ohio

---

11 Permission to reprint the following poems, published originally in *Railroad Magazine*, granted by courtesy of White River Productions, Inc.

Canal Winchester, Ohio

"The Freight Train"

by Harry Kemp

"I saw him grow in sight, I watched him wend;
    Superb, he took the curve and fetched the grade,
Superbly leaped the long-linked cars behind
    The laboring locomotive, serving trade.
With heavy, rhythmic wheels and flying truck
    The hulking boxcar, rolling flatcar, struck
A distant symphony from rails and ties,
    The sounding-board of which were hills and skies…
The freight grew large beside a water tank;
    It took a stance, impatient, while it drank
With a long sigh for the miles it had gone,
    Then, newly gathering resonance, it rode on."

"Night Run"
by Douglas Ward

"The red glare of an open firebox
　　Against a solid black sky;
The starry wonder of God's Universe,
　　As the stilly miles slip by.
The long, lonely shrill of the whistle,
　　The hiss of escaping steam;
The endless cadence of wheels on rails,
　　The creak of a straining beam.
The drowsy songs the night folk sing
　　Along the shadowy right-of-way,
The tender warmth of the 'wakening Sun
　　Caressing a new-born day.
These are the night run's lures,
　　These are the graveyarders' pay;
So give me a call for midnight,
　　For dreamers can't work by day."

"The Invisible Hand"
by Ernest A. Smith

"We were rambling through the foothills
    That stormy night in '23,
A solid mile of dripping reefers and
    The hogger had them rolling free.

Suddenly, the engineer seemed to stiffen,
    And looked 'round to see if he was alone.

He'd felt another hand on his throttle,
    A soft warm hand that was not his own!
The strange hand shoved the throttle closed,
    The latch caught fast as we could see.
The startled hogger next felt the hand
    Upon the brake-valve by his knee.

We ground to a stop beside the River
    Where naught was left but swinging tracks.
In naked fear we looked at each other
    While icy fingers played on our backs.

Together we knelt in that littered deck,
    The hogger, the brakie and ashcat, me,
To give thanks to a watchful Presence
    With the saving Hand we could not see."

"*The Shop* was a great, wide shack with the sun pouring in through the open door and windows all around. Clouds of dust and metal filings danced in the light, and the place was full of the sound of hammering and the grunts and shouts of men wrestling with heavy engine parts. The floor was cluttered with headlights, brass trimmings of engines, flat wheels, and dismembered boilers. It made you feel arrogant and at the same time sad, to walk safely among these crippled hulks, which were usually so full of snorting power." (from) *Treasury of R.R. Folklore*

"Signs o' Spring"
by Leon R. Harris

"Saw a ray o' sunlight peepin' through a winder o' the Shop.
　　Sun don't ever see that winder 'cept in Spring.
It's beneath a big transformer that is belt up by a prop,
　　And the sun has got to twist to dodge that thing.

Heard some fellas on the shop train arguin' bout seeds—
　　Should they plant 'em in the light or dark o' the moon?
Don't know nothin' bout the moon-time,
　　But if they 'ud beat the weeds,

They 'ud better plant their gardens pretty soon.

Got a funny kind of feelin' somethin's happened to my blood;
　　Eyes keep wanderin' toward them open doors a bit.
Drank some sassafras fer breakfast, but that didn't
do no good;
　　Guess I want to go fishin,' that 'bout it.

Tell yer winter woes to Sweeney, I've no time to listen in,
　　Spring is comin' faster than our engines run;
I ain't goin' to church next Sunday. Reckon it'll be a sin
　　Jist to stay out in that April air an' sun?"

"The Pensioned Engineer"
by J.W. Nealon

"Out to the shops on a storage track
    is an old sweetheart of mine.
Battered and worn, faded and shorn,
    The old Nine Forty-nine
Was brand new when I was set up…
    A beautiful sight to see—
And I was the proudest man on the line
    When the M.M. gave her to me.

Today when I saw her, there was nobody 'round,
    So, I spoke to my old-time pal,
And I said in a voice that I know you knew;
    'How've they been treating you, pal?'
The years have been long, since last we met,
    The going's been mighty hard;
My name is now on the pension list,
    And you are in the discard.

Things have changed an awful lot
    Since the year of 'seventy-nine,
When we were pulling the fast express,
    The finest train on the line.
All the old time bunch are gone
    That we knew, both you and I;
Let's hope they're on the payroll
    Of the Roundhouse in the sky.

THE RAILROAD

I'm sitting once more in your cab, old pal,
 As I did in the days gone by;
Your lever bar is out of gear,
 Your water glass rusty and dry.
But I'll be the Fireman and Engineer,
 And I'll open your throttle wide;
And over the rails of memory
 We'll go for one last ride."

"The Old Timer"

by James Shankland

"A hobo sat in the waiting room
    With a shaggy and bowed-down head.
The porter poked at him with a broom
    And found the poor man was dead.
Only a hobo, so the papers read,
    Who'd wandered in out of the cold;
But a hundred things they could have said
    Of the man who was ragged and old.

As a boy he cleaned the signal lights
    Way back when the road was young;
Through rain and snow and the cold that bites
    He saw they were properly hung.
Early and late in the shops he worked
    When first he became a man,
And never a job he dropped or shirked
    But, "I'll do it, sir, if I can."

The day he climbed in the cab,
    Was the happiest day in his life;
That Locomotive became his special care
    And he loved it more than a wife.
The years rolled on, as they always do,
    While older he grew and gray,
And ever as strong as steel, and true,
    He made his run day after day.

They set him down upon the ground
    When his eyes began to fail;
And then for years he hung around
    To hear the singing rail.
And so he died today, I read,
    A hobo left all alone,
As though his dying were a deed
    For which he should atone."

"The Telegraph Operator"

"As a lad, Harry would go down to the station in the little Iowa town and look with pure awe at the telegraph operator.

Young Bedwell had decided that any railroad job was wonderful, because you could ride the trains free to any state in the Union, but the operator's job seemed beyond compare, since he could work for any railroad. Harry could hardly believe it when he was told he could study under the local operator. All the boy had to do in turn was to sweep out, carry coal, keep the fire going in the big pot-bellied stove, take the U.S. mail to the Post office, and do the station's accounting.

In turn he was permitted to sit and copy what the sounders said. He saw the country, and in time he became a station agent.

—(*Railroad Magazine*)

THE DEPOT

The telegraph operator's office was near the center of the depot, with his desk placed well within the bay window for easy track-viewing, both right and left. The telegraph instrument, a typewriter on a small table nearby, the operator's large swivel chair, a round walnut-rimmed wall clock, a large plain calendar, hoop-poles for passing up information to engineers, and a bucket to retrieve coal for the stove; were all hallmarks of the depot. The walls were wainscoted part of the way up, something of a trademark for the small town or country-side depot. The passenger waiting room was on one end of the building; the baggage, mail and weigh room on the opposite end. The invention

450

of the telegraph in 1844, was the beginning of much safer travel for locomotives; giving engineers and station agents greater peace of mind.

It seems that railroad men were unassuming and took for granted their accomplishments; not considering perhaps the wonderful work they were doing to advance the country in providing safe and extensive travel from coast to coast and many places between.

I recall the clack-clack sound of the bamboo pole as it struck the brick platform at the Hobson depot where my dad worked as a telegraph operator. (His dad and brother had life-time careers also with the New York Central System in the Hobson yard shops; a mile or so beyond, and adjacent to the Ohio River.) Often, I delivered lunch to him; just a short walk from our house, and would tarry for a time in that different world of sights and sounds. The only activity I recall was his continual clicking the telegraph key, in silence and not further acknowledging my presence, as I sat behind him near the stove.

It was a treat to see on one occasion however, a massive steam locomotive, in what seemed a full steam pass with freight cars trailing, suddenly appearing just outside the bay window. The engineer leaned slightly out the window, and slid his arm through the loop on the pole that dad held up for him. Quickly removing the slip of paper; tossing pole onto the brick platform, and he was gone. How small the country-side must look to him from his proud height; his distinguished and grand post.

While warming beside a pot-belly stove; a cup of hot cocoa in hand, a Trackman with his quaint and woeful tales, would have enlivened the closing hours of any day:

"A Trackman's Life"
by J.A. Morris

"It's rain an' rain an' rain again, till all the world's afloat,
    An' workin' on this mud-line now, it surely gets my goat;
A kingsnipe on the mud-line in the mud an' slush an' rain,
    The old man's throwin' butterflies from his ever bloomin' train.

There's sloppy joints in Johnson's cut; the track is out of line.'
    'Go, quick! and cut the driftwood loose at trestle twenty-nine.'
The fence was down at Wilson's place when I passed there today.
    And all his cattle, sheep and dogs were on the right of way.

The longest day must have an end, an' men must have their rest,
    An' comes the time, at evenin's close, the time I love the best,
When car and tools are put away, an' I get home once more,
    To see my Maggie's smilin' face beside the kitchen door.

Then I wash up and sit me down to supper, pipin' hot,
    An' cares take wing an' fly away an' troubles are forgot.
Then I smoke up while Maggie clears away the supper things,
    An' I start up the phonygraff an' Harry Launder sings
A Wee Hoose 'mong the Heather" an' "The Bonny Banks o' Doon..."

Bibliography

ABDY, HARRY B. "On the Ohio," Dodd, Mead and Company, New York 1919.

ADAMS, ABIGAIL, *Letter to her Husband.* Boston, 21 July 1776. "Letters of Mrs. Adams, the wife of John Adams." Charles F. Adams, E. Boston, 1848. Reprinted in *The American Reader* by Paul Angle, c. Rand McNally Co., 1958.

_____ *Letter to Her Daughter* (from The White House).

ADAM, KARL, "The Spirit of Catholicism," 1924. "The World Treasury of Religious Quotations." Compiled and Edited by Ralph L. Woods. Garland Books, New York City, 1966

ADAMS, HENRY, (1838-1918) "The United States in 1800," Cornell University Press, 1955. Consisting of the first six chapters of Vol. 1 of "Adams' History of the United States of America During the First Administration .of Thomas Jefferson." Charles Scribner's Sons, 1889.

ADAMS, SAMUEL H. "Grandfather Stories", Random House, N.Y. 1955, [*The Canal Bride*].

ALLEN, ETHAN, *Ethan Allen takes Ticonderoga*, 1775. "A Narrative of Col. Ethan Allen's Captivity, written by Himself." Walpole, N. H. 1807. Reprinted in "The American Reader."

ALLEN, HORATIO "The Railroad Era, First Five Years of its Development," c. 1884, by Horatio Allen, New York.

AMES, NATHANIAL, *An Almanac for the Year of Our Lord Christ*, 1758, Boston. Reprinted in "Time in New England", by N. Newhall and P. Strand; Oxford University Press, New York 1950.

ASHE, THOMAS, "Travels in America performed in the year 1806." New York, 1811.

ATWATER, CALEB "A History of the State of Ohio," Glezen & Shepard, Cincinnati 1838.

AURELIUS, MARCUS (Reign): 161-180 A.D. *Meditations; Walter J. Black Inc. 1945.*

AUGUSTINE, AURELIUS *(354-430)* *"The Confessions of St. Augustine," Random House Inc., 1949.*

AZOY, Colonel A.C.M. *Patriot Battles.* "The Infantry Journal," *Washington, 1943.*

BARCLAY, ROBERT, (1648-1690) "An Apology for the True Christian Divinity of a People called Quakers," 1678. Friends Book Store, 1906.

BARKER, JOSEPH (1765-1843) *Recollections of the First Settlement of Ohio*; Marietta College, Marietta, Ohio, 1858.

BELL, LANDON, An Address: *The Battle of Point Pleasant: First Battle of the Revolution,* October 10, 1774.

BERNANOS, GEORGE, "The Diary of a Country Priest." 1937. "The World Treasury of Religious Quotations," compiled and edited by Ralph L. Woods; Garland Books, 1966.

BIRKBECK, MORRIS: *Letters from Illinois in 1818.* "Notes on a Journey to America, from the Coast of Virginia to the Territory of Illinois." London, 1818.

BLANE, WILLIAM N. "An English gentleman's excursion through the United States and Canada during the years 1822-1823," London.

BOKE, LIWWAT, (1807-1882) "The Journal of Liwwat Boke: The story of an immigrant pioneer woman and her husband who settled in western Ohio." Minster, Ohio: Minster Historical Society c. 1987.

BOTKIN, B.A. and HARLOW, ALVIN F. (Edit.) "A Treasury of Railroad Folklore." Bonanza Books, New York, 1953.

BOURNE, HENRY and BENTON, ELBERT J., "History of the United States," D.C. Heath and Company, New York, 1913.

BOURNE, RUSSELL: "Floating West: The Erie and other American Canals." New York, Norton c.1992.

BRINTON, HOWARD H., "The Nature of Quakerism, a reprint of chapter 11 entitled *Quaker Education in Theory and Practice, 1949.*" Pendle Hill, Wallingford, Penna. 1967.

BROWN, EVERIT, "The National Standard History of the United States," A.L. Burt, New York 1886.

BROWN, WILLIAM H., "History of the First Locomotives in America," Astragal Press, *N.J. 1871.*

BURNET, JACOB, "Notes on the Early Settlement in the Northwest Territory," Cincinnati, 1847.

BUTLER, WILLIAM O *The Boatman's Horn.* "The Old Northwest Pioneer Period, *1815-1840*," R. C. Buley Indiana Historical Society, 1950.

CASTELLIO, SEBASTIAN (1515-1563) "The Luminous Trail," by Rufus Jones. Macmillan Co., New York, 1947.

CHANNING, EDWARD, "A Student's History of the United States." The MacMillan Company, New York, 1903.

CHARLES, WILLIAM E. "Age 18" *A Canaller's Diary.* "Best of American Canals" *V. 5.*

CHURCH, ELIJAH H. "The Early History of Zanesville." From the Zanesville Daily Courier, 1874-1880. Publ. by Zanesville, Ohio Muskingum Valley Archeological Survey c. 1986.

CIST, CHARLES, 1792-1868. *Census Sketches*, 1841 Manufactures.

_____ "The Cincinnati Miscellany, or Antiquities of the West and Pioneer History and General and Local Statistics compiled from the Western General Advertiser"...by Charles Cist, editor, Cincinnati 1844-1845. C. Clark, printer.

_____ 1844 *"Pioneer Mothers."*

_____ Cist's *1859 "Manufacturers and industrial Products." 1859: "Assessing the previous [10] years."*

CLARK, COLONEL GEORGE ROGERS, *Expedition into the New Northwest Territory*, 1778-1779. "America Series Vol. 3: The Revolution." Chicago, 1925.

_____ The Capture of Fort Vincennes.

_____ *Victory at Piqua, Ohio*. Ohio Archeological and Historical Society Publication: "Along the Pathway of a Great State."

CLEMENS, SAMUEL "Life on the Mississippi." (*Mark Twain* 1883) Airmont Publishing Co., New York, 1965.

CLEMENT OF ALEXANDRIA "The Luminous Trail" by Rufus Jones, Macmillan Co. New York, 1947.

COOK, LEWIS, *Memories of One Time Canallers. The Ohio-Erie Canal*: [Articles written for the Columbus, Ohio Dispatch in the 1940s.]

DANIELS, CAPTAIN WILSON, *Memoirs* "Indiana Magazine of History," *June 1915*.

DRAKE, DANIEL: "A Natural and Statistical View, or Picture of Cincinnati and the Miami Country." Printed by Looker and Wallace, Cincinnati, 1815.

DWIGHT, MARGARET VAN HORN, (1790-1834); *A Journey to Ohio in 1810*. 1812 Manuscript. The Ohio Historical Connection's Library.

EASTMAN, MARY REED, "The 1833 Diaries of Mary Reed Eastman," *Vol. 2*, Ms. Schlesinger Library, Radcliffe College.

ELLET, ELIZABETH, "Women of the Revolution," Baker and Scribner, New York, 1848.

EMERSON, RALPH WALDO, *Divinity School Address* "Selected Essays, Lectures and Poems," *July 15, 1838, Simon & Schuster, New York, 1965.*

EMMITT, HON. JAMES. "Life and times of Hon. James Emmitt." By M.J. Carr, Chillicothe, Ohio, Peerless Printing and Manufacturing Co., 1888.

ENCYCLOPEDIA BRITANNICA, *The Erie Canal*, Volume 8, 1964, (R.E. At.) William Benton Publishing Co., Chicago.

EVANS, NELSON W., (1842-1913), "A History of Scioto County together with Pioneer records of Southern Ohio." Portsmouth, Ohio, 1903.

FEARON, HENRY B. "A Narrative of a Journey through America in 1817." London, 1818.

FITE, EMERSON D, "History of the United States," Henry Holt and Company, New York, 1916.

FITZGERALD, COLONEL JOHN, *An Account of the Trenton Expedition.* "The Battles of Trenton and Princeton," by William S. Stryker, Boston, 1898.

FLEXNER, JAMES. *Providence Rides a Storm.* "American Heritage Magazine," December, 1967.

FOX, GEORGE, (1624-1691) "The Journal of George Fox," Capricorn Books, New York, *1963.*

FRANKLIN, BENJAMIN, (1706-1790) "The Completed Autobiography of Benjamin Franklin," Regenery Publ., Lanham, Md., 2006.

FULTON, ROBERT: *Steamboat Trip to Albany*; Letter to the American Citizen Newspaper; September, 1807. Reprinted in "The American Series, Volume 5, 1803-1820." Copyright Americanization Department Veterans of Foreign Wars, 1925.

GALLIA COUNTY, OHIO *HISTORY*: Breckenridge on the French settlers.

GIBBON, FLOYD, *And They Thought We Wouldn't Fight.* New York 1918. Reprinted in "The American Reader" by Paul Angle, Rand McNally 1958.

GLAZIER, WILLARD CAPTAIN, *PITTSBURGH*: "Peculiarities of American Cities." *Hubbard Brothers*, Philadelphia, *1884.*

GUYON, JEANNE (1648-1717), "Madame Guyon," Autobiography. Moody Press, Chicago.

HALL, JAMES, "Notes on the Western States Containing Descriptive Sketches of their Soil, Climate, Resources and Scenery." HardPress Publishing, Miami Fl. 1838.

_____ "The West: Its Commerce and Navigation," Cincinnati, 1848.

_____ "The Romance of Western History", OR *Sketches of History, Life and Manners in the West.* Cincinnati, Applegate & Company, *1857.*

HARLOW, ALVIN, "When Horses Pulled Boats. A Story of Early Canals." Published by American Canal and Transportation Center, 1983.

HARPERS MAGAZINE, *The Lading of a Ship,* in 1877 New York.

HARRIS, THADDEUS M., 1768-1842; "The Journal of a Tour into the Territory Northwest of the Allegheny Mountains in the spring of 1803." Boston, 1805.
(Reprinted in Reuben Gold Thwaites *Early Western Travels:* A.H Clark Company 1904-1907).

HARTLEY, CECIL B., "The Life of Daniel Boone." Porter & Coats, Philadelphia, 1865.

HATCHER, HARLAN: "The Buckeye Country: A pageant of Ohio." G.P. Putnam's Sons New York, 1940.

_____ "The Western Reserve, The Story of New Connecticut, Ohio." Bobbs-Merrrill Co., 1949.

HAVIGHURST, WALTER, "Long Ships Passing": The Story of the Mississippi Waterways, New York, Macmillan 1964.

_____ "The Heartland," Regions of America Book," Harper and Row *N.Y. 1956.*

HEADLEY, HON. J.T. "The Life of George Washington." Publ. by G&F Bill, New York, 1860.

HENRY, GOVERNOR PATRICK, *"Give Me Liberty or Give Me Death,"* 1775. Reprinted in "America" Vol. 3, Chicago, 1925.

HOFFMAN, CHARLES FENNO, 1806-1888: *"A Winter in the West," by a New Yorker.* Readex microprint, c.1966.

HORNUNG, CLARENCE P. "Wheels Across America." By A.S. Barnes, Co. New York, 1959.

HOWELLS, WILLIAM C. "Recollections of Life in Ohio *1813-1840."* Robert Clark, Co. Cincinnati, 1895.

_____ *Reminiscences of Early Manufactures of Southeastern Ohio* in "History of Ohio Counties: Jefferson County."

HOWELLS, WILLIAM DEAN., *Life in the Backwoods,* "Stories of Ohio," American Book Co. Cincinnati, 1897.

HOWE, HENRY, 1816-1893. "Historical Collections of Ohio," Cincinnati, Ohio. Published by The State of Ohio, 1904.

_____ Brown County, Ohio. The John Rankin House.

_____ Jefferson County, Ohio

HUGHES, JESSE P. *"My life as a Steamboat Captain,* published in 'Tallow Light' v. 5-6, Washington County, Ohio.

HULBERT, ARCHER BUTLER, "The Ohio River: A Course of Empire," G.P. Putnam's Sons, New York, 1906.

IERLEY, MERRIT "Traveling the National Road: A Composite of Writers," Overlook Press. Woodstock, New York, 1990.

IRVING, WASHINGTON 1783-1859, "The Life of George Washington," *Vol 2;* Merrill and Baker, 1855.

JONES, RUFUS M. "The Faith and Practice of the Quakers." Book and Publications Committee, Philadelphia, 1927.

JORDAN, PHILIP D., "The National Road," The Bobbs-Merrill Company, Indianapolis and New York, 1948.

KEMPIS, THOMAS A' "The Imitation of Christ" (1441). The New American Library of World Literature, Inc. New York, 1962.

KETCHUM, RICHARD, "American Heritage Book of the Revolution," American Heritage Publishing Co., Inc. N.Y. 1958. [Narrative on *Valley Forge*: "The unseasonable run of shad."]

KILBOURNE, JOHN *Public Documents Concerning the Ohio Canals*, Columbus: I. N. Whiting c. 1832.

KINGSLAND, WILLIAM *Our Infinite Life* 1922, "The World Treasury of Religious Quotations."

KNOX, HENRY: *Causes for the War.* [Reprinted in] "An Ohio Reader,", edited by Thomas H. Smith. Wm B. Eerdmans Publishing Co., Grand Rapids, Michigan, 1975. From: "Statement of Causes of the Indian War," January 26, 1792, Clarence Carter, (ed.). *The Territorial Papers of the United States, 11, (1934).*

LAMB, MARTHA, 1829-1893, *Marietta, The Earliest Settlement in Ohio*, published in "Encore for Two Voices," Washington County Historical Society 1976. (Additional Contributor: Alfred Matthews, 1852-1904.)

LASALLE, SIEUR, *1682---La Salle claims the Mississippi Valley for France.* Illinois State Historical Library, Vol. 1, Springfield, 1903. (Reprinted in "The American Reader").

LAW, WILLIAM, "Christian Perfection," 1726. "The World Treasury of Religious Quotations."

LEE, ALFRED E. "History of the City of Columbus, Capital of Ohio," New York, 1892.

_____ Christian Heyl: *Entrepreneur*

LEWIS, ALEXANDER, "Cincinnati and its People." Ohio River papers....

LONGFELLOW, HENRY WADSWORTH, *Tales of a Wayside Inn*, "Longfellow's Complete Poems," Houghton, Mifflin & Company, 1902.

LORD, JOHN, *Saint Augustine*, "Beacon Lights of History," Vol. 1, New York, 1883.

LUTHER, MARTIN, (1483-1546) *On Romans Chapter 6*, by John Dillenburger, New York.

MACKINNON, J.W. *The Ordinance of 1787*, "Ohio History Sketches," Press of Fred J. Heer, 1903.

McKINLEY, GOVERNOR WILLIAM Address: The *Centennial Anniversary of General Wayne's Treaty of Greenville.* August 8, 1895. "Ohio Archeological and Historical Publications."

MEIGS COUNTY, "Ohio History Book," Pomeroy, Ohio. c. 1979.

MEIGS COUNTY "Pioneer and Historical Society": Pomeroy, Ohio, c.1987.

_____ "Pomeroy: An Historical Sketch of the Village"

_____ Quillin, Uriah, *Flatboating on the Ohio River*, "Log Cabin Reminiscences."

MELISH, JOHN 1771-1882. "Travels in the United States of America in the years 1806 and 1807." Philadelphia, 1812. Published by John Melish... 1815.
> (Reprinted in "The America Series", Volume V, 1925; Chapter titled: *American Ways of Life in 1811*).

MERRICK, George B. *Torch Baskets: Old Times on the Upper Mississippi.* c 1909. Reprinted in "A Treasury of Mississippi Folklore," Edited by B.A. Botkin, Crown Publishers 1955.

MICHAUX, FRANCOIS A. "Travels on the Westward of the Alleghany Mountains in the States of Ohio, Kentucky and Tennessee in the year 1802," London, 1805.

MILTON, JOHN (1608-1674) *Paradise Lost,* The Odyssey Press, New York, 1962.

MOORE, FRANK, "The Diary of the American Revolution," 1775-1781. Charles T. Evans, New York, 1863.

MUZZEY, DAVID S., "An American History" Ginn and Company, 1911.

NAHMAN, RABBI OF BRATSLAV (1772-1811) "Quoted in Judaism." 1961 ('R.Q')

NELSON, S.B., "History of Cincinnati and Hamilton County, Ohio," 1894.

THE OHIO GUIDE. Writers' Program of the Work Projects Administration (WPA) in the State of Ohio. c. Ohio Archeological and Historical Society, 1940.
_____Akron, Ohio _____Hebron, Ohio
_____Portsmouth, Ohio _____Cambridge, Ohio
_____Ironton, Ohio

OPPEL, FRANK, The City of Buffalo, "New York Tales of the Empire State," compiled by Frank Oppel, Castle: A division of Book Sales Inc., 1885.

PAINE, THOMAS, The American Crisis 1775-1776, Boston, 1777.

PADOVER, SAUL K. The Genius of America: Thomas Paine 1737-1809. "The New Book of Knowledge," Grolier Incorporated, 1970.

PASCAL, BLAISE, "Pensees" 1670, Translated by A.J. Krailsheimer; Penguin Books, 1995.

PEATTIE, DONALD, *Bride of Spring: The Dogwood Tree*. Reprinted in Reader's Digest's, "Our Amazing World of Nature," 1969.

PENN, WILLIAM 1644-1718, "History of the United States," Bourne and Benton

PERRY, Oliver H. *The Battle of Lake Erie, September 10, 1813, "Letter to the Sec'y of the Navy."*
Reprinted in The *American Reader* by Paul Angle, Rand McNally, New York, 1958.

PEYTON, JOHN L. "Over the Alleghenies and Across the Prairies." London, 1870.

POMEROY LEADER NEWSPAPER: *Log Cabin Reminiscences*, 1992.

QUILLEN, URIAH, *A Flatboat Trip.* "Log Cabin Reminiscences," The Meigs County Pioneer and Historical Society," Pomeroy, Ohio 1992.

RAILROAD MAGAZINE, Poems by Douglas Ward 1970, Harry Kemp 1935, Ernest Smith, 1966; Leon Harris, 1977, J.W. Nealon, 1968, J. A. Morris 1975 and James Shankland. Popular Publications, Inc., c. White River Productions, Inc.

RANDALL, E.O.M., *The Northwest Territory*, "Ohio History Sketches," published by F.B. Pearson and J.D. Harlor. Press of Fred J. Heer, 1903.

RANKIN, REV. JOHN, *The Underground Railroad: The Rankin House, Ripley, Ohio*. "Howe's Historical Collection of Ohio." (Norwalk, 1896).

READ, REV. "Howe's Historical Collection of Ohio," reprinted in Weisenburger's, *The Passing of the Frontier*. 1825-1850, A History of the State of Ohio, Vol. 111.

RIDELING, W.H. *The Old National Pike*; Harpers Magazine, Nov., 1879.

RILEY, JAMES WHITCOMB, "The Complete Poetical Works of James W. Riley." c.1883. Published by Grossett & Dunlap.

ROBINSON, SILAS, *One Rafter's trip to Cincinnati*. "Meigs County Pioneer and Historical Society," Pomeroy, Ohio 1992.

THE ROCHESTER HISTORICAL SOCIETY, Vol. XV111:
> *Travelers to the Genesee Country:*
> Basil Hall: "Captain Basil Hall, Travels in North America in the years 1827 and 1828." Edinburgh, 1829.
> James Boardman, "America and the Americans" (London, 1833)
> William Mackinzie., "Sketches of Canada and the United States" (London, 1833).
> De la Segra. "Published. in Watt Stewart: *A Pilgrimage through New York State in 1835*." New York History, October 1938.

SCHAAF, MORRIS. "Etna and Kirkersville" The Riverside Press, Houghton, Mifflin and Company, Cambridge, 1905.

SCHNEIDER, NORRIS. "The National Road, Main Street of America." Columbus, Ohio Historical Society, 1975.

SCIOTO COUNTY, OHIO: "Newspaper Abstracts and Historical Reminiscences," 1866-1869.

THE SCIOTO VALLEY: *The Journey and Occupations.* From "Pioneer Sketches of Scioto County, Ohio."

SCIOTO COUNTY, *The Town Artisans of Early Portsmouth,* "History of Scioto County, Vol. II" Nelson A. Evans.

SEARIGHT, THOMAS B.: "The Old Pike: A History of the National Road." Uniontown, Pennsylvania: c. The Author, 1894.

SHAW, RONALD: *Erie Water West:* "Canals for a Nation: The Canal Era in the United States." 1790-1860. University Press of Kentucky c. 1966.

SIBLEY, WILLIAM G. 1860-1935: *Memories of the Upper Ohio River Activities between 1860 and 1890.* W.G. Sibley, Chicago Journal of Commerce. "An Ohio Archeologic and Historical Society Publication."

SOCRATES: (470-399 B.C) *Trial and Death of Socrates*, "The Apology of Socrates" from *The Dialogues of Plato*," Translated by F. J. Church. A.L. Burt, Co, New York.

STIVERS, ELIESE B., *Ripley, Ohio, Its History and Families.* "Sesquicentennial Historical Committee," 1965.

_____ FRANK GREGG, "A Noted Historian." Observations regarding the Ohio River.

STRONG, CYPRIAN, *A Discourse at the Celebration of the Anniversary of American Independence,* July 4, 1799. "Passing the Torch of Liberty to a New Generation." The American Vision, Inc. Georgia, 2009.

TALLMADGE, BENJAMIN, *The Brooklyn Retreat.* "Memoir of Colonel Benjamin Talmadge," *New York, 1858.*

TATUM, SYBIL, *Account of the Journey of Sibyl Tatum and her parents from New Jersey to Ohio in 1830,* Independence, Ohio.

TAYLOR, R. "*An Early Settlers Journey to Northern Ohio,* Cuyahoga County, Ohio Number V111.

THACHER, JAMES, *A Military Journal during the American Revolutionary War from 1775 to 1783.* Boston, 1823. Reprinted in "The American Reader."

THALHEIMER, M.E., "New Eclectic History of the United States" *Van, Antwerp, Bragg and Company, 1881.*

THURSTON, GEORGE: *Pittsburgh As It Is,* 1857.

TRIPLETT, COLONEL FRANK. *Conquering the Wilderness* or *New Pictorial History of the Heroes and Heroines of America.* The Northwestern Publishing Co., 1888.

TRYON, ROLLA AND LINGLEY, CHARLES, *The Winter at Valley Forge,* "The American People and Nation." Ginn and Company, Boston, 1929.

TRYON, WARREN S. 1901-1989 *Over the Alleghenies; John Peyton's Stagecoach Journey in Ohio.* "A Mirror for Americans: The life and manners in the United States. 1790-1870" as recorded by American travelers, University of Chicago Press, 1932.

VAN FOSSEN, WILLIAM H. "The Story of Ohio," The Macmillan Co., New York, 1937.

WALDO, DR. ALBIGENCE, *Diary of a Surgeon of the Connecticut Line: Valley Forge 1777-1778.* "The Pennsylvania Magazine of History and Biography," *Vol. XXI, No. 3,* Reprinted in "The American Reader."

WASHINGTON. GEORGE, *Washington Bids his Army Farewell*, "America, Great Crises in our History told by its Makers," Vol. 3; issued by the Americanization Department: Veterans of Foreign Wars of the United States, Chicago, 1925.

WATSON, HENRY C. *Lexington and Concord*, "Camp-fires of the Revolution or The War for Independence." Philadelphia: Lindsay and Blakiston, 1853.

WAY, FREDERICK "Pilotin' Comes Natural," Farrar & Rinehart, Inc. New York, 1943.

WESLEY, REVEREND JOHN, "Wesleyan Theology" *Sermons* Lane and Scott, New York, 1850.

WHITTIER, JOHN G. "The Complete Poetical Works of John Greenleaf Whittier." The Riverside Press, Cambridge, 1894.

WILLS, WILLLIAM H. *A Southern Traveler's Diary* in 1840. "Southern History Association Publications" Vol. 7, No. 6. November, 1903.

WOOLEY, MARY E. *On the Meaning of Life*, 1932. "The World Treasury of Religious Quotations."

WEISENBURGER, FRANCIS P., *The Passing of the Frontier,* 1825–1850. "A History of the State of Ohio," Vol. 3, Ohio Archeological and Historical Society, 1941.

"The Diary of the American Revolution by Frank Moore"

The following newspapers had articles reprinted in *The Diary*

Pennsylvania Evening Post

New York Journal

Clift's Diary, Gordon

Pennsylvania Journal

Upcott V

Eliot Manuscript

New Jersey Gazette

New York Gazette

Viator, Boston Country Journal

Pennsylvania Packet

New Hampshire Gazette

Virginia Gazette

Pennsylvania Gazette

Rivington's Gazette

Dunlap's Pennsylvania Packet

Freeman's Journal